May 2023

Dear Mary,

So glad we were at Magnificat and have gotten to know one another as friends as adults!

With love,
Mary Pat

As written in a preeminent sixteenth century
Irish book, Ineen Dubh is noted to be,
"like the mother of the Maccabees
who joined a man's heart
to a woman's thought."

From *Annals of the Four Masters,*
Sixteenth Century Ireland

Dark Queen
of Donegal

Mary Pat Ferron Canes
with
JR Foley

PEN WOMEN PRESS

Library of Congress Control Number: 2021924282
ISBN 978-1-950251-07-0 (paperback)
ISBN 978-1-950251-08-7 (hardcover)
ISBN 978-1-950251-09-4 (electronic)
First edition
Printed in the United States of America

Published by
National League of American Pen Women, Inc.
PEN WOMEN PRESS

Founded in 1897, the National League of American
Pen Women, Inc. is a nonprofit dedicated to promoting the
arts. NLAPW, Inc., 1300 17th Street NW, Washington,
D.C. 20036-1973
www.nlapw.org

Acknowledgements

This book would not have been written *or* completed without the work and insight provided by David Canes. David was awarded a Hewlett Tri-College Grant from Swarthmore University to live among Catholics and Protestants in Northern Ireland before the Good Friday Agreement. His honors thesis related to that endeavor, and his book *North of the Border* captured the attitudes and violence of Unionists and Nationalists in Northern Ireland that had continued since sixteenth century Ireland. David also helped edit this book for its historical accuracy.

A grand thank you also goes to the O'Donnell Clan Association. Their dedication and research have been indispensable. Attending the most recent Clan Gathering in Donegal, Ireland, I spent days at the major sites in this book while listening to scholarly presentations. A highlight was a concert inside the restored Donegal Castle where the musicians performed on ancient instruments. I hope to have captured the power and presence of Irish music in the book.

A librarian and editor, Julie Arnold went beyond professional proofreading and shared suggestions that made the manuscript ready to send to publishers.

The many offerings of the National League of American Pen Women proved a source of much encouragement. "10 Steps to Completing Your Novel," a multiple-day presentation by award-winning author Maureen Stack Sappéy, led to significant progress in this book.

Appreciation goes to the Pen Women Press team at NLAPW headed by Lucy Arnold. They worked together to bring the completed manuscript into a finished book. The book cover illustration by Debbie Patrick captures so well the Dark Queen at her Scots-like castle in Ireland.

Thanks go to Lydia De La Viña Foley who accompanied her spouse JR Foley to Ireland more than once.

And special thanks are due to Mike Canes, who willingly took multiple trips to Ireland, as did our children and grandchildren, to trace their Irish heritage.

Historical Characters

Ineen Dubh MacDonnell, Queen Consort of Hugh O'Donnell

Hugh O'Donnell, King of Tyrconnell

Aodh Ruadh "Red Hugh" O'Donnell, Son of O'Donnell King and Ineen Dubh

Donal O'Donnell, Son of O'Donnell King & Irish wife

Sioban O'Donnell, Daughter of O'Donnell King & Irish wife

Rory O'Donnell, Son of O'Donnell King & Ineen Dubh

Nuala O'Donnell, Daughter of O'Donnell King & Ineen Dubh

Manus O'Donnell, Son of O'Donnell King & Ineen Dubh

Caffar O'Donnell, Son of O'Donnell King and Ineen Dubh

Marie O'Donnell, Daughter of O'Donnell King & Ineen Dubh

Margaret O'Donnell, Daughter of O'Donnell King & Ineen Dubh

Alex McSorley MacDonnell, Foster son of James MacDonnell

Agnes Campbell, Mother of Ineen Dubh

Mac Sweeney Doe, Foster father to Red Hugh

Hugh Maguire, Cousin of Red Hugh O'Donnell

Niall Garbh O'Donnell, Cousin of Red Hugh O'Donnell

Feach O'Bryne, Irish Firebrand

O'Clery, Hereditary Scribe of O'Donnells

Mac an Ward, a Bard

Hugh O'Neill, Earl of Tyrone

Rose O'Neill, Daughter of Hugh O'Neill

Turlough O'Neill, King of Tyrone

Elizabeth I, Queen of England 1558–1603

Sir John Perrot, Lord Deputy of Ireland

Sir William Fitzwilliam, Lord Deputy of Ireland

Sir Richard Bingham, Lord President of Connaught

Sir Nicholas Bagenal, Queen's Marshall in Ireland

Family Trees

O'DONNELL

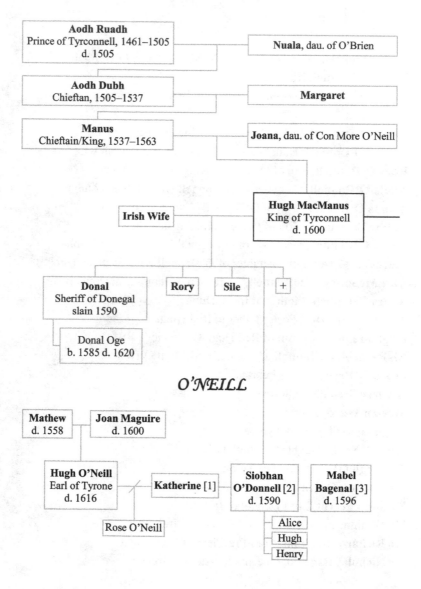

Aodh Ruadh Prince of Tyrconnell, 1461–1505 d. 1505	**Nuala**, dau. of O'Brien
Aodh Dubh Chieftan, 1505–1537	**Margaret**
Manus Chieftain/King, 1537–1563	**Joana**, dau. of Con More O'Neill

Irish Wife — **Hugh MacManus** King of Tyrconnell d. 1600

Donal Sheriff of Donegal slain 1590 — **Rory** — **Sile** — +

Donal Oge b. 1585 d. 1620

O'NEILL

Mathew d. 1558 — **Joan Maguire** d. 1600

Hugh O'Neill Earl of Tyrone d. 1616 — **Katherine** [1] — **Siobhan O'Donnell** [2] d. 1590 — **Mabel Bagenal** [3] d. 1596

Rose O'Neill

- Alice
- Hugh
- Henry

Family Trees

CAMPBELL & MACDONNELL

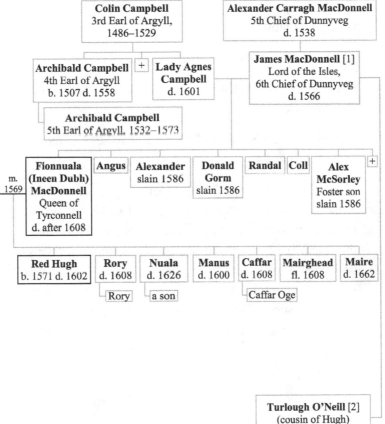

Dedication

To these special people—*all* of whom are descendants of the O'Donnell Clan.

Mary Foley Ferron and John R Foley II

Brandice Wrone, David and Aran Canes, Nicole and Bryan Jack Foley

Grandchildren Sarah and Davita Wrone, Lucas Canes, and Dylan Foley

Mary Donohue and Nellie Foley, granddaughters of Rose O'Donnell. Rose was the first O'Donnell relative to be born in the United States. It was Mary who kept the tale alive throughout her one hundred and five years of life—as well as Nellie. Rose's father, Sir Anthony Hugh O'Donnell, married Jenny Scott, a niece of Sir Winfield Scott. Thus, this American-born Rose had an Irish O'Donnell father and a Scots mother, also—just like one of the main figures in this tale, retold.

Contents

Dark Queen
of Donegal

I

Mongavlin Castle
Michaelmas 1586

In a pleasant drizzle, a noble Scots woman, her purple mantle reaching her boots, inspected a new claymore with a detail of her Redshanks when she heard a scream.

"Mother!" yelled a lad's voice, turning all their heads toward her castle's iron gate in the wall that rose above the river Foyle.

It was her son Red Hugh running to her, red hair tossing like a horse's mane, green mantle flaring, a look of great pain and grief in his eyes. A certain dread pierced her heart. Dropping the claymore, she raced to catch her son, her long black hair falling from its hood and her high cheekbones flush from the afternoon's chill.

"Mother!" He halted, catching his breath. "They are all dead!"

"Jesus, Mary, and Joseph, *who*?"

"Slain!" her son shouted. "Your brothers—their wee ones—thousands of Scots!"

She wailed, squeezing his shoulders.

"Donal Gorm and Alexander and their families—three thousand Scots."

Then she noticed the other Alex, her cousin Alexander McSorley, in his belted plaid, walking up the bawn. Tall as any MacDonnell male, his eyes in his rugged face as sky blue as her own. She felt sudden keen relief he was not the Alexander Red named.

"Ineen Dubh, dear Ineen." He greeted her by the pet name her father had given her, *Dark Daughter,* for her rich dark hair. "'Twas in Ardnarea. Near the southern border of Donegal."

"Don't tell me!" she cried out. "'Twas *Bingham* did it! Bingham and his English."

"Aye," said Alex. "'Twas Bingham. Doing the Crown's will. Bingham enforcing the English queen's efforts to a complete conquest of Ireland."

The captain of Ineen's Redshanks started to her side but at her signal desisted. There was no need to guard her so close when she was with her cousin. The bare-legged Redshanks were Scots mercenaries recruited from Inveraray and the Isles.

"I told them, I told them and told them—if you are not in Scotland or the Isles, come to this kingdom, stay in Donegal or any place in these lands!" She crossed herself, closed her eyes, dropped to her knees, royal mantle spreading on the muddy ground. She raised her arms high to the darkening clouds and keened, keened as though a chorus of banshees joined in her keening; but no tears came, her grief and despair sinking too deep for tears.

Red and Alex gripped her to raise her to her feet but she needed no help.

"Donald Gorm! Alexander!" she lamented. "Brave, glorious fools! How hard we rode together in the glens."

When she looked toward the hills beyond her castle, a mist was beginning to shroud them. The castle, Mongavlin, perched above the west bank of the Foyle, dominated three thousand acres of autumnal woods and heathery hills in northwest Ireland. A gift from her husband the O'Donnell, King of this land, when they married seventeen years earlier, and she became the Queen of Donegal. Mongavlin was a tall, narrow tower of the Irish kind, ringed by a wall; but, as a Scots noble, she had added the sharp stone cone atop the tower, Scots-fashion, to make it her own.

"Let me go after Bingham," her son urged. "'Tis raiding I've done since I was twelve."

"Red, Red, Red!" Ineen hugged Red tight, all but burying her face in the wind-whipped mess of his ruddy hair. "You have but fourteen years."

"Mother, let me get him!" her lad pleaded. "I have almost fifteen years."

"Someday you will, Red Hugh," she said. "You will rid the land of Bingham and of his minions. The prophecy of

Holy Columcille tells us so. Already, harpers strum your deeds."

"Time I am bloodied in battle," Red raised his voice. "And for your brothers! And three *thousand* Scots!"

Then his mother, holding in her grief, let burst her fury at the dead. "Your father would give them all the land they needed to plant near Donegal, his seat of power, or anywhere else in Tyrconnell lands, son. They threw it away to fight for strangers—to die! And all their women and their wee ones with them!"

"You warned them not to go near Bingham's land, my Ineen," said Alex, "and they flicked your words to the clouds." He held her face against his shoulders and the wet shag of his blond hair.

"You're all I have left," Ineen managed to say. "Yourself and my Red Hugh."

Gently but firmly, Alex eased her back on her own feet, reminding her of other sons, Rory, Manus, Caffar and her daughters Nuala and the two wee girls and the O'Donnell himself; and her brother Angus, Lord of the Isles, who had the sense to remain in Scotland.

"Aye, and not to mention my widowed mother, Agnes. Still a noble Scots Campbell. 'Tis a hard blow, too hard." Ineen bent her head and could say no more. Alex sighed, but when she looked up at him again, she asked, "You come from my O'Donnell? At Castle Donegal he is?"

"Aye. At his seat of power."

"And what is my husband doing about this slaughter?"

"He mans the gap."

"Aye, of course. He mans the gap."

"Maguire does not think Bingham will cross the river Erne into your kingdom," said Alex. He turned toward the Ulsterman coming up just behind him, whose castle was near where the Erne divided Bingham's Connaught from Tyrconnell.

"Maguire?" For the first time Ineen looked at the massive man with bushy brown hair glibbed over his eyes. He was first cousin to Red Hugh.

"'Tis a grim visit I pay you today, Ineen Dubh." Parting the glib from his eyes, the sub-chieftain of Fermanagh frowned. "I come as kinsman and friend."

"This news comes from you?" she asked sharply. "Surely, some Scots escaped to your castle?"

Maguire shook his head. "Ah, from peasants only. This news."

"You have not gone to verify it?"

"Burke's land, Ineen."

"You mean Bingham's," she said.

"Soon enough 'twill all be Bingham's," said Maguire. "Bingham's and his English."

"O, this is all the doing of that illegitimate ruler across the sea!" Ineen spun around. "She orders Scots out of Ireland and then 'twill be all Scots out of Scotland."

Alex McSorley placed a calming hand on her shoulder.

She turned to Maguire, "You heard nothing of Bingham before my brothers . . ."

"To the Burkes the Scots came, not to me," Maguire lamented.

"My brothers slaughtered, thousands of Scots, while you remained in Enniskillen?"

Maguire took a mild tone in response to her rebuke. "And how am I to stop it after it's been done?"

"Maguire did not know of your brothers' march, Ineen," said Alex. "Nor did I."

"Aye," was all she could answer.

"I know now," Maguire went on, "your brothers marched to Mayo at the invitation of the Mayo Burkes. If they had stopped at Enniskillen on the way, I'd have warned them. If my spies knew anything of it, I would have alerted you."

Holding apart his glib, he looked straight into Ineen's eyes. "I can tell you that any rebellion by anyone, anywhere, against Bingham was already put down before—before your brothers arrived. Of Ardnarea I know only the ravings of peasants."

Ineen clutched the gold cross that graced her neck as she asked for details. Maguire told her what he could. Bingham had burst out of the woods as the Scots rested for a meal by the river Moy. His men posted on the Moy's far side killed all who tried to flee across it, turning the river into blood.

"'Twas a sheep slaughter," Maguire concluded. "I doubt it lasted an hour."

Ineen clung to Alex. "So—none?" she asked Maguire.

He shook his head, stared at her, and said, "I keep Bingham out of Fermanagh; I do not spend my men trying to shove Bingham out of Connaught, where he is president by the Crown's orders. Ulster alone is most free of Saxons. Your kingdom of Tyrconnell is freest of all."

Ineen raised her voice. "How could this happen? Bingham would destroy our kingdom and then destroy all of Ulster. And you know that the Crown favors Donal O'Donnell, that son of O'Donnell's by another wife. And the English queen wants that son to succeed his aging father by primogeniture. If that occurred, it would keep Red Hugh from becoming king."

After a pause, Ineen mentioned, "Who will bring my brothers and their people for a proper burial?"

Maguire heaved an impatient sigh. "To step onto that field at Ardnarea is never to leave it!"

"And so, my brothers are left for the rooks to feed on! Rathlin Island all over again, Alex McSorley MacDonnell, again and again, only worse. Worse than six hundred of my kin massacred."

"Dear God, 'tis still a deep wound, Rathlin," said Alex. "Always with me."

Ineen grabbed her son's hand. "You are half Scot; your brothers and sisters are Scots as much as Irish. That treacherous ruler in England has Mary Queen of Scots under house arrest and now this slaughter!" She looked at Alex. They were both cousins of Mary Stuart; Ineen had served in her court at Holyrood. "Does that English queen mean to kill us all?"

"Never!" cried Red Hugh. "Never will we let them!"

"Aye!" echoed the Redshanks. Alex clapped Red's shoulder. Maguire cleared his throat. Ineen gazed at the Foyle winding its way north.

Alex moved closer to Ineen. "Give me your hand . . ."

She reached over to touch Alex, and he surprised her by dropping a medallion in her hand.

He whispered, "The MacDonnell medallion is for you to keep for Red Hugh. Thanks be to God, my father gave it to me before he began thinking of submitting to the English."

"So sad he even thinks of it." Ineen looked at the words engraved upon it: *God is our hope*. She kissed it. "Was thought to be lost when my father died."

"But my father was able to find it off the body of his brother," said Alex.

"'Tis yours, Alex," she said.

"No," he answered. "For you to give to Red Hugh when the day comes. Now put it away."

She placed it in a pocket inside her mantle, then spoke in a loud voice. "Where is that claymore?" she asked her Redshank captain.

Captain Crawford gave it to her. It was a two-handed claymore just come to her from Argyll across the water in Scotland: thick, tempered, high carbon steel with steel pommel and out-angled cross-guard. Its grip was of wood covered in fine black leather.

"You do not mean to go attack Bingham, Ineen," said Alex. "'Tis defense we must plan, not offense."

"If Bingham were here, I would go at him." *Someday,* she thought. *Someday . . .* she knew in her bones. *Until then and beyond, Tyrconnell must stay free that Red Hugh O'Donnell become king.* "I cannot bear this atrocity and do nothing."

"Let *me* go after them, Mother!" Red Hugh reached to grip the claymore's hilt. His mother moved her hand to his; and with his other hand, Red rubbed its fingertips on the glassy smooth steel of the blade. "Alex and me. We'll avenge your brothers."

With the steady strength that only a powerful arm could exert, his mother gently eased the claymore out of her son's hand. He reluctantly let go. After passing the claymore back to her captain, she took her son's head in both hands, staring into his gray eyes as though held by a spell.

Alex reminded him, "Your time is coming, right enough, Hugh Roe O'Donnell. But take heed. Your uncles, my foster brothers, did not heed anyone."

"Tyrconnell is free," Red Hugh proclaimed, "and shall stay free."

"And you, Red Hugh," his mother said, "have a prophecy to fulfill."

"The prophecy!" said the lad, his gray eyes brightening with a streak of sunlight in the clouds.

For a thousand years the prophecies of Columcille, an O'Donnell ancestor, had been recited, but from the birth of Red Hugh O'Donnell, one prophecy resonated:

"When Hugh fathers Hugh
And both Tyrconnell rule
The younger shall all Erin rule
And drive out the Gall."

The *Gall*, the stranger, the foreigner who raided and devastated the land of Ireland, yet never succeeded in exterminating the Irish themselves.

"Your hair is as red, my son," his mother mussed it, then allowed a hint of smile, "as the bright burning red comet that lit the skies the night you were born."

"The comet of a king," Alex smiled. "But before becoming king, a man must be his king's successor, his Tánaiste. Is this your intention, now, Ineen Dubh, to see your son's name brought before the *urri*s, the under-kings, and be named his father's Tánaiste?"

"Tánaiste is it already, Mother!" Red looked at them both, astonished. "What about Donal?"

Ineen stared at her son and raised her voice, "Donal is *not* the prophesized one. You are. And don't you ever forget it!"

Ineen had never kept it secret from her son or anyone else that her husband the O'Donnell had long promised to promote for the Tanistry his Scottish wife's firstborn. The complication was O'Donnell's son Donal by his deceased first wife, a fully Irish woman. Donal was moreover his father's Seneschal, in charge of financial and domestic affairs, including justice, in his father's lands. Donal was very capable and widely respected by the Crown; in fact, all but successor himself.

"Is it himself who is hinting this matter to you?" asked Alex to break the tension.

"No," she said as an afterthought. She was too discreet to say more in front of her Redshanks or Maguire. But the ailing O'Donnell was aging, and rumors carried news that he was becoming senile though he manifested no intention of stepping down.

"I'm thinking," Alex breathed, "'tis not too soon to approach *himself* about this."

Hearing this turn of the discussion, Maguire excused himself to attend to some of his men back by the gate.

Ineen took a few pensive steps to one side, Alex and Red Hugh following. "In a few days, at Michaelmas," she lowered her voice almost to a whisper, "the celebration of harvest and the feast of Michael, who thrust the evil one from paradise. At the festivities up north at Rathmullen *himself* could begin encouraging nobles to agree to Red becoming Tánaiste."

But before Ineen could say more, Maguire walked up again. He cleared his throat. "My men, milady, have had a long ride."

"Of course, Maguire," she said. "They must eat and drink."

Ineen called to her servant Annag, who poised near the castle doorway to hear what was going on. "Order oatcakes and salmon, mead and wine aplenty for all present."

As Ineen moved into the castle, a picture grew clearer for her: Red Hugh, Tánaiste, then king at last, atop the Rock of Doon in the stone footprints of the first O'Donnell *ri*, taking the white rod of kingship and vowing to defend his people. Suddenly she felt a composure the emotions of only moments ago did not let her expect.

"You must eat too, Ineen," said Alex, interrupting her thoughts. "Be assured all that can be done is being done. O'Donnell sent for Tyrone, and—"

Ineen whirled on him. "My husband sent for *Hugh O'Neill*?"

Alex looked at her, startled. "Aye."

"And *Hugh O'Neill* is on his way to Donegal?" She motioned Maguire and his men into the great hall.

"He might be there already!" Alex added.

"What is O'Donnell thinking? He might as well have sent for Bingham himself!

Hugh O'Neill is the most Saxon Irishman in this whole isle!" she nearly yelled.

Her son looked from his mother to Alex, perplexed.

Even in England it was well known that Hugh O'Neill was married to Red's half-sister Siobhan, who was Donal's sister.

"O'Neill is O'Donnell's son-in-law and dear friend," reminded Alex. And Donegal is your husband's seat of power and where he should be now."

Ineen said, "Hugh O'Neill dresses Saxon. He was raised by the English!"

"Ineen! 'Tis O'Donnell's business to call on him—a fellow Ulsterman to boot. Your husband is the king, my cousin, and you are *his* queen."

But Ineen once again called Annag. "Fetch my riding outfit!" She ordered Captain Crawford, her most valiant Redshank bodyguard, to bring up horses and torches. "We ride for Donegal!"

"I'll ride with you, Mother!" Red said with excitement.

"You stay with Alex, Red Hugh." She dropped her voice. "Your father needs you to succeed him. The prophecy must be fulfilled."

It was beginning at last, what Ineen long hoped and never neglected to prepare for. There would be battles with those supporting the false queen across the Irish Sea. That queen forbade naming of tanists, forbade inauguration of Irish kings, according to Brehon law and ancient usage. She ordered their books burned; their harpers killed. She meant to destroy and bury everything under English law. The ancient prophecy was no longer something for the time to come. It was for *now*. For the defense of the kingdom of Tyrconnell, for Ireland, it must be fulfilled soon. And her husband must do his part.

There was not a moment to lose. Red Hugh O'Donnell, named in the ancient prophecy, must be named his father's Tánaiste before it became too late to be his father's successor.

II

Donegal Castle
September 1586

*I*neen galloped south up the Foyle till the river split to the west at the tributary Finn, where she chose the north bank because its paths, muddy as they were, ran clearer and straighter than those through the thick heather on the other side. The north bank, however, along walls of oak and pine, took them closer than she liked to Castlefinn. Castlefinn remained a threat to the O'Donnell and therefore to Red Hugh, for the sons of Conn O'Donnell believed their father should have been the O'Donnell king. She pulled the hood of her black mantle tight round her head to disguise herself further and rode without banner and only a detail of her most trusted Redshank bodyguards.

"Captain Crawford, pass Castlefinn without halting for any reason," she ordered.

Eighty of Ineen's thousands of Redshanks were named Crawford, the tallest found in Inveraray, whom she had recruited by way of her cousin, the Earl of Argyll. And more than one Crawford was a captain.

The rain posed no problem and often thinned to a Scotch mist, though not for long. At Drumboe Abbey they crossed the Finn, which curled on northwest.

Then they turned due south, and thanks to cloudy light lingering beyond the mountains, they did not have to fire their torches till they reached the Gap at Bearnasmor, the main pass between the north and south. From Bearnasmor it would not take long to Donegal Castle, the O'Donnell's seat of power.

The wind kept Ineen's eyes in tears. At moments, as she remembered her brothers' boisterous laughter, tears were not from wind alone.

But the wind and rain in her face, and the sure-footed speed of her horse, helped to clear her head. Ardnarea was more than a warning of what could come, and the more she rode the more convinced she became that Alex McSorley was right. It was defense they must plan right now. Bingham and his Saxons must never be permitted to cross the river Erne. It gave her a somber smile to think of Queen Maeve, ancient queen of Connaught, riding north to battle the Ulster Red Branch. Ineen Dubh was reversing the direction of fierce old Maeve's ride.

And Alex was right that now too was the time to press O'Donnell to urge his nobles to name Red Hugh Tánaiste. Her son's youth was not a serious matter. Red Hugh as Tánaiste would involve Ineen and thousands of Redshanks that she and Alex brought in from the Isles and Inveraray. They would be more than a match for Bingham. More than once, she loosened one hand from her reins to touch, through her mantle, the MacDonnell medallion—now hers to keep for Red Hugh. The rugged noble feel of it to her fingers seemed to promise the hope she held for her prophesied lad.

"We slow to a canter," Captain Crawford said, torch in hand, as they followed the noisy little stream through the Gap.

It was a pitch-black night, with only a pale moon behind high clouds, when they rode out the other end. But it was also a short ride the rest of the way to Donegal Castle, with many a flicker in the dark from the doorways of peasant huts. Soon enough there were pinpricks of light above the trees from slit windows of O'Boyle's castle across the river Eske, until the tall square shadow of Donegal loomed where the Eske rushed into rapids. There were also random sounds in the dark, cries of night birds here and there, a dog's barks, even strains of a pipe and thudding bodhran, a voice jumping to clapping hands. So peaceful an evening to such a horrifying day.

Ineen's one immediate hope, that she could see O'Donnell before Hugh O'Neill arrived, was dashed when she found too many horses gathered outside the Donegal bawn, and in the bonfire light, a banner blew with the "Red Hand of Tyrone." She gave a horse-boy her horse and ordered the castle gillies to give Captain Crawford and his men *Uisce beatha*—whiskey, hot and plentiful.

She entered the ground floor then hurried up the spiral stairs in the castle's southwest corner to an upper floor with O'Donnell's private bedchamber where he met with important nobles. Stretching their legs before the turf flickering in the fireplace, O'Donnell and O'Neill were talking of the Scots and the English queen.

Ineen halted, hearing the voice of Hugh O'Neill: "She is more and more distressed at your Scottish connections, let alone your Spanish ones. And I don't have to tell you, you know very well, that Queen Bess wants every Scot out of Ireland."

At that Ineen stepped fully into the chamber. "Am I to get out of Ireland, Husband?"

If the two men had been startled by rapid footsteps up the stairs, they were even more startled to see who entered the room.

"Ineen Dubh, by all that's holy!" cried her husband, the elder of the two, building painfully to his bare feet, rocking in his saffron tunic, kilted up at the belt, to embrace and steer her toward the turf fire.

By the fireplace, the chamber looked like a smaller version of the great hall, with its fine oak trestle table and chairs against the walls, on which tapestries hung. Toward its far end, a grand bed with tall oak pillars supported a canopy of rich burgundy. Wardrobes for husband and wife stood against the wall and a wooden trunk at the foot of the bed.

"O'Donnell!" she answered, tearing off hood and sodden mantle, flinging it onto a silver wall sconce. Her purple riding tunic, usually roomy, clung wet against her.

"Completely unexpected," her husband started to say. "O, my dear woman, what sad, terrible loss you bear." He enveloped her in his strong arms.

She hugged him, trying with all her strength to hold back her tears.

"Thank you, my good man." Ineen plucked the tunic away from her skin as she moved from his arms into the warmth of the fire. Her hair, wreathed in loose braids for the rugged ride, now fell in a black cascade to dry.

Age had not curtailed O'Donnell's energy, when he wished to show it off. Tall and stout as a mountain ash he stood, despite the three decades he had on his thirty-one-year-old wife. His beard was immense as a sloebush and surprisingly black, though white-streaked, as was his hair, still full to the shoulders. He boasted a great glib. At the moment his hair was tied back from his eyes by an embroidered band of blue and red.

For nearly a quarter of a century he had been the King of Tyrconnell. Good king that he was, he did not let any malady force his abdication as it might have, for by tradition no king in Ireland was permitted physical infirmity, let alone lost potency.

The second noble, now also on his feet, bowed, lifting a knee in greeting in the Irish manner. "More than I can say how distressed I am," said Hugh O'Neill, "at this . . . calamity for you, Ineen Dubh."

Ineen nodded, "Do not use my pet name, Sir Hugh. 'Tis not a night for such familiarities."

O'Donnell looked at his wife with discontent. "Ineen! 'Tis no way to address your son-in-law."

"Your son-in-law, O'Donnell. I mean only to keep O'Neill's respect. How is your wife, Siobhan?"

"Ineen, Ineen," O'Donnell sighed, knowing Ineen's displeasure that O'Donnell's daughter from his first marriage married the Earl of Tyrone. "Not even such devastation can sweeten the barb in your tongue. But enough of this."

Ineen looked over at O'Neill, noting the white Saxon ruff atop the grey Saxon doublet and the trim goatee in contrast to O'Donnell's beard. Hugh O'Neill wore trunk hose puffed out like a silver-gray cow's bladder about the waist, not at all bare like O'Donnell's, gleaming in the firelight like silk. The removed boots themselves stood close to the fire. He surely appeared raised by the English. The Earl of Tyrone, entirely! O'Neill could be Saxon in speech and in deed or Irish when he wanted, but it was nothing to waste another breath on this night.

"You are soaked through and through, wife, and now so am I. Dermot!" O'Donnell called his devoted servant.

Dermot, who waited just below the turn in the staircase, appeared promptly, wearing simple tunic and trews.

O'Donnell ordered, "Send Brigid to bring fresh garments for Ineen and fire up a bath below."

Ineen rang handfuls of her damp tunic, smoothed pleats, then said, "I can wait to bathe. A cup of hot mead will be sufficient."

O'Neill and O'Donnell had been on the floor, lying on freshly strewn rushes before the fireplace, each with a pewter mug of ale, before standing up to greet Ineen. O'Donnell now took oak chairs from the walls and made a circle of three in front of the turf fire.

With a nod of thanks, taking her seat, Ineen said, "I wish to be alone with my husband, but first, Hugh O'Neill—tell me what you have been sharing with my O'Donnell."

But, as Dermot reappeared with the cup of hot mead, it was O'Donnell who answered. "I'll tell you what Tyrone has been telling me," he declared, restless on his chair and glancing with obvious preference at the rushes on the floor. "He sent to Dublin for permission to find and retrieve your brothers' bodies for you and for the sake of Ulster's peace. Then they can be given a burial—somewhere among Scots. That he has been telling me."

Cup arrested before her lips, Ineen looked at O'Neill, who sat up straight on his chair, holding his cup with both hands. "Catholic burial," she managed to say.

"Catholic indeed," said O'Neill. "They are Catholics."

"But you . . ." Ineen did not finish what she was about to say. She was touched. She recovered: "If their bodies—

any of their bodies of their women and children—are returned to Ulster for burial, I shall be grateful."

"'Tis grateful you should be, woman, that O'Neill is even trying to do that," said her husband, taking a good swallow of ale.

"Grateful I am, Hugh O'Neill."

"I do not pretend it will be easy to accomplish," said O'Neill. "I have reason to believe the Lord Deputy, Sir John Perrot, will be amenable. But he and Bingham hate each other." For the moment it took Ineen to respond to this, O'Neill added, "Perrot does not favor Bingham's savagery, and there's a strong rumor he's trying to have Bingham removed from Ireland."

To this strange news, all Ineen could think to say was, "But that horrific Ruler across the sea favors Bingham and what he does to us!"

O'Neill considered: "Both Bingham and Perrot have had her favor."

"You mean she favors the one who kills my people and the other who stands by to watch."

"Your tongue, Ineen." O'Donnell caught himself. "'Tis your grief speaking."

"Perrot is not our friend," Ineen countered. "Look what happened, Husband, when you trusted him and let two hundred of his soldiers come into *our* lands. Women ravished, fields ruined, villages torched, and almost nothing done to punish them!"

"We sent them out of the kingdom," O'Donnell answered. "And MacSweeney Doe, a great sub-chieftain, punished them."

"Perrot nearly sent in hundreds more troops," O'Neill added. "He was persuaded not to."

"You persuaded him," O'Donnell held up his cup to O'Neill.

Ineen held up hers. "For that I am thankful to you, Sir Hugh."

"Sir John will listen to reason," O'Neill said, with the fingers of his free hand making the universal sign for accepting consideration. "He keeps his word."

Ineen stood up, placed her cup on the trestle table near her chair, and moved to one side of the slit window where the tapestry hung. A gift from King Philip of Spain, Red Hugh's godfather, for the baptism. Woven in Madrid in fine intricate threads, it depicted a holy man, kneeling among silver rocks, cloaked in red and gold, with white birds caught in flight along wool borders of forest green and sky blue. Glimmers from the turf and flickering tall, floor candlesticks allowed only intermittent glimpses of the magnificent needlework.

Ineen raised her voice, "Bingham would burn this cherished tapestry if ever he crossed the river Erne and attacked Donegal Castle."

The O'Donnell cautioned his wife. "There is further news. Tell her about the letters, O'Neill."

"What letters?" Ineen asked, turning away from the tapestry.

"Your letters, my dear," O'Donnell said.

"My letters!" Ineen stifled a gasp. She looked at O'Donnell, then at O'Neill.

"The news of Ardnarea in Dublin," said O'Neill, "also claimed letters from you were found among your brothers' effects." He paused. "Including letters inviting them to come to Ireland."

"My brothers were coming anyway." She advanced on O'Neill, as though to pounce. "I told them to settle here. How often I pleaded with them to do so, even to come here to Donegal, the strongest place in our kingdom."

"What you said in the letters matters not to Dublin or the Crown, only the fact that they found letters from you on your Scots kin."

"How else can we defend Donegal and the rest of our lands from Perrot's men and the likes of Bingham?" Ineen turned and paced.

"Donegal or elsewhere, you keep bringing in Scots. That's what Dublin, and the Crown, care about." O'Neill's tone was warning.

"'Tis sure I am, my Ineen," said O'Donnell, "you know our own men can put up a very strong defense."

"Scots or no Scots," said O'Neill, "all of Ulster, both Tyrconnell and Tyrone, may not be able to hold off the Crown."

"Scots help." Ineen Dubh asserted.

"In truth, at this time, Scots do not help," O'Neill cautioned. "If they continue to come in and fight local rebellions against the Crown, it will only aggravate the situation. Do you think the English queen forgets that your father spoke ill of her and supported your kinswoman, Mary Queen of Scots? Or that you served in the Stuart Court?"

"Well she remembers," Ineen responded, arching her back, proud of her time at the Stuart Court. "And I am a queen, too."

"If Scots keep coming in, I can tell you what the Crown will do!"

Ineen jabbed her finger at O'Neill. "Well you know what Saxons can do. Because you, you yourself, did it in Munster. With Sydney, who ordered the massacre on Rathlin."

"Ineen!" cried O'Donnell.

"Sydney," said O'Neill, "did not order that massacre, Essex did. But, yes, Munster is precisely my point. And Rathlin, and now Ardnarea. We must never forget, *but* we must recognize how these came about."

"My aunts, uncles, and cousins were hacked and burned and drowned at Rathlin!" Ineen clutched at her gold crucifix, glaring at him. "And my brothers and their families hacked and drowned at Ardnarea."

"And that is what must not happen in Ulster," O'Neill answered.

"The reason entirely why I have ridden here," Ineen said.

"And entirely why I have," O'Neill went on. "Mind you, I take no pleasure or pride in the memory of Munster, when I was young, and foster son to Sydney. All the forests gone. No fields. No villagers. East to west, nothing but ashes. Children with green mouths from eating shamrocks and they died all the same."

"I will not have these free lands reduced to ashes," said Ineen.

"Dear Lady, nor will I! And more than Scots alarm the Crown. Spain, too, and your son Red Hugh's godfather, King Philip."

"A mighty king," said O'Donnell, raising his cup.

Ineen gazed again at Philip's tapestry as it glistened in the dark.

For decades, Tyrconnell and Spain had traded fish for wine, a commerce so warm and prosperous the king of Spain agreed to have a proxy stand for him at the young O'Donnell's baptism.

O'Neill continued, "The Crown fears Spain will come to Mary Stuart's aid, and perhaps France and the Pope as well—and use Ireland as a base to attack England, depose Elizabeth, and put Mary in her place."

"Mary *is* the rightful Queen of England," Ineen affirmed.

Ineen watched O'Neill's expression. He returned her stare but chose not to bite the bait.

Ineen sniffed and drank from her cup. "So, *do nothing*, you tell us. For myself I cannot do nothing."

26

Suddenly suffering the weight of the day and the ride from Mongavlin, she felt all but suffocated. Putting the cup aside, she dropped into the sturdy oak chair, clutched the crucifix again, and pulled at her hair.

"My concern is Ulster," said O'Neill, "not Mary Queen of Scots. Ulster remains the last free province of Ireland. Your lands and Tyrone must remain free, and the part I play with the English helps keep it that way."

"So, we must give the Crown assurances, is that the way of it?" O'Donnell asked.

"You once promised Dublin your son Rory as pledge," said O'Neill.

"Never!" said Ineen, glaring at her husband.

"Nor do I advise it," said O'Neill.

"A pledge is worth ten thousand men at arms," said O'Donnell, "but I did not, and I will not, send Rory."

"Or any other son," declared Ineen.

"One way to keep Bingham and the English out of Tyrconnell," said O'Neill, "is no more Scots."

"I rode here to do something about Bingham," Ineen countered. "At the very least to put more men on the river Erne, from Ballyshannon and the bay all the way to the Lough Erne."

"Put your Redshanks on the river Erne," O'Neill replied, "and Bingham *will* invade."

"Scots, we could hold in reserve," Ineen said, thinking quickly, then looked at her husband. "We will have the MacSweeneys send men."

"Donal shall post his men," said O'Donnell. "He is my Seneschal. And the Crown respects him."

This took Ineen by surprise; she had no mind at all to promote her stepson Donal's interests. Yet, there flitted past her eyes a thought—that any Donal men lost to Bingham on the Erne meant fewer Donal men at all. There it was.

"There shall be no invading of Connaught," O'Donnell declared, pounding his mug on the trestle table.

Looking at Ineen, O'Neill replied, "The Crown does have a favorable view of Donal. To the Crown, Donal is the eldest living son of O'Donnell, and if your husband is to have a successor, Donal they will support. That should stop Bingham from crossing into Tyrconnell, at least for now."

Ineen said after some thought, "Put Donal's men along the Erne. We are all in agreement."

O'Neill felt relief that his diplomacy did not fail. "*Sláinte*," he toasted and raised his cup.

O'Donnell echoed him, raising his own.

Ineen raised hers. But she said, "May we be alone, husband?"

O'Neill took a deep breath and excused himself. "A long two days I have ridden here from Dublin, with only a brief night's rest."

O'Donnell said Dermot would see O'Neill to a bedchamber. "And at first light we shall hunt for deer. I will send Donal his orders this very night."

But O'Neill declined, saying he must ride home to Dungannon in the morning. His last words to Ineen: "Again, I express my own sorrow for your great loss."

Ineen caught her tongue, seeing O'Donnell's stare. She answered, "*Codladh.*" *Sleep well.*

O'Neill gone, Ineen said to her husband, "We must discuss an urgent matter."

"What urgent matter is this, then? More urgent than my sending a messenger to Glencolumbcille so that Donal readies his men?"

"That you must do and send even more than one messenger, given what has happened," Ineen demanded. "I shall wait here for you!"

When the O'Donnell came back, he moved close to his wife, who straightened her back, looked up into his gray-green eyes, and grasped one bed curtain to open it. She also took his hand and held it. It felt warm as she long remembered it and said, "First, I thank you for sending Alex McSorley, and our Red Hugh, to inform me of what happened at Ardnarea."

"'Twas not my wish to burden our son with Maguire's message, but you know Red Hugh. He would not let a moment go before he rode off to tell you."

"'Tis of our son I speak."

"Yes?" O'Donnell replied and frowned.

"I ask you to fulfill your solemn promise and summon the *ur-ris* to urge them name our Red Hugh your Tánaiste."

O'Donnell stared at her. He did not pull his hand, but she felt his forty-six years of strength in it.

"I shall urge the naming of my Tánaiste when the time is proper," he said.

"I did not think to ask it now, but when Alex mentioned . . ."

"Alex McSorley!" O'Donnell raised his voice, pulled his hand from hers, and scowled.

Ineen met his look with steady, searching eyes and knew better than to try to take his hand again for the moment. "The time is now, my husband. Consider what just happened across our southern border."

"Is that what Alex McSorley said?"

"What I say—when I hear what English have once again done to my kin and more so."

O'Donnell said nothing immediately. "Terrible this slaughter. But may I ask, what about it makes this the proper time to gather nobles and urge them to name a half-Scot at that?"

"A half-Scot!" Ineen was even more shocked than offended.

"I promised," he raised a hand to quiet her retort, "to do all for Red Hugh when the time is proper. Alex McSorley does not decide that. I do. The time shall be proper when I say it is."

"What do you mean, half-Scot!" Ineen said. "That is not something you have brought up to me ever. And on this night of all nights?"

"You heard O'Neill. Red is half-Scot, you are a Scot, and I love the both of you more than my own heart. You yourself say we must keep our Scots in reserve. Naming a half-Scot lad at this time is not keeping Scots in reserve."

Ineen took a deep breath, and, letting it go, held her tongue a moment. "I heard O'Neill. The Saxons are not about to invade unless provoked. Naming Red might annoy the Crown, but it will not provoke them."

"Oh, it won't, my dear! They not only tell us not to bring in Scots, they tell us not to name Tánaistes or indeed not inaugurate O'Donnells or, for the love of God, keep harpers. At what point will they not be provoked?"

"I'm thinking of the men of this kingdom." Ineen spoke in a measured voice. "If you mean to keep the peace . . . the sub-chieftains respect Red Hugh. They know the prophecy."

"Keep the peace! That the O'Donnell does, first, last, and always! I have kept the peace in our kingdom these twenty years since Farsetmore, and no other *ri* in all of Ireland can make that boast," O'Donnell responded.

"And now 'tis less easy than before," Ineen said, realizing she must employ other tactics. She walked over to her wardrobe, selected a fine linen night shift, and removed her dried riding clothes. Then she began to pull the shift over her head, catching her husband's eye.

"Even in the worst of times, you are a beautiful woman of thirty years, Wife," he whispered.

Outside rain fell, drubbing the limestone, snuffing the little light slipping through the slit window from bonfires and torches below. Light in the chamber was failing from the candle melting on the table and the dwindling flame in the turf.

Ineen sighed.

"A fine son, our Red Hugh, no doubt of that," O'Donnell said.

"Only *he* shall be your named successor," Ineen pleaded. "Not Donal."

"And what of my Donal?"

"You promised 'twould be Red."

"Aye, aye! But my Donal is a man of Ireland, my Seneschal, my oldest living son. He keeps the cattle whole, keeps the *ur-ris* in line, your very thought—he shall keep the Erne secure. And Dublin, so 'tis said, regards him well, not least because his mother, God rest her, was Irish. And not raised in a Scottish court. He will keep Saxons out. He will help keep the peace for now."

"Hugh—" she began, but caught herself. She kept her tongue quiet, yet clear: "Donal does not command the Scots."

"Nay, you do!"

"And for near twenty years you have welcomed them most generously, Husband."

"Ineen, you know the clan wars that break out when a king dies, or even when a Tánaiste is agreed upon and named."

She listened.

"A clan war," O'Donnell went on, "is the very thing the Saxons will intrude upon. Peace we keep and peace we shall keep."

The Scots keep the peace, she so wished to correct him. With one hand she tugged the bed curtain half open. She lowered her head. "Ardnarea," she began.

"Ardnarea," O'Donnell breathed, and grabbed the bed curtain, opened it further, then restlessly moved back and forth.

Ineen looked up at him, held her hand against his chest, then moved it to his wrinkled face. In a voice sunk to a whisper, she said, "Hugh McManus O'Donnell, you must call the nobles and urge naming our son, before any more time is lost."

"Ineen Dubh, you have had my promise these fourteen years. O'Donnell keeps his promises. Leave me the time to gather nobles. I shall urge naming Red Hugh O'Donnell when the time is proper, and not before."

"Thank you, my love." She kissed his firm lips, a kiss he returned.

"Come," said he, taking her hand. "Let me comfort you. And God have mercy on us."

III

Inch Isle
December 1586

*A*lex McSorley, Ineen's cherished foster brother, always plotted for the unexpected when he brought Redshanks from Scotland and the Isles into Tyrconnell to add to the thousands Ineen brought over the years from Inveraray.

More Redshanks built up Ineen's forces supporting Red Hugh's claim to become his father's successor. This time Alex was bringing four hundred Redshanks in thirty boats, including six horses, pack donkeys, and a few oxen and oxcarts to haul additional crates of claymores, halberds, and a few muskets. Ordinarily Redshanks agreed to only three months' service in Ulster—the summer months—but as Saxon forces pressed deeper into Ireland, nearing Tyrconnell, Ineen Dubh insisted on hiring winter replacements, for higher pay, with inducements of farmland.

A number were becoming permanent, planting themselves in Ireland.

And *fubun,* forget Hugh O'Neill's warnings. Ineen would be pleased! So, when the rough, sunny seas began to darken and run high as a squall roiled into a storm over the preferred landing beach on the Inishowen shore at Kinnigoe Bay in Ireland, Alex promptly turned the boats south toward the secondary beaches. Even the strange clarity of the light south of black rain was no more ominous than on any earlier crossing. Suddenly, winds reversed and, instead of blowing them southwest, seemed to suck them due south toward Lough Foyle. It took a greater effort than usual to keep pointing the boats toward landfall on Inishowen above the mouth of the Foyle. There was always something different about each crossing. But they made it, this time with the loss of only one yoke of oxen and two donkeys, thrown overboard to keep their boats from capsizing.

"The weapons are saved!" cried Alex McSorley with a laugh to the cheers of his men. He jumped from boat to beach, his blue and green tartan catching the wind. He preferred to land in Kinnigoe Bay, northwest of the cape stretching above the western side of the Lough, for there were beaches on the east and south sides of the cape, which were easier to see from spyglasses. But here they were below the cape, and directly across from the O'Neill—not Hugh O'Neill, but his contentious cousin, the reigning O'Neill of Tyrone himself, Turlough Luney. Turlough Luney was so wary of the O'Donnell that he enlisted English troops to augment his own. So, these few hours were precious for Alex to move troops quickly far down Inishowen into mainland Tyrconnell before Turlough Luney ventured troops into O'Donnell country to cut them off.

The two hundred Redshanks committed to Ineen, and led by yet another Captain Crawford, went straight south toward Derry and Mongavlin with a letter from Ineen's surviving brother Angus, Lord of the Isles. The other two hundred were slated for the three MacSweeneys to the west and to O'Donnell himself at Donegal to the southwest. Alex McSorley's intention was to take them west to Lough Swilly then south and up to MacSweeney Fanad at Rathmullen as fast as they could travel. But travel was questionable this night, in intermittent snow squalls. Although two hundred were able to march swiftly to Lough Swilly and a ways down beside it, Alex insisted, "Halt here in this snow-crusted field! We will build campfires for the men and bed the officers in peasant huts."

It was there that Merriman, an English captain and newly appointed Crown Sheriff, led a detail of Saxon and Turlough Luney's troops and found Alex early next morning. Merriman was accompanied by Hugh McDean O'Gallagher, leader of the Castlefinn O'Donnells, who were still determined the next O'Donnell king be one of their own.

It was later said that Merriman had only one hundred and sixty soldiers, mostly Turlough Luney *kerne* armed with pikes and lances, but some Saxon regulars, too, helmeted and clothed in mail like the captain himself. They would have been outnumbered by two hundred Redshanks left. Merriman recognized this and took precautions.

At first light, Captain Merriman moved in, quietly seizing the Scots' oxcarts and crates of weapons. Then he dispersed a few of his men, armed with swords and pikes, among the low-burning campfires of the sleeping Redshanks and the huts sheltering officers. For brief minutes they removed weapons lying about the sleepers, though not any swords attached to the Redshanks.

Then with a broadsword banging on the wood of a cart, Captain Merriman and his men roused the Redshanks, crying out, "Gold will be yours! Gold for all! If ye follow instructions!"

Redshanks jumped groggily to knees then feet, grabbing for weapons that were not there. Snow again began to fall on noses.

"Listen well!" Merriman called in the flame-light of one campfire where he swung bags, "Three gold pieces to every man who goes back to Scotland today!"

He repeated and repeated this. Every Scot was to march back immediately, and upon arriving at the boats under Merriman's escort would, for the "inconvenience," be recompensed with three gold pieces each. Setting down one bag at his feet, he reached into the other, held up his fist, and shook jingling coins for all nearby to hear.

Cries went up all over, confused and hostile, to the answering shouts of Merriman's men, "Gold! Gold!"

At this point Alex McSorley broke out of the hut where he and others had been sleeping, swatting Saxon guards aside. Nobody attacked him, and it was later said this restraint was an element of Merriman's strategy. He was able to maintain the advantage of his outnumbered position, thanks to surprise and promises of gold, and to avoid swift losses to his own men by instructing them to back off if struck at, but not far.

"Hold the line until I signal to give combat," Merriman said.

Alex quickly appreciated the situation. "Who are ye?"

"Soldiers of Her Majesty, the Queen of England and Ireland," came Captain Merriman's reply, a kerne holding a torch by his bearded face. Merriman pushed the torch aside and stood in front of the campfire, eyes and beard in half-shadow.

"Captain Merriman, is it?"

"Aye, Alex McSorley MacDonnell, we are merry old friends."

"You have killed more MacDonnells than you have married, old man."

"Ho, true enough, young Scot!"

"'True we are noble Scots," Alex responded.

Merriman held up one of his bags. "And to the Isles you shall return—with gold and Her Majesty's compliments."

"Nay," said Alex, raising his voice to stentorian pitch for the ears of all the Redshanks in the field. "Your queen is not *our* queen. Here, in free Tyrconnell, we shall find wealth far beyond mere pieces of gold."

"Without weapons you shall find nothing at all."

"Armed we are," Alex shouted.

"No match for our broadswords and pikes or for your claymores and halberds, which now are ours, too," the Crown Sheriff said.

Two helmeted Saxons, in the light of the torches, lifted two two-handed Scottish claymores in mock salute, laughing.

"Note well," chuckled Merriman, "you could have been slain in your beds, with your own weapons. But that was unnecessary. Now, however," turning to the Scots crowding in from the field, Merriman raised his voice, "Scotland and gold—or your blood on the snow!"

Alex McSorley might well have noted that Captain Merriman talked a wee too much for a man who thought he had an easy upper hand.

"I propose," said Alex, "to spare you your gold, and us our blood," raising his voice again, "by single combat! You vanquish me, and we all go back—free and unmolested—and you keep your gold. But I vanquish you, and you all go back—across the Foyle, with your gold—and with your lives. You too, Hugh McDean! How dare you be riding with the English? Go back to Castlefinn where you belong, or you'll be deemed a traitor in Tyrconnell!"

Merriman, still standing backlit in front of the campfire, took a moment. "Very well. This may be a quite satisfactory resolution. But an Englishman fights in breastplate and helmet."

"My Scot's tartan is armor enough." Alex moved to a wide space, limbering wrist and arm with practice swats and thrusts. Then, not Merriman, but one of the tall Saxons stepped forward, gripping a great sword, point down, as though it were a giant six-foot dagger.

"I challenged *you*!" Alex pointed a broadsword not confiscated at Captain Merriman, who remained in front of the campfire, one eye and beard flickering in the torchlight.

"You challenged the Crown. So, you fight the Crown's champion," said Merriman.

The Saxon tipped up the massive sword in laughing salute, then charged and swung. Alex skipped aside, the great sword slamming so hard that his own sword broke, but not before checking his opponent's swing so that the sword landed against Alex's ribs instead of his neck. He fell, but the Saxon stumbled. Alex pulled a long dirk from its holster above his wounded ribs, then drove it home into the Saxon's groin and rolled aside as the man fell. The dirks could not be taken in the night, being worn in a holster on the bodies of the Scots.

"Claymore!" shouted Captain Merriman to another tall Saxon, but before he could take it to finish off MacDonnell, Alex was seized by two of his men from the peasant hut.

They dragged him in a rush out of the firelight into the last of the night's darkness.

Merriman cried, "Soldiers, pursue them!"

Because the field of campfires round which the Redshanks had bedded for the night was on the slope of a long, wide hill rising gently to a ridgeline, it commanded in moonlight and daylight a fine view of Lough Swilly in the near distance, even to Rathmullen on the far shore. Just off the near shore lay a large hilly land called simply, in Tyrconnell Irish, *Inch,* or "Isle."

Captain Merriman might have been distracted by the easy success of his gambit in capturing the crates of claymores and halberds. It is unlikely, though, after years of campaigning against Scots, stealing their cattle for the Crown, that he actually forgot that one of the most prized weapons of a Scot was the long, often serrated dirk kept in a holster up the sleeve and under the arm. Maybe he assumed the tactical surprise in slipping pikemen about each campfire would minimize the effectiveness of any smaller weapons his force would not be able to confiscate. A calculated risk, perhaps. He had placed mailed Saxons as guards at the peasant huts, such as the one Alex McSorley and his lieutenants had bedded in. Maybe it was the clever stroke to offer gold rather than to start slaughtering Redshanks outright that beguiled him. With the ruse of accepting the challenge, then substituting another for himself, Captain Merriman perhaps did momentarily forget about the many odd dirks.

When Alex McSorley, fallen wounded, pulled his own dirk to stab his assailant, his lieutenants pulled their dirks and threw aside their guards, who were momentarily entranced by the spectacle of single combat.

Merriman left kerne, not even mailed Saxons, in charge of the Saxon horses. Of these Alex's lieutenants made short work. They slapped the horse they lifted Alex onto, which galloped off downhill. A savage sky began to lighten, but horse and Alex were able to disappear against tree lines, although the sound of hoof beats did not.

"I'll go for Alex!" shouted Hugh McDean to Merriman, and ordering his men to their horses, took off. But on the field of the campfires Redshanks now pulled dirks or raised what broadswords had not been collected. At first Merriman shouted orders to slaughter as many Redshanks as his men could lay hands on, and the few minutes given up to the battle gave Alex McSorley enough time to put distance behind him as he galloped for the shore. It could not have been an easy ride and must have taken all his strength and heart not to fall from the horse. He must have realized, too, that his right leg was cut as well as his left side.

There was no bridge or causeway from mainland to Inch, only boats; and although one boat was later found not far from where Alex dropped off his horse, either he did not see it in the reeds, or he did not think he could reach it and push off in time. Sliding off the horse, he rolled across the little icy mudflat into the water not fully frozen and used his arms to haul himself the short distance until he reached the reeds of Inch. Two peasants fishing nearby heard the splashes as well as the cries from the battle, and ran over to pull him onto the shore.

"Bury me!" Through chattering teeth Alex tried to say as his fingers dug at the frozen mud. The men soon understood. "Cut a reed!" he then managed, and "keeners, keeners." One Islander told the other to bring more people, blankets, and spades.

Once, as a lad, to frighten his cousin Ineen and her brother Donny Gorm, Alex had the other Alex, Alex Carrach, bury him in a shallow grave, under loose dirt, with a hollow reed to breathe through. The other Alex then fell to his knees and keened loudly. When Ineen ran up, Alex McSorley, hearing muffled voices raised, stuck his hand out of the dirt and Ineen and Donny Gorm screamed for all the glens in Scotland to hear.

Up the hill Captain Merriman now took a dozen Saxons from the battle and, with a couple of unlit torches, rode to join Hugh McDean below. The terrain made them descend dales and ride slowly through woods into clearings and up rises. When they reached the shore, they found Hugh McDean hacking bushes, looking for any boat he might find; his men held the reins of a riderless horse.

"Look," Merriman pointed. On the island across the way, tiny figures were running around.

At last, the boat Alex McSorley did not use was found. With several bodyguards, Merriman and McDean pushed out in it, torches lit, and, after stepping into the mudflats of Inch, sent the boat back for more men.

Merriman's and McDean's ears heard the keening before their swords hacked a path through a long high thicket of dwarf tree and near frozen shrub.

"There," McDean pointed.

In the graying air they saw dark figures in excited activity low to the ground which, as they came upon it, were women kneeling and keening over a patch of earth. More women waddled up, and a number of men moved around, heads lowered. The patch of earth was a mound of soil strewn with rushes.

"What grave be this?" Merriman demanded.

"'Tis a dead man. God have mercy on him."

"Died in the rushes," said another man.

"God have mercy," said the captain. "Her Majesty cannot."

Unsheathing his broadsword, with both hands Captain Merriman plunged it deep into the grave, pushing and twisting, to a sharp muffled sound from under it. The kneeling women shrieked and leaped to their feet. The other Saxons jumped in and pulled them away, beating them with their swords. The nearby men, running to the women's aid, grabbed the Saxons, who slashed at them, and two or three fell wounded.

"Halt!" cried Captain Merriman, withdrawing slowly his sword, whose muddy blade dripped red in the flickering torchlight, with the fresh blood darkening the fresh snow. The Saxons halted. The women broke away from them and fell upon the grave, keening wildly. The peasant men, tending their wounded, backed off.

Quickly, the grave was dug up but the body left where it was found. With both hands Merriman chopped and sliced at it. Then he bent over and, by Alex's matted hair, swung the bleeding head wide of his own body. "Bring me a bag of some sort."

Hugh McDean, eager to respond, given the demise of Ineen's cousin, tore a short mantle off one of the women, whose scream got her thrust aside by a soldier.

Merriman handed him the head and Hugh McDean raised it high. "Look you on the head of Alex McSorley, cousin to that troublesome Scotswoman, the Dark Daughter. Troublemakers be damned!" He covered the head with the mantle and, whipping round the head-heavy mantle like a sling, slung it over his shoulder.

"Mind you, Inchmen," added the English captain, "Her Majesty has forbidden Scots to set foot in Ireland." He raised his sword. "This time you yourselves are spared! Ha!"

With that the captain and his men ferried themselves back to the mainland of Inishowen. They left the Islanders to rebury headless Alex and raise their keening as high as they liked.

Hugh McDean kept hold of the shrouded head as though it were treasure indeed, knowing it would be presented to Lord Deputy Perrot at Dublin Castle where, after being plunged in a bucket of hot tar, it would be spiked upon the castle gate.

"When they spike this head on the gate of Dublin Castle," he laughed to Merriman, "A blade they shall twist in the heart of that Scottish one, Ineen Dubh, that Dark Daughter."

IV

Whitehall
London, Winter 1586

As fierce waves washed across the Irish Sea to England, the English queen with golden crown topping her imperial head awaited her Irish envoy. Dressed in a golden gown adorned with jewels, she moved arms embellished with puffed sleeves of pure white that went well with her red hair. She intended to be most attractive to her Henry Sayer when he arrived at Whitehall, so she appraised herself in a gilded mirror. The reflected figure pleased her despite Elizabeth's fifty-three years. For twenty-eight of them she had been the English queen.

Her vanity was a source of amusement among her courtiers.

"Your Majesty," Alice, a lady-in-waiting, looked for an opportunity to gain favor. Alice was herself carefully dressed in creamy satin, in a gown meant not to outshine her

Queen. "Your coloring, your brow, your expressions . . . you of all your father's children most resemble him."

Elizabeth saw no irony in the lady's flattery; she chose to hear only what she wanted. Yes, she must be her father's child, despite cruel aspersions to the contrary. Else why would she of all Henry VIII's children be a living reminder of him with her fair face and red hair? And her father knew that, for he reinstated her right to the throne when she was but ten years old. Still, the London whispers surfaced periodically, salting again those wounds buried deep within her. No, she was not a "Little Whore" any more than her mother, Anne Boleyn, had been the "Great Whore." Nor a witch. Her mother's sixth finger was barely noticeable and meant nothing. It was but superstition concocted by Papists.

Buoying herself with the thought, Elizabeth swept across the room to take her seat upon the raised dais from which she gave audiences. Her mood hardened at a memory of her half-sister, Mary Tudor, sitting in the same chair as the queen. Elizabeth remembered with bitterness that just because Mary's mother, Katherine of Aragon, had been her father's first queen, it did not make Mary more legitimate than a daughter of his second queen, Anne Boleyn.

Elizabeth brooded. Those who still honored Mary Tudor now looked to Mary Stuart, Elizabeth's own cousin, as lawful heir to the throne of England—such treason she must always guard against. The Catholic, Mary Stuart of Scotland, a mere granddaughter of her father's sister Margaret, lusted for Elizabeth's crown—as she lusted after every creature with a codpiece—when, after all, Elizabeth was Henry's rightful heir.

But suddenly an announcement went out, "Sir Henry Sayer, Envoy to Ireland."

Courtiers stepped to the sides, forming an aisle between them. Henry Sayer dashed down that aisle, parchment in hand.

"My Queen," he beamed, bowing when he reached Elizabeth, "it seems you grow more beautiful each time I see you."

"My Badger!" She flirted openly with her envoy.

Tall and courtly, Henry Sayer returned her gargoyle gaze with one poised to convey both respect and affection. The queen was attracted to Sayer. With his height, golden hair, and light, confident manner, he was, in fact, irresistible to women. This day he had donned a black velvet doublet glittering with gold buttons. His long hose complemented shoes with golden buckles. He was not one to take his sovereign's favors for granted. He had attained his office owing to the patronage of one of Elizabeth's favored earls. Henry Sayer's present privileged access to her and his acquisition of that signal mark of favor, a pet name, he won by himself. He balanced an adroit management of discerning flattery and advice based on studious political acumen. He assured the monarch that he was *of value* to her, surrounded as she was by mere sycophants.

"O, my Badger! My astrologer warned that some sort of occurrence bodes not well for England. An evil omen.

Assure me that it has nothing to do with Ireland—that dark and savage island?" Elizabeth's voice rose coquettishly.

Henry was not inclined to act on omens or superstitions or even prophecies, yet he knew Elizabeth was deadly serious despite all her claims to being Protestant, though she came to the throne a Catholic.

He coughed, vying for time, what with the mustiness of the Privy Council. Elizabeth's trinkets, especially the exquisite yet dusty rug that had come from far-off Turkey, provided an excuse to cough, long and deep. He grasped at a proper reply. "As to that, Your Majesty, I beg to plead my ignorance of astrological signs, not to mention what they portend."

Elizabeth rose from her dais. "Listen! Rumors abound about that son of the Scotswoman, Red Hugh O'Donnell. It is said that he is an impetuous sort, full of believing some prophecy attributed to him—one that Scots mother of his promotes. And his father, O'Donnell, still has not given our cattle rent since he married that Scots wife. And there may be an attempt to have Irish nobles gather and proclaim Red Hugh Tánaiste against our expressed outlawing of that institution."

"My Queen, this Red Hugh has all the impetuousness for which he is known. Hugh O'Donnell has not given any trouble for many years."

"And the Crown, after all, only goes after what is rightfully ours. Still no cattle rent from the O'Donnell since he married that Scotswoman. It is she who threatens any accommodation with The Earl of Tyrconnell," Elizabeth raged.

"O, Your Majesty, you are right. But O'Donnell promised to pay his cattle rent." Henry did not add that he would likely never pay it.

"But that ancient prophecy—swirling all about—and in that vile land that is part of *my* kingdom: *Hugh born of Hugh shall be a King in Ireland and banish conquerors.* What do you say to that?" Elizabeth raised her voice.

"I know of the prophecy of which Irish bards sing— *When Hugh is fathered by Hugh* . . . They've been singing that for centuries. But let me . . ."

He changed the subject. "I bring victorious news. The Scot, Alexander McSorley, cousin of Ineen Dubh, the mother of the Hugh of prophecy, was slain on Inch Island."

"Tell me more, Badger. A noble Scot slain is welcome news." Her Majesty sat down.

"As told by those who witnessed the event—Saxon and those Irish favoring you—Your Majesty, this Alexander was bringing Redshanks in from Scotland against your expressed command. He immediately sent many to his cousin, the Scotswoman, at Mongavlin before our Captain Merriman entrapped him. The Scot Alexander proposed to fight a duel. If he prevailed, the Scot would proceed with the rest of his mercenaries to Donegal. Severely wounded in the duel, he nonetheless swam to Inch Isle and hid in a false grave. A claymore penetrated that grave, piercing the body, killing Alexander."

"Would that all my captains could succeed as Merriman."

"And, Dear Majesty, the leader of the Castlefinn O'Donnells, Hugh McDean, took part in this. He came with Turlough O'Neill's Irish and Captain Merriman, our own Crown Sheriff. I can further report that Alex's Scot's head is spiked on Dublin Castle, black as any rebel."

Elizabeth reached her arms toward Henry Sayer. With a wide smile, she patted Henry. "Well done. Ridding Ulster of Scots is the only way to reduce it to obedience. The head of such an infamous rebel, especially that Scotswoman's cousin, pleases me. Yet that vile woman still has a brother alive, Lord of the Isles."

"Take little notice. The Lord of the Isles' problems are in Scotland." He proffered his parchment.

She took it and glanced over it. "Captain Merriman must be congratulated on the demise of Alex McSorley. This satisfies me." Her Majesty smiled. "Tell Dublin to keep their eyes on this Hugh McDean. He may be of more use to us." She set aside the parchment.

"Yes—and recall that Alexander McSorley is cousin of Ineen Dubh by way of his father being Sorley Boy MacDonnell, who has submitted to you."

"This adds to my satisfaction," she replied.

Henry nodded. "Alex's slaying along with Bingham's annihilation of Scots at Ardnarea, including two of Ineen's brothers, is proof of the success of your policies."

Queen Bess took a moment to enjoy this information before standing up again and addressing Sayer, "But the Scot that stirs up the most trouble in Ireland—she is still there—that Scotswoman, that wife of the O'Donnell who calls herself a queen and mother of that son of prophecy. That vile Scotswoman was raised in the Stuart Court."

"This is true."

"More results, my Badger. I want more results. Therein depends Ireland's reformation. I want the Scotswoman stopped. Her prophesized half-bred son contained."

Elizabeth went on and on about the Scots. After she put her cousin, Mary Queen of Scots, under house arrest, the Scots became the lodestone of her every thought. Courtiers all knew her harangues by heart.

She added the Spanish. "The King of Spain, that Papist Philip's mastery of the high seas allows him to collect friends—and godchildren—as well as treasure the world over and one is the Scotswoman's son. Accursed idolaters! They all bow east to Rome, to a Pope who has the temerity to declare *me* excommunicate—*me*, Defender of the Faith and by the grace of our Lord, Head of the Church of England! I should excommunicate the Pope, if only he were English! Strip *him* of legitimacy!"

By this point, as always, she was shouting.

Although he had yet to touch on the main purpose of his audience, this tirade, familiar as it was, left Henry Sayer wondering whether the opportune moment had slipped away. "Your Majesty, that Philip is godfather to O'Donnell's son is but by proxy." Sayer stepped back, prepared to speak when his Ruler stomped her feet.

"You courtiers," she yelled, "move back! Stop your loud chatter. Is this not my Privy Chamber? I command privacy with my envoy."

Swiftly, the crowd melted to the farther edges of the chamber, gentlemen to play drafts or checkers at tables in the corners. Most ladies whispered the latest court gossip along the walls.

When it quieted some, Henry smiled. "Dublin has received happy reports that Ineen's mother, Lady Agnes, has worn the taffeta gown you so generously sent to her. She is a Scot and wife of Turlough O'Neill, who boasts of the great honor done his wife. It is no small thing to have such a woman in Ulster as Lady Agnes Campbell, and who is closely related to the Earl of Argyll."

"Don't I know that."

"But the mother is entirely unlike her daughter. They are as different as sky and mud, if I may say, Your Majesty."

"Ha! Indeed, Badger."

"Let me give you an example of how distant in temper and in loyalty that mother and daughter are, although living only a few miles that separate them geographically. Lady Agnes and her daughter Ineen, when they do speak, are known to shout at one another across their borders—and not always in pleasantries."

With that Her Majesty threw back her head and laughed as she sat back down.

"Further," Henry Sayer continued, "Lady Agnes' husband, Turlough, has assured your Lord Deputy in Ireland, Perrot, that he is foursquare with England. I can vouch, with one reservation, that this is almost certainly true of our Hugh O'Neill, the Earl of Tyrone as well."

Elizabeth frowned. "What reservation about Tyrone?"

"Oh, only that as each vies to demonstrate loyalty to Your Majesty, their rivalry occasionally unsettles the peace."

"But it does not spill into the rest of Ulster?"

"Neither man has strong enough footing in his part of Ulster to concern the rest, much less pose a nuisance to the Crown."

"This seems hardly a serious reservation. What have you not told us yet?"

"It is a mere cautionary note, Your Majesty. A general observation. Loyal as Tyrone has continually shown himself to be—and, as I say, strategically weak as his position in Tyrone remains—in my judgment it is necessary for Dublin to make sure he does not forget all he owes the Crown. Education, civilization, lands . . ."

"So? Stop yammering."

"But as I know Your Majesty is certainly aware, even the most loyal subjects, if they have spent a great deal of time in Ireland, sometimes fall victim to the attractions of savage Irishry. And he *is* married to that daughter of the O'Donnell, Siobhan, from O'Donnell's first marriage to an Irish wife."

"How many times must I hear that? What *are* you telling me?"

"When President Bingham of Connaught scored his great victory over the Scots at Ardnarea, Tyrone hastened to Donegal Castle—whether a coincidence or already planned."

"And O'Donnell's wife?"

"She arrived from her castle at Mongavlin, so our spies tell."

"Did they resolve a conspiracy against us?"

"We have no direct knowledge of what they discussed. It is certainly known that O'Donnell's wife was in a rage about our victory even more so as her brothers were among the Scots, and their wives and children. Whole families of Scots," Henry said. "But yet we do not know yet of her reaction to the recent beheading of her cousin Alex. Though devastated, she will be in even more grief."

"Spare me that Scotswoman's griefs. How many times must I remind you that *we think it necessary* that the service begun in Ulster for the expulsion of the Scots and the reducing of that country to obedience should go forward?"

"To do that and more, in the humble opinion of the Dublin Council, it is necessary to approach Parliament to release more funds for our Irish Administration." Sayer shuffled his shoes, as he was wont to do. "Turlough supports our English troops—even includes O'Donnells with him, especially Castlefinn ones."

She nodded but not so much as to threaten her crown. Then she laughed again. "That sot, Turlough O'Neill, is easy enough to control. And the Earl of Tyrone is given two thousand marks, which, I dare say, he would not want to forfeit. But bloody saints, that wife of O'Donnell wears a sluttish mantle, though once she served at a royal court. See how easily the Irish influence such behavior."

"Sadly, they do."

"The only money that we are prepared to release to our Irish Administration is for enforcing laws against those shameless mantles and exasperating glibs of hair hiding eyes of savages. Beastly creatures. So, *so* easy to whip those mantles open and go at it like dogs. And the Romish religion is outlawed. Remind Dublin of that! And don't neglect to burn Irish books and hang their harpers!"

Elizabeth had never once set foot in Ireland, nor did she intend to do so.

It took all his startled mastery of manners for Henry not to stammer in response. Would he ever get used to his queen's mercurial wit and temper, to the way she continually kept everyone off balance? It was her policy, of course, but at times it preyed on him that something else more disturbing was involved.

As though on cue, she winked. "Loyal as Tyrone has continually manifested himself—and, as I say, strategically weak as his position in Tyrone remains—in my judgment he should be watched closely. Suggest that we may find it needful to cede more Tyrone lands to Turlough O'Neill. Just suggest it, nothing else. I like Hugh O'Neill, you know. Unlike the other Irish he dresses Christian. Tell him to stay away from that Scottish wife of O'Donnell. And to keep an eye on Donal O'Donnell, that full Irish son of O'Donnell. We favor him."

"Yes, Your Majesty." Sayer bowed.

"Furthermore, demand O'Donnell pay his cattle rent. That Scotswoman's son of prophecy may have to be taken as a pledge for his mother's and the O'Donnell's loyalty. O'Donnell has sent no pledge."

Henry stifled a gasp. Not about a pledge being sent. Young pledges were one thing and sons of chieftains and kings a rather a common occurrence. Yet even the hint that Her Majesty would consider taking the son of the *King* and *Queen* of Tyrconnell sent alarm bells ringing.

"*Now.* I have a particular office I wish to invest in you."

"Yes, Your Majesty?"

She smiled and wiggled her fingers with their rings and jewels of various splendors, highlighting the glory of her years as reigning Queen of England and Ireland. "There's a bear-baiting at the Bear Garden at Bankside. You will attend with me."

Bear baiting was Her Majesty's favorite entertainment, though not one of Henry's. Bears, chained or let loose in the arena, baited dogs sent in to go after them. Yet, Henry bowed. "As you wish."

He tried to remember everything she had said to him, not at all certain that she committed herself to more funds for Ireland. The consequences of the suggested gambit—seizing the O'Donnell's and Ineen's prophesied son—loomed far more dangerous than Her Majesty realized.

She took his arm. "Badger, do not think I will send bears after you. But that Scotswoman, now that would be such a pleasant amusement."

V

Donegal Friary
Christmas of the Stars 1587

Snow glistened silver in the torchlight that illumined Donegal Castle where, inside the great hall, the harper played soft melodies for *Christmas of the Stars,* or "Twelfth Night," as the English called it.

That brought Ineen little cheer this year. The Feast that celebrated when the Magi found the Child King could not snuff out her flames of grief for Alex. Her pain burned constant as the Christmas candle. She still saw Alex, headless in the dark and cold of that ill-fated grave on Inch. She imagined his blackened head on that accursed royal castle.

The only thing that brought her from Mongavlin to Donegal was her husband's promise to tell Red *this night of all nights* what he had always promised to do: put forth Red

Hugh's name before the nobles to proclaim Red Hugh his successor.

Not even the *presepio* she treasured—the venerable Nativity stable with infant Jesus, Mary, Joseph, angels, and three kings that graced the mantle above the turf fire and brought from Rome years ago on Manus O'Donnell's pilgrimage there—comforted her. Draped in a full-length mantle, black as the turf in the fireplace, she went to the window slit and looked out at the darkening sky where so few stars shone. *Let that not be an omen,* she prayed. *The prophecy must go forward. I must remain resolute.*

The angle of the window gave Ineen a direct line of sight to the distant snow-laden roofs of Donegal Friary that spread out above the river Eske. She saw dwindling figures walking along the river path, her husband and her son, Red Hugh, and their Redshank bodyguards, strolling to the Friary with Red Hugh's wolfhound keeping up with them. Ineen turned away and shook out her rosary, praying that O'Donnell keep his promise this night and that Donal not be there.

Crunching through the snow, O'Donnell and Red Hugh reached the Friary gate and entered near the refectory. Snow overhung the Friary buildings like the edges of an altar cloth, breached in its center by a tall square bell tower surmounted by a great crucifix with ice-dripping arms.

The O'Donnell smiled and swept his arm toward his son, then directed the bodyguards to wait behind. "Son, this is one Friary in Ireland *not* dissolved and ravished by the English. 'Tis the heart of true faith, our Donegal Friary, with the best library left in this entire island. Were I not the O'Donnell, a Franciscan I'd be."

"Father," said Red with a smile, "you have too many children for that."

"Aye, son. But someday that may come to pass. Many of my forebears retired to a friary when the proper time came. Now we head toward the high crosses in the churchyard near the river where so many of our ancestors are buried."

A tiny edge of the bay was visible only a bowshot away, and the wind off the river blew new flurries against them. O'Donnell pulled back his hood to give his whitening locks the freedom of the wind. Streaks of bright saffron rippled on the gray waves of the river from the setting sun bristling in the trees on the icy bank opposite. Tugging tighter the dark fur mantle that covered him all the way to his boots, O'Donnell looked to see his son pulling back the hood of his own mantle of fine green wool.

Red's hair caught snowflakes like the thick little flames of a torch. He peered back into the darkening clouds but could make out only a single star or two for this night of stars. The wind in the trees made a high, running river sound but left the air down by the river itself gentle, clear.

The O'Donnell smiled and swept his arm toward the snow-capped crosses. "Ye know that the O'Donnell serves the living souls of all our lands. So, it is. But he serves all the Cinel Conaill, all the way back the thousand years to Conall Gulban and his father, who was the father of us all,

Niall of the Nine Hostages. Well to remember our forebears, for a grand part of who we are is what we remember."

Just then, chapel bells chimed the first summons to Vespers, urging O'Donnell to hasten words he promised his wife.

"Son," he pronounced, "I shall put your name for my Tánaiste to the nobles at Kilmacrennan soon. Are you prepared to be my Tánaiste, to succeed me, Hugh Roe O'Donnell?"

"Your Tánaiste, Father?" Though he was expecting this entirely, Red felt his breath taken away. "Now?"

"Now, you ask? Soon. Are you not prepared?"

"Sure, Father, entirely. Have you not, and Mother, been preparing me for years?"

"I tell you this eve as between you and me only—and your mother. Not be for some months yet. After Michaelmas I'll put it to the nobles formally."

"I—I thank you, Father."

"Thank me later, you have much to do beforehand."

"Aye."

"I tell you now," O'Donnell went on, with a glance he could not help in the direction of the castle, though it could not be seen from where they stood. "You have much to learn, and Donal will help with that."

"But Donal . . . Sure, haven't I learned from him already? Mother tells me I must watch myself around Donal, that there be rumors that he is my father's son but born of an unknown Irish woman. And that Donal thinks he should be your Tánaiste. And that the English like Donal. Mother wants me to train with her Redshanks, and with my foster father MacSweeney Doe."

With the sound of Red's raised voice, his dog, Scotty, began to bark.

O'Donnell sighed. He looked toward the river and the bay, and then at Red Hugh and admonished him, "Donal is my oldest living son, my most loyal Seneschal all these years. He is twice your age, has twice your years, a man strong and valiant enough to be O'Donnell himself. Yet when he was but your age, I gave my word to your mother, that the babe of prophecy—the babe she insisted we name Hugh Roe—would one day succeed me. I do not deceive myself it will go hard for Donal that I put your name to be my successor."

"Father, Mother says the English favor primogeniture and, as you say, Donal is your oldest living son."

"That she likely says. But Donal is full Irish and I do not expect him to be drawn over to the English. However, you shall be returning to MacSweeney after this night's festivities. I will think about your further training."

Red peered over at the friars' graveyard, with their small, simple crosses befitting holiness and humility, unlike the tall crosses of the O'Donnell kings.

Then father and son walked. O'Donnell cleared his throat as the air turned colder and drifting snow blew their way. "Son, I know well the evil brothers can do," he said, "especially when they're sons of different mothers. My brother Calvagh overthrew our father, Manus O'Donnell, and chained him in a dungeon. I had to defeat Calvagh in battle to free our father. Many souls went down in the kingdom to put that evil right."

"I would never do that to Donal," said Red, alarmed.

"I intend to ensure it. Never treat Donal in an inferior manner. You may need him as your Seneschal, Red."

"As you say, Father. We are, after all, half-brothers." Red said. "We have ridden together on raids."

"'Tis true," his father said.

This all brought an uneasy feeling upon Red, especially as his mother was very wary of Donal. "Sure enough, I shall keep Donal as Seneschal."

They walked now in silence to the entrance to the church. Snow began to fall thicker, hastening the darkness of this January evening.

The bells continued to toll as they reached the church. Scotty found his corner by the entry kept swept clean just for him. The O'Donnell and his son went into the church. It was not large like a cathedral, but there was an altar and three chairs—two plain and one ornate, for the O'Donnell, and room for the nobles to stand. The white gravestone of their ancestor, the great Hugh Roe O'Donnell, lay at the altar's foot, with standing room on either side. There were side chapels as well for smaller congregations. Faint daylight came through in the blues and reds of the window arched above the altar, but the dimness was aglow from the flames of stout candles.

"We have little time, son. Give me your hand," O'Donnell commanded, "I already hear the rattle of the friars' beads." With only a little difficulty, O'Donnell unsheathed his sword. Its hilt, forged in a Celtic cross, gleamed and glinted in the candlelight. O'Donnell rested it on the marble burial stone of Hugh Roe the Great and set the hand of his son Red Hugh on the beams of the cross. "Promise that when you become Tánaiste, you will honor my wishes and even more so when you become king."

"*O'Donnell Abu!*" Red affirmed.

"*O'Donnell Abu!*" proclaimed O'Donnell.

"*O'Donnell Abu,*" Red repeated.

Then the O'Donnell resheathed the sword. He bowed his head, looking at the altar.

Friars processioned in, infusing the twilight with a rich trace of incense, their chanting voices rising and falling in shimmering dark.

The O'Donnell prayed that he had done the right thing. That he must do what he long promised his Scottish wife. And yet, he thought of his son Donal.

When O'Donnell and Red Hugh walked together nearer the altar, they had no forewarning of what soon lay ahead for them both. And for that matter the Friary in which they now prayed.

VI

St. Patrick's Day
17 March 1587

Bagpipe skirls hit such a high, sweet plaintive note that O'Donnell inhaled the day's clear air.

"A fine Feast Day entirely," he chuckled.

"Aye, Husband," said Ineen. "And with wisdom and strength you have kept these lands under true Brehon law." Ineen stood beside her kingly spouse in a satin mantle that rippled in the fair winds, as green as the newly growing grass of March. Her dark hair, free of a hood, flowed beneath her shoulders.

Also mantled in festive green and with a golden collar, O'Donnell hugged his wife close. "Would I ever forget now the Feast of St. Patrick? Himself brought us the faith a thousand years ago when Brehon law was law *throughout* all Ireland."

"Aye," she said.

Her husband stood straighter than in many months. No symptoms of age betrayed him. His broad face was wreathed with white and through his glib his green eyes sparkled with pleasure and pride. He was among the most generous and hospitable kings, an esteemed value of O'Donnells.

On a grassy rise, not far from Donegal Castle, the O'Donnell and Ineen were bathed by a fresh sun breaking the spring sky into white clouds. They watched the hills and dales on both sides of the Eske fill with nobles and peasants, hills that loomed above fields and woods and meadows atumble with purple heather.

The low roar of the river seemed a musical instrument to accompany bagpipe and bodhran. The tents of Ineen's Redshanks sprouting over hill and dale in the thinning mist sang to the breezes from the bay.

"Your words, Husband," she responded, "are as true for your dear friend O'Neill's Tyrone as for our Tyrconnell."

"Ach, 'tis no day to be getting into that, woman. And does anyone need to remind me, that so much is *strictly* forbidden by Saxon law, including this hurley game that the lads will be playing? Why, the English might declare all my fish forfeit if they hear about that!"

"You have never been one to shy from danger." His wife smiled.

"Sure, I have never shied from *you*!"

Ineen stepped back but slipped her slender arm through his. "Truly a bright day, husband, with our children all home to celebrate."

The *birs*, spits of iron, were firing up to roast the lamb and beef for the festive meal, and cauldrons of stews sent out the aroma of fresh herbs. Mead, wine, and whiskey were placed and replaced upon the refreshment tables alongside silver bowls of honey and platters of oatcakes, cheese, and loaves of bread.

Without a further word, husband and wife awaited the forbidden game of hurley in which O'Donnell had once excelled. The shouts of Red and the lads drew their attention.

A hurley pitch had been marked out in the fallow field below the rise.

Watching, Ineen had to fight back an impulse to run and divert Niall Garbh, son of the now dead Conn O'Donnell, Hugh O'Donnell's brother and great rival. The sons of Conn were certainly among the men of the clan who believed they had cause to be the O'Donnell's successor. Riding up with the Castlefinn O'Donnells was their brother-in-law and leader, Hugh McDean, as though being in on the slaying of Alex McSorley meant nothing.

Outraged, Ineen turned to her husband.

Before she could speak, he gave her a look. "Woman, 'tis I who am the king. Hugh McDean must be welcome—to keep the peace here and the clans united."

She knew this was not the occasion or the place for retaliation. So, Niall Garbh and his brothers *and* Hugh McDean, who was there when Alex was beheaded, *had* to attend. Yes, all true, but Ineen would not leave them unwatched. She fingered the MacDonnell Medallion, always pocketed with her. She had to maintain the strength and the wisdom to carry on as long as the O'Donnell lived and Red advanced.

O'Donnell interrupted her thoughts. "Ineen, let us step closer to this game."

Ineen glanced again at her son, his ruddy hair blowing in the breeze. "Let it go forward," she heard herself echo her husband's words.

"Did we bring our hurley sticks?" Niall Garbh laughed to four of his brothers, who were dismounting.

"What have you here?" Niall Garbh, three years senior to Red, strode up and down the side of the pitch. "No hurley for your dog, Scotty? Are these any odds for Cuchulainn? It should be three fifties against one if this is a fair game for a champion."

The hurley players laughed. They all knew the first mighty deed of the boy hero, Cuchulainn, champion of ancient Ulster. The first morning he stepped on to the hurley pitch at Emain Macha, he single-handedly routed a hundred and fifty of the renowned boy corps of the Red Branch and fifty of the Red Branch warriors themselves. Then, for sequel in the afternoon, he killed himself a trio of giants.

Niall Garbh, hair black and straight as a rook's wing, tossed his satin mantle, fastened by bejeweled brooch, onto the ground. He called out to an impressive figure in black and gold mantle. "Donal! I say, Donal O'Donnell, you mighty Seneschal!"

Donal regarded the hurley game from further along the slope. As Seneschal, he had made all arrangements for the day. The second time his name was boomed he turned his head slowly.

"We are challenged to the field of combat, Donal!" bellowed Red. "Sons of Conn against sons of Hugh!"

The Conn O'Donnells' laughter sliced the sharp, dark look Donal gave them.

Then Donal swept his arm toward the tents with a gesture of immense lordly dignity and whirled off his satin mantle. "If a thrashing you desire."

The Conns roared again.

"Did you bring your hurley stick?" Red Hugh cried out to Donal.

"Bring me a hurley stick," Donal shouted. "A plain stick will do."

Red gave Donal a plain stick. They tossed the cowhide ball, the *sliotar*, and the game began, Donal jumping in to give it first whack toward the Conns' goalposts. The action kept most eyes on the pitch even as a rider galloped up the lower slope of the rise and halted to dismount beside the O'Donnell. The rider appeared as breathless as he was excited, whispering urgently in the O'Donnell's ear.

"*The English!*" cried O'Donnell's wife.

O'Donnell turned Ineen aside along with the rider, facing away from the hurley game. Outcry was heard and some hurley players halted to look at them. Red Hugh, holding his stick up like a sword, left the pitch and ran up the hill to his parents.

The others on the pitch paused and watched. After a moment, Donal handed his *caman* to another player and, without running, followed his half-brother up the hill.

O'Donnell, with but a glance at Red, continued questioning the rider in a low voice, with a nod or two, as though the message was nothing of great import.

"Anyone killed?" O'Donnell asked, showing no excitement.

The messenger took the hint, calmed his breath, shook his head. "Don't know."

"If only cattle they've taken," O'Donnell said quietly, "we will get them back."

"Who stole our cattle?" said Red in a loud whisper.

His mother nudged him, but O'Donnell did not look at him. Red mouthed at his mother, "*Bingham?*"

Ineen frowned but gave him a look that told him, *Listen!*

For months, Bingham had been demanding cattle for the Crown. He knew well that since the O'Donnell married Ineen Dubh, the *ri* of Tyrconnell had ceased paying cattle rent.

O'Donnell asked the messenger, "Saxon only?"

"Nay," the rider breathed. "Connaught scum. Perhaps no Saxons."

"I'll see that these cattle are not distrained, Father," said Donal, stepping forward. "'Tis my office as Seneschal. Where are they?"

Red looked at Donal. "I'll ride with Donal!"

"Nay," said their father with deliberation. "Red Hugh!" O'Donnell pointed a warning finger. "Keep your voice down."

Red shut his mouth and, with a restrained stamp of foot and crossing arms, looked away.

"No going after *distrainers*, seizers of our cattle?" Donal frowned.

Ineen, keeping both Red and Donal in her glance, held her tongue.

"A distraint of cattle," said O'Donnell, "is just the thing to spoil this fine feast day. I'll not to be abused by cattle thieves, especially scums or blackguards. I have called for St. Patrick's festivities today. I want no word of this raid to spread, though it will be well heard of later."

O'Donnell then glanced about to see the many eyes on him. Some Redshanks had gathered, looking up expectantly at the foot of the rise.

O'Donnell raised his hand and voice. "Some distant cattle raid, nothing to concern us." Under his voice he said, "Donal, send one of your men to alert O'Boyle. Then meet me in the castle, in my chamber. Don't hurry nor tarry."

Donal went off at a saunter, appearing unconcerned, shrugging and shaking his head to inquiries.

Once Red overheard that Donal was going, even though that be Donal's position, he protested, "But, Father—!" as though something precious were being taken from him.

O'Donnell looked at Red. "Plenty of time for you to complicate your days with small bothers like cattle thieves."

"Small!" Red said. "No cattle raid is small!"

"Red!" Ineen warned.

Red gave her a face but held his tongue.

"'Tis a matter," his father addressed him, as though to teach a lesson, "of a few men to ride to Ballyshannon and report back. Donal will gather some of his men. It is his responsibility. Given that this raid is so near our border, he can access the situation. You go back to your hurley game. Say that fields have been burned over . . . a matter of checking cattle."

Red went back down to the pitch, trying to keep the disappointment off his face.

As Ineen crossed arm in arm with her husband toward the castle, Red's mother turned back on her son a long, anxious gaze.

Niall Garbh strolled up to Red.

"What's it all about?"

"Oh, cattle."

"Aye, plain it's all about cattle. Surely no affair of mine. Are we on with hurling?"

"Later, I'm thinking."

"Well, now. The Conns have surely put it to the sons of the O'Donnell. Hail us if you want a rematch."

Red looked at him and then looked away.

Niall Garbh went back to his brothers. He gestured, said something that made them laugh, and as a bunch they lay down their *camans* and walked off toward a table with *uisce beatha.*

Owny O'Gallagher and the other lads ran up.

"You know," Red spiked their questions, "'tis a fine day for riding. I'm thinking let's go!"

"Riding!"

"I haven't had me mead yet!" mock-cried Kieran MacSweeney.

"I think," winked Art McGroarty, "he means the sacred water of life."

"Plenty of mead and whiskey later, lads. Go! Let no one mind you, but get your horses and," he peered round, "lead them into the trees over there," he nodded to the east. "But once you're in, go to the Ballyshannon road, where we meet up."

"What?" said Owny, whose home was indeed Ballyshannon Castle.

"Aye," Red whispered. "Your cattle were raided. I don't know, but sure enough Saxons are behind it," he proclaimed. "Quiet we must be, and not look in any hurry. But we can't waste time."

"Do we bring our horse-boys?"

"No, leave the horse-boys. 'Tis St. Patrick's Day, after all, tell them. We're just going for a little ride."

"We stow our *camans* with the horse-boys!" said one lad. "Let them play!"

That got a round of *ayes*.

"Red," said Owny, "certain I am me father is already after any blackguards."

"Certain I am, too. We're just trotting down to have a look."

"Oh," one lad rubbed his hands, "sounds good!"

"Who's for hurling," Red smiled, "when good action is afoot?"

It turned out to be much easier to get away without drawing notice. People were streaming in over the meadows and Donegal hills and both sides of the river. Within half an hour nine lads and their mounts crossed the Ballyshannon road, east to west. They waved greetings to a group of peasants coming up the road, but they were a hurrying, grim-faced lot. The man in the lead pointed a warning finger back down the road: "Raiders at Ballyshannon!"

Owny O'Gallagher fired questions the peasants could not answer, then turned to Red.

But Red said, "We sneak up to Ballyshannon. If there are Saxons, they might have guns. We're after spying cattle, lads, but we'll see what else turns up." He headed into the woods.

Owny kept urging a straight ride, but the others followed Red, and Owny was not about to take the road alone. It did take more time than Red had patience to pick their way horseback through the trees above the Friary. They could have reached the beaches much faster by cutting through the Friary fields, but they would have been seen, too.

Once upon the firm mud of the river beach, however, they had clear riding till it swerved in a cape out into the bay, at which point they had to turn inland again. But on the beach Red halted till his friends caught up.

"We go first to Ballyshannon, Owny, to find out what's what. We need to sneak, but I want to get there before Donal's men or O'Boyle's, so we cannot tarry." He drew his sword and raised it high. "Who rides with me today," he cried, "rides with me when I'm the O'Donnell!"

The lads cheered.

"*In Hoc Signo Vinces!*" Red cried.

In using the phrase, "In This Sign Conquer," Red referred to the Latin device circling a cross that Constantine, while still a Pagan, saw in the sky before the Battle of the Milvian Bridge. That victory made him emperor. Only a few centuries later it became the device on the O'Donnell coat of arms after St. Patrick used his own staff to trace a cross on the shield of Conall Gulban. The saint himself conferred their clan motto.

"For St. Patrick we ride!" Red yelled, breaking into a gallop.

The lads followed.

"*O'Donnell Abu!*" Red raised the battle cry.

VII

Cattle Raid
March 1587

Red Hugh led his detail due south for the ten-mile ride to Ballyshannon, along abundant fields of oats, golden corn, and barley plants, as peasant girls, working naked in the warm fields, yelled, *"O'Donnell Abu!"* The lads waved, then turned back into verdant woods near the road.

The sunshine, so golden bright and warm at Donegal, paled and clouded over, as though whipped by all the pines and birches they rode through. When they heard chapel bells tolling, Red signaled the lads to follow Owny as he broke back toward the road.

The first peasant huts near Ballyshannon that they passed appeared intact, and the rear bawn and tower of Ballyshannon revealed nothing. But a clamor could be heard, and the lads trotted round to the river gate, which was thronged by peasants and kerne holding back with pikes.

They recognized Red and Owny and some of the women cried out to them, "Fires ahead. Cattle have been raided."

Up by the riverbank toward the river itself, the lads saw burned huts still smoking. O'Gallagher Redshanks, directing the kerne, motioned the lads through the gate to the castle. As they passed through near Ballyshannon castle's tower, they saw two mercenaries, one with a cup poised to throw, standing over a trussed-up peasant with angry eyes and bloodied cheeks.

One mercenary asked, "Are ye connected to Bingham?"

No answer came.

Because the border could not be left undefended even for a great feast at Donegal, O'Gallagher and his men, remaining at Ballyshannon, enjoyed festivities within the bawn and up in the hall. The gate was barred, of course, the tower manned, archers on watch upon the walls. But perhaps the spirit of the feast, not to mention its most convivial spirits, got the better of the watch. Although they did report afterwards what seemed an unusual number of peasants wading the ford up toward the lough, it was St. Patrick's, so they thought no more about it.

Only a little while later when they heard shots and a thunderous splashing, cries and yells, did they see the drove of cattle floundering across the ford to the south, men whipping them. Some cows fell under, bobbing up with dying bellows.

"So, is it you lads are the reinforcements O'Donnell sends?" Owen O'Gallagher, father of young Owny, asked Red Hugh as he stood outside his castle.

"Nay," said Red. "Donal's and O'Boyle's men are coming. We came to assess the situation, to lend a hand. 'Tis well, O'Gallagher, you are the man in the gap at Ballyshannon."

"We shall scout the blackguards," Owny said to his father.

Owny and Red exchanged an excited glance.

"By your leave, O'Gallagher," Red announced, "Let Owny and the rest of us ride south to spy where the cattle are."

"You think me daft, son? 'Twill be your heads on my head if aught happens to you."

"No, no," said Red. "Nothing will happen. We only spy. We've all been on cattle raids, I mean. We know better than to attack the blackguards without sufficient force with us."

"You know better, do you?" O'Gallagher roared. "But your father has no idea that you are here. O'Donnell did not fully get the message I sent. No one has yet come. There's no getting these cattle back if we do not track them. And now! McAteer!"

"Aye, sir!" A lean, tall man with a ragged blonde moustache and short beard stepped forward, throwing back his long green mantle to stand naked legged in a great kilt of green and blue plaid. McAteer was a Redshank, among thousands, who came to Ireland with Ineen when she married

80

the O'Donnell. McAteer eventually settled in Ballyshannon and rose to become Captain of Redshanks. He boasted a small castle of his own nearby, where he lived with his wife and five children.

"Only go with these lads to see where the cattle be." O'Gallagher said.

Red first rode on a cattle raid at twelve years, with O'Gallagher himself and McAteer with him, when they raided O'Rourke.

"Do not let one of these lads out of your sight," O'Gallagher instructed McAteer. "For if a single hair of a single head of theirs suffers harm, you have me, O'Gallagher, to answer to and surely Red's father, the O'Donnell."

As the lads flocked off, Red and Owny and McAteer with them, they paused beside one of the mercenaries attending the captured raider.

"Balloughshee, they are to hold up!" the raider finally said, with a sneer and a chuckle.

"The fairy mound!" Owny grinned.

"'Tis the Good People he's saying stole the cattle?" laughed Red.

"Blackguard Irish entirely," the peasant answered, "but Englishmen hired them."

"Bingham!" said Red with anger and elation.

"Fools!" McAteer frowned. "They soft in the head to steal O'Gallagher's cows and pen them only a hop and skip down the way?"

So off they went, grabbing a good share of mead on the way. Fording Lough Erne, riding with McAteer and Red in the lead with no more than short swords and torches against the early dark, they took the bayside road to Bundoran, south of Ballyshannon. Only a hundred head or more of cattle had been rustled, it turned out, more insult than injury, but insult that could not be left unanswered. The raiders should have been hours ahead of them, yet it was not long before the party halted. A few straggling cows grazed what grass survived the general trampling, and not a raider was in sight.

"I ken what's up," McAteer turned to address the lads. "No collecting the Crown rent, 'tis blow flies sent to disrupt the feast day."

"I don't hear anything up ahead," said Red.

"Balloughshee is a few miles on yet," said Owny.

"Aye," said McAteer, peering west at the bright glare lingering in the cloud cover above the bay. "But here we leave the road. 'Twill soon enough be sundown."

"We must hurry," Red Hugh said. "Donal will be coming with some of his men, and we must settle this before he arrives."

An hour or so later, they hitched their horses to slender birches below the east side of the hill of Balloughshee. Balloughshee rose in a bare knob above the forest. Twilight had turned to dusk, and from the other side they could hear a low general moaning and occasional male shouts. McAteer and Red took Owny with them up to the crest to see what could be seen in the small pass hemmed in between the fairy-mound and the lower knob across the way.

Not only was the moaning of cattle louder to their ears at the top of Balloughshee but the shouts and laughter of men keener. The three could barely see the cattle, not directly, but from their seething in the dark, dimly illuminated at the head of the pass by two campfires, which winked black and red as shadows moved back and forth.

McAteer pointed at the foot of the pass where the head of the herd had to be.

"List!" McAteer said.

They listened, and to the lads' surprise, they could hear lowing and hoofs moving back along the road toward Ballyshannon.

McAteer said, "Those blackguards don't know how to conduct a cow raid. I wager no guards are posted down there!"

"You mean the cows are heading home?" asked Owny, excited.

"They're raiding themselves back to Ballyshannon!" Red covered his mouth not to laugh too loud.

"Sometime fools make a small raid to try them out."

"McAteer!" said Red, "We can raid them all back. And we're not really raiding. We're just helping the cows home. We have to slap one of them on the arse and away they all go. But we must do it fast before these blackguards catch on, wherever they are."

McAteer considered. "Not raiding, you say. O'Gallagher said nothing about doing aught but raiding."

"I'll tell him you said that!" Owny laughed.

"Your heads are on my head and O'Gallagher's."

"We don't raid," said Red again, grin clear, though in the dark none could see it. "What would the Good People of Balloughshee do? A bit of fairy trickery."

"Magic, is it!" said McAteer with what could only be a thoughtful smile.

"If the Good People swooped down," said Red.

"Torches!" said McAteer.

"Aye, torches!" echoed Red.

They talked, Red and Owny having difficulty keeping their laughs stifled. In a moment between them, Red Hugh and McAteer had a plan to which they eagerly agreed.

"Only as many cows as we can manage," McAteer laughed.

The most important thing, besides getting away clear and well, was to hem the cows toward the ford so they did not all run into the Erne and perish in the water.

"I think," mused McAteer, "we are not after getting all the cows home. We're after spoiling the blackguards' day. And their pay!"

In the trees below Balloughshee, Red detailed the plan to the seven lads. They would use their torches. At best, three torches would wave on each side to make a gauntlet for the cows to gallop through.

"The dearest task," McAteer asserted, "one lad to ride hard the cows and the bulls back to Ballyshannon, rouse drovers and round them up to build fire breaks to lead cattle to the ford."

As no one volunteered to miss out on the fun at Balloughshee, Red Hugh whipped his arm about till it fell on someone: Liam, who protested, but the other lads urged and praised him for the "most dangerous" task, without which nothing could succeed.

"No time to lose, then," McAteer said, striking fire into Liam's oil-soaked torch. "But 'twixt yourself and cows, lad, save yourself!"

Red put Owny in charge of a far team. "The fools have let the cows get the better of them and start trottin' home. Don't be trampled."

"O'Gallagher orders I don't let you, Red Hugh, out of my sight. So, you stay in my sight. Up we go!"

McAteer and Red reclimbed the hill, but not far, and edged over to the front. They had to feel their way carefully not to slip. The pass was dark but alive with restive, jammed-in movement and the grunting and snorting of cattle. No nearer sounds could be made out. With their own torches soaked, flints in their hands, the two looked back and forth down the pass for the signal that the other lads were in place. Although his mantle was wool and his hood on his head strung tight against the steady wind, Red was impatient to light their torches and get the adventure going.

They were near the entrance of the pass, the cattle below them so close it would take nothing to get to the nearest one. "As you say, lad," said McAteer, "set one a-going, the rest do follow. Wave the torch at a cow's arse like a wand."

"Are you forgetting," Red retorted, "we have raided together before and with O'Gallagher?"

"Aye, sure, and how could I be forgetting that?"

Peering for the signal, at last Red saw three then four sparks in the dark. He and McAteer watched. The sparks on the far side waved and the ones on the near side waved.

"Signal enough," said McAteer. "Won't do to have cows run back and find their raiders." He struck fire into Red's torch. "You take the honor, young O'Donnell."

Said Red: "'Tis the Good People of Balloughshee bringing these cows." He dropped his voice— "*O'Donnell*"—then raised it: "*ABUUUU! O'Donnell ABUUUU!*" He waved the torch and slid down the rock. Playing the flames over the nearest hindquarters, the lad provoked an immediate, terrified *moo!*

"Keep waving," McAteer said, "but *stay* here." Then McAteer squat-walked to the end of the rock and jumped. Whirling his torch like a sorcerer, he plunged into the midst of the confused cows, slapping hindquarters, pushing, whistling, cow-calling.

Suddenly feeling stung, knowing his friends were waving torches as close to the cows as McAteer, Red slid to the spot where the Redshank had just jumped. He jumped himself, landed square, and ran to the edge of the herd.

The cows were getting turned this way and that toward the open road, heads bobbing in the flame-light, picking up speed one after the other. Slapping cows, Red looked for space to plunge among them like McAteer but knew better than to take a stupid risk. His arm was suddenly wrenched and yanked behind him.

"Is it my head you want spiked on Ballyshannon gate, O'Donnell?" McAteer was behind him, not in front. "If ye must be a hero, be it on your own head, not mine. You stick like wax to me. Time to bring the cows home."

"Ach, we've done a wonderful thing, McAteer, rescuing these cattle. I shall tell my father what you have done," Red said.

"Just tell him I hate blackguards!"

It took even longer to return to Ballyshannon than any of them expected. The road of thundering cattle kept Owny busy. Others walked horses through woods and dark fields. Then rain began to fall.

They stumbled out of the woods soaking wet, ragged, dirty, and utterly exhausted into a night of drizzle loud with the roar of cattle reaching Ballyshannon. The drovers were already there, ready to take charge of the cattle.

McAteer climbed onto a nearby horse, and Red followed suit.

Then out of the drizzling black came the flickering torches of the O'Donnell, Red's mother, and Donal.

Ineen almost jumped off her horse to run up to Red Hugh. "Hugh Roe O'Donnell," cried his mother, "what in the name of Jesus, Mary, and Holy Joseph possessed you!"

The O'Donnell strutted up to stand by his wife. "By St. Columcille and St. Patrick, himself," his father began, "Hugh Roe, I did not authorize—"

But O'Gallagher, hobbling up, cut in, "Where is Owny O'Gallagher?"

"On his way," said McAteer from his horse. "Along the bay."

"I told you no raiding!" O'Gallagher shouted.

"I forbade Red to go on this raid," O'Donnell roared.

"There was no raiding," Red informed his father and O'Gallagher. "The cows were trotting home already; we gave them but wee encouragement. We saw no blackguards at all."

"'Tis true?" asked O'Gallagher.

"Aye, true," McAteer affirmed.

Then Donal rode up and seized the reins of Red's horse. His eyes in the torchlight flickered, blazing. "You know distraining cattle is for me. Did you think of that?"

"No," Red started to say. "'Twas no raid."

"No raid, it was. A slaughter altogether—slaughter by drowning." Donal said.

"Drowning?" Red looked steadily at Donal. "Cows . . . into the Erne?"

"Many," the O'Donnell himself answered. Then he said, "Enough, Donal! Your brother was almost lost and is found. He is alive and that's all there is to it for now."

Red hastily dropped off the horse, which a horse-boy ran up to lead away. Red suddenly could not look his father in the eye, but the old man embraced him, weeping.

Tears burst from Red's own eyes. "I had to, Father," he stammered. "My heart—I could not let those cattle get away. No one was here, and so much commotion. I wanted to try to locate the raiders; instead, we found only cows."

The lad's mother, still at her husband's side, now reached her arm round her son.

"Mother—" Red started, but his mother's hand stopped his lips.

In the torch flicker they stared at each other, then she embraced her firstborn. In gratitude, in bewilderment, and not without anger. She hugged his sweaty hair, blazing red in the torchlight. She held him out to look at his face, at the victorious gleam in his eyes, when with a catch of breath, she turned his face. "You're bleeding!"

Red touched the side of his head and tried to see his wet fingers.

"Tree branches. I've never been so knocked and scratched in the woods."

"Trees?" She shook her head and buried his head against her.

He tried to say more but his mouth was pressed against her wet, warm-smelling mantle. When she released her grip a little, he got out, "Mother, I never forget our kin killed by the English and blackguard Irish. No vengeance enough for Alex for me to catch cows, and for your brothers."

"Ach," she said.

"Bingham.'Twas surely Bingham's minions encouraged this raid," Red asserted.

"Leave Bingham for now! Oh, Red, Red—did it ever occur to you, you could be riding into a Bingham trap?"

"But Mother," he began.

"Listen to what I tell you. Obey your father!"

"Aye. Mother, I—"

"Yes, yes, yes, my Red!" She hugged him tight, blood and all, so he could not answer, and tried to control a shaking beginning to steal through her limbs. Then she realized she was pressing Red against the pocket under her mantle holding Alex's Medallion. The thought pierced her heart, with a pain strangely sweet. All the years of losing family: father, aunts, uncles, cousins, her dear Alex, brothers—and now would her impetuous, valiant young hothead of a son of prophecy, Red Hugh, storm himself to an early grave beside them? The tears suddenly burst in her, but in the night and the increasing rain she could hide them, if not the stifled sobs.

Red Hugh O'Donnell was coming into himself. He was everything she hoped for, so much so she now feared for him. The blood on his face would not always come from trees. It was beginning. She hugged him tighter. "Ah, Red, Red, let me hold you a little while longer."

VIII

Donegal Castle
February 1587

The O'Donnell and O'Neill were sharing news, and nonchalantly O'Neill temporarily set aside his Saxon ways and his clothes, as did his father-in-law. In the cool of night, flames blazed in the fireplace in O'Donnell's chambers. Three fat beeswax candles glowed in the darkened room, adding to moonlight visible through slit windows. Flamelight played on the Ulstermen's legs as they lay sipping flagons of wine. Hugh O'Neill related a tale he had pieced together from his English sources, one to which he was eager to know his father-in-law's reaction.

"But as the Dean of Peterborough begins to speak his exordium, Mary, the Scot, cuts him off. 'Mr. Dean,' says she, holding high a crucifix, outcrying the Dean's voice, 'I shall die as I have lived, in the Roman faith. All you pray for me is but vain.' And with that her black gown drops to the floor, and underneath she's wearing crimson silk."

O'Neill chuckled. He knew much of the intrigue surrounding the execution of Mary Queen of Scots.

"Aye, a martyr's crimson." O'Donnell mused. "And the Dean of Peterborough, one of the English queen's favorite preachers surely had to deal with that. Ach, what irony. Ineen will delight in hearing that! Crimson silk, was it?" O'Donnell repeated. "Surely, a martyr's crimson."

"Then," O'Neill continued, "she puts her head on the execution block, and the headsman lets fall." He paused, put the flagon to his moistened lips. There was the sound of drinking and breathing. "But the Queen, Mary Stuart, intrigued even after the headsman struck. She'd prepared one last act of defiance for her cousin Elizabeth. When the headsman picks up her head to swing it before the assembly and cry, 'Long live the queen!' all he picks up is a handful of wig. And Mary's head escapes and hops off the block onto the dais."

O'Donnell rolled nearer his friend, laughing with vigor. "She had venom, she did, Mary Queen of Scots. Ineen loved her for that."

"I fancy she will find this true tale to her liking." O'Neill put forward his flagon. "Sláinte, my dear friend. You've always the best of Spanish wines."

O'Donnell returned the gesture to his younger friend.

Easily but carefully, O'Neill shared, "'Tis said that there is a great outcry in Scotland and the north of England, and even Spain, France, and Italy, for the English queen signing the warrant to kill her cousin queen."

"Aye. Ineen was a pot boiling over when she heard. She marched straight to the Friary and ordered the Franciscans to say Masses for Mary. She will do the same at many a church in Scotland. You know she holds her father's blood on the English queen as she holds the blood of every one of her Scots kin slain, and her cousin Alex's, especially. His tarred head spiked there on Dublin Castle gate for gawkers."

"The Crown is well aware of your wife's views. Your Ineen is not someone I would want holding anything against me," O'Neill said.

"A great shame—the Scottish queen's execution. And Mary Stuart had but forty-four years on this earth," O'Donnell said, "and I myself have forty-seven long years."

O'Donnell, silent for the moment, stared directly into the fire, thinking of Ineen, whom he missed when she was off to Scotland to procure more Redshanks. And with the killing of Mary Stuart, O'Donnell experienced a sense of foreboding.

"Ineen has been rumored to keep even larger numbers of Redshanks at Mongavlin as well as those at her fort at Carrigans and those kept here at Donegal?" O'Neill asked, breaking into O'Donnell's thoughts.

"Aye, at Mongavlin and Carrigans," O'Donnell responded. "And those given to me."

"You know," Hugh O'Neill mentioned, "I happened to hear that Turlough has slipped a few back to his Castle at Strabane. It comforts his Scottish wife, your own Ineen's mother, despite Agnes Campbell's gifts from Queen Bess."

"Aye, Lady Agnes is reverent toward Her Majesty," the O'Donnell said. "And Ineen has Redshanks enough to handle any of her mother's."

"Aye, my friend. And for me to be 'the O'Neill,' the king in Tyrone as you are king here, Turlough must cease to be king and chieftain in Tyrone."

"Sure, and that will soon happen, my friend."

Think on this: Ineen's kinsman Sorley Boy, her father's own brother, submitted to the English crown. And when in Dublin, he saw where his own son, Alex's, head is spiked."

"Sorley Boy!" O'Donnell breathed, as though to sigh. "Now there was a man in the gap. He watched from a distant shore as his kin were slaughtered on Rathlin, where he'd sent them for safety with English assurances."

"Aye, he was a man who once championed his Scots." O'Neill nodded.

"But to keep his lands, he submitted. Ineen has harbored a rage over that. But Sorley Boy is an old man with Alex slain." O'Donnell drank and stretched his legs, fleshed out by his years. "My arm is still feared by all in the kingdom. There is no stranger in Tyrconnell but a new wind at the door."

"Indeed, all Ireland knows the might of the O'Donnell."

"I have performed services for the English queen; but less so with Ineen as my wife," O'Donnell said. "But I do not submit. I submit to no man born of woman."

The darkness hid the expression on O'Neill's face as he noted that for O'Donnell it certainly was not a question of never submitting to a man. But not for the first time did O'Neill wonder just how much O'Donnell submitted to Ineen Dubh.

"Your lands are free," O'Neill said for O'Donnell to hear. "The freest in all Ulster. But you must be cautious. It's not been easy for me to stem Dublin's outrage. Not only is it feared that Red Hugh is your presumed successor—for word of the prophecy spreads across the Irish Sea—but Red Hugh's impetuousness and bravado have been noted in London. Pay your cattle rent to calm the Crown's concerns."

"God bless Red. He takes account of English assurances being broken. Strong as Cuchulainn. He can ride the wildest horses with ease. Red is a lad who will submit to no man, no one, save his mother. But I will continue to warn him. It would be an ill thing to have the English planted in Tyrconnell as they are in the south and in Connaught, with that Bingham. And recall that Donal is my Seneschal, and the Crown takes a liking to him."

"Nonetheless, keep in mind that Elizabeth wants her cattle rent. That would be a step in satisfying her." O'Neill hoped what he said was true. "Lest you have the likes of Saxons upon you, again, pay your cattle rent!" O'Neill raised his voice and turned his own face from the fireplace to look at O'Donnell.

He was doing what he was supposed to do, what England wanted him to do despite his indulgence in this Irish custom. But in a deep corner of his mind, he admired O'Donnell.

O'Donnell smiled and said, "I shall call for more wine?"

"Aye," O'Neill said as a friend, as a son-in-law. "There has been talk, you know, among the English, that your son Donal should challenge Red Hugh to become your successor. He has a few years on your Red. The Crown prefers him to Red and wants to establish the rite of primogeniture in Ireland."

O'Donnell responded, "No, Donal knows his place as my Seneschal and that I have given him Glencolmcille Castle."

Turning on his elbow and setting his flagon aside, O'Donnell addressed the shadow of the other man earnestly. "There is an honor that I want to ask you. There is time, but not much, and I have brought no black man, no negotiator or go-between, here to mediate this."

"*Black man, a marriage negotiator*," O'Neill exclaimed. "I'm already married to your daughter, Siobhan. What need do I have a matchmaker!"

"Aye. I'm after knowing that my Red wants the hand in marriage of your lovely daughter, Rose."

Silence.

"Glory be," O'Neill exclaimed. "Isn't Ineen negotiating for him to have the hand of a princess in Connaught?"

"Aye, but Red will not hear of that."

"Sweet is your hand in a pitcher of honey. So, it's on the road for a wife that Red wants, are you!"

"You have the right of that," O'Donnell said.

"Well, Rose is not like her mother from a marriage thankfully annulled, or how could I have married your dear Siobhan?"

"Rose is sweet as honey herself. And any daughter of yours is bound to be a fine wife, Hugh. It's Ineen that you must win. She has intentions that Red marrying the princess in Connaught would be more strategic."

"If your Red Hugh prefers my Rose, my bet is on Red marrying Rose O'Neill."

They both laughed with gusto.

Hugh O'Donnell's heart jumped. Could it be possible that O'Neill would unite his clan with the O'Donnells through marriage once again?

"Be aware, my dear friend and father-in-law, that any further alliance with you is something that the Crown *will not want*—especially a marriage between Red and any daughter of mine!"

"Likely not. But this is free Tyrconnell where the O'Donnell makes the decisions, not London."

"Surely, you will pay your cattle rent then. Allay suspicions."

"A night of other thoughts, son-in-law."

"I won't even count the cattle. I'll give you a hundred droves for such a marriage," O'Neill said with enthusiasm.

"Grand. I'll speak to Ineen. You can send your Black man to Mongavlin to negotiate. My wife will listen to her son's heart." O'Donnell raised his flagon of wine, once again, in toast. "Sláinte!"

"Health to you!" O'Neill toasted. Firmly he kissed O'Donnell on the cheek, in the Irish way of friendship.

O'Donnell returned the kiss.

O'Neill said words often spoken by bards:

" 'Twas given that no O'Neill
Fight his brother O'Donnell.
Didn't an O'Neill die of grief long ago
For his brother, King of Tyrconnell."

"Aye, by uniting Red and Rose, O'Donnells and O'Neills will become preeminent in all of Ulster." O'Donnell smiled.

IX

Betrothal
Donegal Castle 1587

As O'Donnell and O'Neill sealed their exchange, a couple huddled against the far wall in the shadows of a flaming bonfire. They had slipped out from the castle and if they had escaped the attention of some eyes, they had not escaped O'Neill's horse-boy's, whose gaze had often lingered on the face and figure of a girl he could never have. He shot one sharp jealous glance at Rose O'Neill and Red, who would not leave her alone.

But Rose O'Neill did not seem to want to be left alone. She had come with her father from Dungannon. Siobhan, her stepmother, stayed back at Dungannon with the wee children and, to Rose's delight, Ineen was not at Donegal but Red Hugh was.

In the shadow of the wall, Rose leaned against Red, only to start whenever his hand touched her waist, to his amusement. He touched her waist, touched her shoulder, touched her cheek till she almost shivered and he laughed, but she smiled, too.

"I am blind in the dark, Rose O'Neill. Only my fingertips can see your beautiful dress, Saxon though it may be."

"Then I shall stand out in the bonfire for you to see."

"Oh, the bonfire is too hot. Here, it's cool."

She jumped and yelped, slapped his hands, clapped her mouth, laughed and touched him lightly. He wiggled his fingers deeper into her waist until she sprang free. For the first time in his life, Red Hugh found himself falling so in love that he could admire a girl despite her English style of dress.

For Rose O'Neill was the product of her father's English influence. Her small waist was so easy to hold, and she was so delightful to look at in her layered, golden gown, with a neckline surprisingly low. Rubies sparkled all along it. They caught the glimmer in Rose's blue eyes. Her hair, with touches of red, hung loosely at her shoulders in wave after wave of gentle curls. She looked so unlike Red's mother and sisters. Though each of them was lovely in her own way, their gowns fell straight to the ground and their necklines did not dip so low.

Red liked the sniff of rosewater about Rose. He liked to slide his cheek against the soft white skin of her pretty face and to touch her rich curls. For some time now his mother wanted a betrothal for him with the daughter of the Earl of Clanrickard in Connaught. Red had never met the daughter, but he had known the daughter of O'Neill ever since childhood, and if before he had given little thought to an unseen, unknown girl in Connaught, now he gave none.

"My face is burning from this bonfire. Let's find a cooler place."

"And your face will stop burning in a cooler place?"

"I'm thinking that it may burn more pleasantly. There is a cool hill outside the wall not far from the river Eske."

"I'll wait for you here, Hugh Roe. You may come back for me when you are cooler."

"Ach, no! No! I'll never find this cool place if you don't take me. You must take my hand. We can view Donegal Castle and all that surrounds it better from the there."

Rose tilted her chin in a pantomime of deep thought. "And that is what is expected of me as a proper visitor?"

"Entirely! Entirely!"

"And you will not misbehave?"

"I shall not misbehave as we shall be betrothed!"

"Oh, Red, you are truly impetuous. This is the first I've heard of this," she cried as they walked toward the gate. "Betrothed is it already?" Rose teased.

She was thrilled, happier than she had ever felt before. Was this love? Was she in love with Red . . . ? In Red she had found all she ever dared to dream and more. He was the most handsome youth in all Ulster. And not even in Dublin had she ever seen anyone more handsome, despite fancy doublets. Scarcely could she catch her breath. Betrothed! They were so young when they danced and played at her father's wedding to Red's half-sister Siobhan, but she liked him even then. She was not at all sure what Red's intentions really meant, but his words delighted her. She shivered as she passed into the dark beyond the gate with his hand clasping her eager one, several red deer leaping across the rolling ground not far from them.

They reached the crest of the hill. The smell of sheep, herded in for the night, lingered. Red threw his rich blue mantle on the ground to make a seat for them on the dampened ground. Rose sat down beside him, clutching both of his hands, her heart beating wildly.

"You squeeze my hands so they cannot possibly misbehave."

"Your tongue misbehaves, Red. How dare you speak betrothal?"

"How dare I?" He slipped one hand free and around her waist. They leaned their heads together. "We O'Donnells never speak about such things lightly. I would marry no one without a church wedding and with priests there, like Siobhan and your father married. But, Rose, I can pledge myself to you without formal betrothal, you know that! My father knows of my love for you and this night is arranging with your father to negotiate arrangements as soon as possible."

"And your mother?" Rose moved closer to Red.

"She will not deny me, even if she has other plans. I told her last fortnight how much I care for you. My mother will come around."

The cards were stacked in his favor, Red reasoned. Red's father welcomed another bond with his friend O'Neill. O'Neill would not stand in the way of his adored daughter, Rose. And according to Irish custom, they need not wait for formal announcements. Informal alliances among couples were considered a source of strength. In Ireland, such alliances were often sufficient for questions of betrothal or marriage to be put aside as hardly necessary. This was the rub. Red looked upon Rose with fierce love and wanted both—the ancient ways and the church wedding.

"So, I am your betrothed."

"Aye! And Rose, Rose," Red implored, "You feel as much as I do, I know it. I'll surely see to a proper church wedding."

A deep breath shuttered out of the girl. Betrothal! She was caught between her growing desire and the English influence in her upbringing. Yet, she did not think of Red like that. Wasn't he promising a church wedding?

"You Irish wait for nothing," she said, but so low that she thought he could not hear. But he had.

"Are ye thinking that I am like my grandfather—though I never knew the fellow? He fancied dressing like Henry the VIII and had five wives. But he did have nineteen children, after all. And 'twas him who wrote *The Life of St. Columcille*."

"O, Red Hugh, I know Siobhan is married to my own father. But you Irish—"

"We Irish! You are more Irish than I am, Rose O'Neill, and you best remember that, if you will be betrothed to me. I am half Scottish, and don't think that my mother ever lets me forget that. And you—you are wholly Irish, despite your father's ties to England. You wouldn't want me to marry the Clanrickard princess?"

He kissed her ear. She dipped her head to his shoulder.

"The O'Donnells and the O'Neills will be twice united. Tonight, my Rose, tonight be Irish, my love."

"I can't say how Irish I will be with you this night, Red Hugh."

He kissed her lips. Her lips answered eagerly.

"I pledge myself to you, Rose O'Neill, for now, for forever."

"I—I, too, give my pledge to you, Red Hugh," Rose breathed.

"Then I have two great Roses." Red held her and sang from "Rosaleen" that the O'Donnell poet was composing:

"The heart in my bosom faints
To think of you, my queen.
My life of life, my saint of saints
My dark Rosaleen.
My own Rosaleen."

The couple stayed on the hillside until the silver string of dawn stretched sweetly through the darkness. They gave no thought to ways their love would ignite flames from Dublin across the Irish Sea to London.

X

Whitehall
Horse-time, Spring 1587

*T*he English queen rubbed her hand along a small prayer book that hung from her waist cord. "O Badger, this year proves so troublesome. Imagine . . . Mary Stuart beheaded. I wept when I heard." Her voice rose. Her egg-white complexion composed an image of mourning, and her black dress, minus a chain of jewels bordering her cleavage, furthered an impression of grieving the death of her cousin, Mary, Queen of Scots.

"I threw that Puritan Davison into the Tower for stealing the death warrant and executing without my permission. It's made me a regicide! It's played right into the hands of the Scots loyal to Mary, to Philip of Spain and his Pope, and to the Papist Irish." She dabbed constantly at perspiration, as though she herself had not signed the death warrant.

"No one forces my hand, least of all a mere secretary. Is it any wonder I wear black!" She managed to compose quite well this image of grave concern, but the spark in her shrewd glance escaped all pretense.

Henry Sayer stood before his queen, warm and clammy in his darkest doublet and black hose, not in mourning, certainly, but aware of her moods in the wake of the execution of her cousin queen.

She snatched from her envoy the latest dispatch sent from Lord Deputy Perrot. "*And* we are informed of more and more rumors about that Scotswoman's—that other Scotswoman's—son's name being put forward to be successor to O'Donnell and put before the nobles to eventually become king."

"At Kilmacrennan, there's to be a gathering of nobles after Michaelmas. So, it is rumored." Henry explained, with deferential nods to avoid appearing to correct her. "It is the way these Irish do it. A king-to-be cannot be named a successor, merely agreed upon by the nobles."

The queen stared at him. "We care not how these savages do what they do. And what they do is outlawed. Furthermore, that Donal O'Donnell should be successor by primogeniture. And he might learn to follow English law."

"Of course, Your Majesty." He bowed his head.

"As though a savage ceremony could reassure us! How often must we remind the Irish in our other kingdom that the custom of naming a Tánaiste is forbidden," she sneered the word, deliberately mispronouncing it with a long *a*.

"And your law is obeyed in all other parts of Ireland, south of Ulster."

"South of Ulster!" She spat the words.

"And in Ulster as well! That is, in regard to the Earl of Tyrone, and even the O'Neill himself, Turlough O'Neill."

"*All* of Ireland must be made to obey us."

Her envoy was about to say "Tyrconnell" when he remembered she refused to call the far northwest of Ireland by any name but Donegal—the one by which it had been lately shircd as an English county . . . though it still lacked a permanent sheriff. And the O'Donnell's Scots wife saw to it that he ignored such a move by the Crown.

Elizabeth had cleared the Privy Council to address her Irish envoy alone, ejecting the few card-shuffling courtiers and all but one lady-in-waiting, retained to forfend salacious gossip and to embroider. Never ventilated, the room reeked with a too-familiar musty smell. Beneath her gown the queen wore eight layers of clothing. Even the perfumed handkerchief she put to her mouth to freshen her breath and the ever-present scent of rosewater did not dispel the odor. She strayed often to a mullioned window to gaze upon the Thames, not so distant that boats and boaters could not be discerned.

A bright thought itself felt like a little fresh air. "There may be an astute way to make this savage custom work in Your Majesty's favor," her envoy said.

"How, if it flouts Her Majesty's law?" Elizabeth stamped her royal foot.

"It is well known that the Earl of Tyrone wishes to succeed his cousin Turlough as the O'Neill."

"That's true."

"He'd likely want to become the O'Neill king, with or without the savage ceremony. He will be the strongest of any contenders for the office, and the Crown will dominate all of Ulster up to the river Foyle."

"So? We know this already." The queen dismissed the comment.

Henry approached.

"Come, come, Badger," she shook the dispatch, "to the point!"

"It's considered by Dublin that O'Donnell's eldest son by the Irish woman—and Donal being full Irish—might be willing to succeed his father. He is older and his father's Seneschal in charge of justice as well as other significant administrative duties. He might be more than willing to cooperate with *us*. Become the Crown's Sheriff."

The queen nodded. "I like to hear such good things."

"Donal is much older than Red Hugh," Henry Sayer stressed again, before his queen interrupted him.

"Philip of Spain is that Red Hugh's godfather, is he not?"

"By proxy. Donegal Bay fish is a favorite of the Spanish court," Sayer reminded her.

Elizabeth interrupted him, "Philip is raising a hue and cry all over the continent about Mary Stuart's . . . fate."

Henry Sayer wanted to say the relations between O'Donnell and the King of Spain were purely commercial, but he knew this would not do, so he took a new tack. "Philip has hundreds of proxy godsons; I frankly doubt he has the faintest idea who Hugh Roe O'Donnell is. All reports indicate O'Donnell's friendship with Spain is only . . . with its wine."

"We are not persuaded."

Suddenly Elizabeth grinned, shifted the subject with a barb in her glance. "Donal *might* be worth our efforts! Even under their savage Brehon law, a stronger contender can still win the chieftainship away from a Tánaiste even if one's nominated." Elizabeth's voice rang with enthusiasm.

"Yes," Henry replied. "And it's known in Dublin that Donal does function responsibly in running the courts and enforcing the laws, though, of course, they be Brehon laws at this time."

"Those barbarian laws for those wild Irish. As our Sheriff, he would have to administer English laws!"

"That is true, Your Majesty. Sheriff rather than successor may be just what is needed at this present time."

"I shall consider this," Elizabeth said. She smiled.

Henry smiled, too.

Then her face clouded. She peered again at the dispatch, which she shook in his face. "This says the half-breed son of that Scotswoman is already betrothed to Hugh O'Neill's daughter! You know of this?" she yelled.

Henry Sayer lowered his head. "Dublin hears only of a *possibility* of another alliance between O'Neill and O'Donnell."

"Possibility!" the queen snapped. "This goes beyond what reached Walsingham's ears heard only days ago."

Henry surprised himself by how vigorously he shook his head in contradiction of his queen.

"I pray you put that aside, Your Majesty. Dublin has more timely information than Sir Francis. The Scotswoman desires Hugh Roe to marry a daughter of one of the Connaught nobles. Besides, the lad's much too impetuous— he rode out on his own to try to thwart a silly cattle raid by some Irish brigands. O'Neill is too cautious to want him for a son-in-law."

"Mark this, Henry Sayer!" Elizabeth yelled, "That Scotswoman served in the Stuart Court. Her relative is the Earl of Argyll. The Crown must make certain that the Scotswoman's son does not marry any daughter of Hugh O'Neill."

Sayer stiffened, a chill on his spine at her use of his full name instead of the pet name.

"There is to be *no* successor named in County Donegal," she declared, "and *no* other marriage between any O'Donnell and any of Hugh O'Neill's offspring. One marriage alliance between Hugh O'Neill and O'Donnell is already more than one too many. There will not be two!"

The envoy frowned. He did not like dealing with Elizabeth when she was in a foul mood. So, the honor of a private audience had been greatly diminished.

"Is this all, Your Majesty?"

She turned to give him a steady, considering eye.

"Perrot must do more," she said, "and we demand *results*!"

Henry bowed, uncertain what to say, since nothing could be done without considerably more money. The queen resented every coin that went to Ireland.

"Ireland is a dagger pointed at England's heart. Now with the execution of Mary Stuart, that Scotswoman and the thousands of Redshanks she keeps bringing in against our decrees will be too eager to welcome the Papist Spanish!"

It was hardly the first time Henry heard Elizabeth use that phrase, "Ireland the dagger." But the urgency caused him to step back.

She wiggled her finger for him to come closer. "Tell Perrot he must find a way to deal with this Donal of the O'Donnell. He would profit by English primogeniture. My father permitted a man who converted to the new faith to keep his lands. This Donal should be reminded of that. And a sheriff must suppress outlawed customs. This might be well to his liking. This has merit, Badger."

Her envoy contained the happy sigh that nearly escaped him. "I shall tell Sir John all you have said," he breathed. "There is one more thing, though, I should like to divulge to him."

"What thing?"

"The wars in the South of Ireland have put a great strain on the Crown's treasury."

"Not a farthing more!" Bess glared at Henry.

"Understood, Your Majesty." Henry Sayer looked off.

111

"What is it?"

Henry started, "Your Majesty—"

But his queen moved closer, her lips at his ear, the rouge on her cheeks nearly rubbing onto his cheek, and with a throaty whisper no one else could have heard, she said, "Tell Sir John Perrot that Scotswoman's son is not to be left at liberty a day more. I want him taken pledge, for that Scotswoman's loyalty and O'Donnell's. That will resolve two dilemmas at one stroke, and hardly a farthing spent."

Henry attempted to display no shock, but all his objections held his tongue. He steadied his hands. "N-no nobles electing him Tánaiste," he stammered, "and no wedding to Tyrone's daughter."

"And Henry," she said, fixing his eyes. "Not a word of this must reach Hugh O'Neill."

"He's most loyal to Your Maj—"

"Not a word." She placed her trembling finger on his lips. "I want no chance of word reaching the O'Donnells. No one but Perrot is to hear of this."

Henry cleared his throat, wondering how to speak with the queen's finger on his lips, but she released them. "But how—how does Your Majesty wish Sir John to accomplish this?"

"Sir John is clever. More to the point, he is Lord Deputy. If he wishes to remain so, he will find a way. And without delay."

The queen's envoy continued to stare at her in surprise, then recovered. "I understand," Henry Sayer answered, as

112

though this could well bring forth the very dagger the queen most dreaded.

He went on smoothly, "It is a brilliant policy, Your Majesty. The Irish are always taking pledges among themselves to assure peace. And now, by your leave . . ."

He bowed and began to scrape toward the exit, but before he managed two steps backward, he saw the queen's hand reaching out to him.

"If Mary Stuart were alive today, the court would dance tonight. Ah, Henry, we must not let her death defeat us. You shall leave promptly on the morrow to make my command to uncivilized Ireland. For the moment, though, you shall join *us* in quenching our thirst with civilized London beer."

Henry Sayer let the queen's hand linger at her pleasure before bowing once again.

"I shall not play the lute myself," Her Majesty smiled. "We shall listen to another play it. Mary's feet would not have been stilled at my death. Mine will be merry though hers now are stiff."

XI

Plotting in the Pale
Dublin Castle, Summer 1587

I rritated, Sir John Perrot, the Lord Deputy to Ireland, turned his cold, clean-shaven face on her Majesty's envoy. "So, Elizabeth is outraged at the betrothal of O'Neill's daughter Rose to Red Hugh O'Donnell. That the young Red Hugh may well be named his father's successor by the nobles. And at the Scotswoman's recruiting of Redshanks." He paced his chamber. "Am I to seize Red Hugh O'Donnell and keep his mother restrained without enough men to pluck a berry from a bush?"

Henry Sayer had delivered the queen's message to Perrot with a grim face as he set aside his feathered cap. He spoke few words.

Deep and rich, Perrot's voice sounded loud even when it was not raised, as it now was. "If we were properly outfitted with troops here in Ireland, neither that son nor his mother would be a fodder for our talk. Did Her Majesty comment with respect to the fact that I struck Sir Nicholas Bagenal right in the Council Chamber?"

"No. Such tales are best kept in Dublin. If and when Queen Bess hears of it, she may ignore it or . . . that tale may give her pause."

Perrot towered over Henry Sayer, who was of middle stature, as the Lord Deputy reread a statement from Elizabeth's missive. "She's always saying much the same thing as she wrote in this missive:

'The O'Donnell's wife is gone into Scotland with intent to draw thence great companies of men which doth plainly demonstrate their intention . . . to burst into open action.'"

As Perrot read the latest parchment, Henry waited in discreet silence.

Suddenly Perrot thundered, "So, I am to surmise that the English are to push into Tyrconnell? And that though Queen Bess has refused my plea for troops—not willing to spare a man from the coasts of England?"

"I am certain," ventured Henry, studying his nails, "that Her Majesty is in mind of your great success in bringing Sorley Boy to submit to the Crown without a great number of troops. And to think he submitted after riding into Dublin Castle and seeing the blackened head of his own son, Alex McSorley."

Perrot kept pacing. "The men who cowed Sorley Boy but a year ago are now dead, or maimed, or vanished to the South. Every deserter I capture I am obliged to hang, when the much more efficient policy would be to march them west—over the mountains, through the bogs. They'd die for their treason right enough. England sends me her dregs and expects them to triumph like the angelic hosts."

Trying to make sense of Her Majesty, Perrot shook his head. His unusual height made the room seem a child's miniature of a castle chamber. At nearly seven feet he might well have been the tallest man in Ireland; certainly, the most powerful. Sayer had not exaggerated to the queen. By Perrot's hand, as a soldier and as a diplomat, he had conquered almost all the great chieftains of the North. Those whose lands he had not subjugated had yielded him immense respect and cooperation. Sir John was a hard man but fair; when he took a chieftain's bribe, he gave good service, but never to the prejudice of the Crown. Half of every bribe went into the land, but half went to the Crown's army, which lacked sufficient funds from Whitehall. Having served as president of devastated Munster, Sir John learned that if the Crown were to extend its rule without a similar devastation, it would cost dearly in men and treasure. She must treat the chieftains as sovereigns, not savages. As a result, he had achieved more than any Lord Deputy before him, including the illustrious Sydney. Perrot knew Ireland as no Englishman ever had. If some of the chieftains could elect an *ard ri,* a High King of all Ireland, that High King would be Sir John Perrot. The rumor, which he did nothing to quash, that he was a true son of Henry VIII, did not harm him. Bastardy meant nothing to the Irish, sonship everything.

There could, of course, be not a breath about kings and kingship; worse than treason, it would be folly. But there was such a thing as princely folly as well, and one of its many heads was willful ignorance. His half-sister, the queen, knew next to nothing about Ireland. She scoffed at the Irish as savages. And she certainly would not listen to advice from a bastard brother—or acknowledge him as that.

"Her Majesty demands quick results," he said finally, "and does not wish to hear a word about possibilities. She demands victory with few troops and less money."

Henry reddened, his pulse quickening. The Lord Deputy had just come perilously close to defaming the English queen to her own envoy. "I am certain," the envoy hastened to interject, "Her Majesty dispatches to Ireland only the very best men she can find."

Perrot glanced sharply at him. "Would," he replied, "that they lasted as long as I!"

"Indeed," Henry nodded.

"I'll give you a letter for the queen." The tall man resumed his martial pace, sweeping up and down the floor, a tower in black and crimson. "I am no more pleased with the O'Donnell's wife and son than Her Majesty, though the O'Donnell himself might be approached were he not rumored to becoming feeble. Ineen Dubh continues to solicit Redshanks. No sooner have I expelled Redshanks than Ineen Dubh goes to Argyll and brings them back to Tyrconnell. And mind you, she commands and pays her Redshanks personally."

"Elizabeth knows that, but news of more and more Redshanks will not be pleasing to her. But may I remind you that she calls O'Donnell's wife the 'Scotswoman.'"

"She's the one who does," Perrot said. "Many, and not only English, think her nickname Ineen Dubh or Dark Daughter, fits her perfectly, even in Donegal."

"Ineen wishes Tyrconnell never to be referred to as County Donegal," Henry reminded him.

"I will call it Donegal though it lacks a permanent Crown Sheriff. We do not need worry about Ineen regarding that at this time," Perrot replied.

"Nonetheless, my Lord Deputy, her Majesty has some thoughts on that. She likes the possibility of Donal O'Donnell to become Donegal's Crown's Sheriff."

"I have no doubt, but it is of no urgent importance. Might her Majesty be pleased, however, to hear the rumor that Hugh O'Neill may set aside his O'Donnell connection—his wife Siobhan? 'Tis said he's already taken up with a daughter of Turlough Luney's," Perrot said with a chuckle.

"'Twould be nothing new for the Earl of Tyrone," Henry Sayer replied, although revealing a surprised expression.

"I am certain," Sir John gave a hard laugh, without mirth, "he means to outflank Turlough by doing this. He wants to replace him as the O'Neill, though Queen Bess has outlawed that term." Sir John shrugged. "But whether O'Neill or O'Donnell, whether Redshanks today or Irish troops tomorrow, it matters not. I have quieted Ulster, but going after Red Hugh or his mother will stir it up."

Henry Sayer was known to respect Sir John Perrot very highly, and he, like others, knew that it was dangerous for any courtier to be too successful in his service to the queen. He listened to Perrot.

"If not by force, then how," Perrot asked, "are we to seize Red Hugh or stop that Scotswoman, his mother?" He answered his own question. "We are left with guile, are we not? The mountains of Tyrconnell are as wild and remote as Scotland."

"Could not Captain Bingham be given the task?" Sayer began.

"Bingham will be removed from Ireland before this month is out. To the Netherlands."

That proved news to the envoy. Henry swallowed his surprise. "Guile, you say?"

"Why, I should very much prefer that the Scotswoman's son come to us," Perrot commented. "I . . . could invite him and his mother or father to a banquet. One can always catch an Irishman in his cups."

"But has Red Hugh not already received, and declined, such an invitation?" Henry made a gesture of puzzlement.

"Very well. Then perhaps—take the banquet to him."

"To Tyrconnell?" Henry asked.

"Yes, but not to Donegal where the O'Donnell's primary castle is, if it can be helped. How most efficiently, would you say?"

"Our queen demanded that The Earl of Tyrone must be kept out of it. I thoroughly agree with Her Majesty's caution to me," Sayer answered.

"How . . . ? How? How am I to successfully take a pledge from wild north of O'Donnell's lands?" Perrot returned to pacing. "A pledge is useful only if alive."

"By sea?" Sayer burst out.

"Excellent!" Perrot stopped abruptly. "I have Tyrone's own information that the O'Donnells, who presently are scattered about what they call their kingdom, will come together again for Michaelmas celebrations in a most convenient place up north—Rathmullen, on Lough Swilly. MacSweeney Doe, after all, is Red Hugh's foster father."

"Of course," Henry said. "The festivities are to be hosted by another MacSweeney, MacSweeney Fanad, at his castle." This was sounding more and more fantastic.

"No storming of the castle," the Lord Deputy said. "But at Michaelmas MacSweeney Fanad holds a fair. Spies indicate Red Hugh will attend," Perrot continued. "One of those beastly coyne and livery affairs, the vassals hosting their lord like sheep feasting the wolf. In any event, it will be a great gathering of O'Donnell sub-chieftains, with not only Red Hugh but likely his mother and father."

"So, you shall contrive to cater the Michaelmas banquet?" the envoy said and smiled, thinking what a glorious report he could make to her Majesty if all succeeded.

"Precisely. Let's say a merchantman with a hold full of Spanish wine—"

"Spanish wines!" Henry reminded him.

"Burgundian, Rhenish, it won't matter. A hold full of wine—and soldiers." Perrot grinned.

Henry Sayer laughed. "That I would love to see, English soldiers serving wine—and irons!"

"Nicholas Barnes the vintner owes me," Perrot confided. "The O'Donnells shall be invited to a banquet of roast goose and apples and rounds of Spanish wine. God's providence might deliver all three O'Donnells to our table. That Queen of Donegal would truly be the most valuable catch of the netful."

Henry Sayer suddenly had a misgiving. "Do you think her Majesty means taking all of them at once?"

"To bind the mother, yes. Quite enough. Folly to overreach, but one can daydream. Even snatching the half-breed son will be more than enough to stop his Scots mother bringing in Redshanks."

The two men regarded each other. Another misgiving struck the envoy. "Kidnap! That's a dangerous gambit, strictly illegal, even impolitic, and tantamount to confession of failed authority in securing pledges."

"Without troops to enforce authority . . ." Perrot's eyes flared with determination.

"Understood completely, Lord Deputy. The Crown is being pressed by necessity—the threat from Scotland and

Spain and such a gambit would not be unprecedented, but . . . such desperate ventures most often fail."

"Who knows? It might even spark an uprising. But that will happen in any event if the Scotswoman's son, Red, is not seized."

Henry Sayer felt his lips trembling.

"And even success can be dangerous," Perrot said. "After all, the man who carried out Her Majesty's signed warrant to execute the Queen of Scots is now in the Tower of London."

For a moment both officials stood silent.

Perrot then returned to his desk. He dipped his quill in ink and wrote on parchment:

"For O'Donnell if it would please Her Majesty to appoint me to go thither this summer. I will make O'Donnell and his MacSweeneys deliver in what pledge I list: or otherwise, if it please Her Majesty, I could take O'Donnell, his wife (who is a great bringer in of Scots) and perhaps his son by sending thither a boat with wines."

Perrot took his parchment and handed it to the envoy. "Give this first to Walsingham. As Her Majesty's principal secretary, he will be able to bring it to Elizabeth's attention in a most fitting way."

"This is your reply to Her Majesty?" Sayer asked in undisguised dismay. "You wish her to think the situation in Tyrconnell and even the entire province of Ulster is so desperate that success depends on a very chancy ruse?"

The Lord Deputy stood near Sayer and fixed him with his coldest, most disdainful glare. "Yes. And if Her Majesty so greatly fears a Scotland made out of Ireland, the Spanish landing here, and does not believe that an impoverished and depopulated army is not forced to wager for victory with just such chancy stratagems, then she is invited to conduct a royal progress to Ireland. Thus, to behold her other Kingdom."

XII

Kidnapping at Lough Swilly
Michaelmas 1587

As Michaelmas festivities proceeded in and about Rathmullen, a Spanish merchantman, with square sails on his vessel, dropped anchor in the sunny, dark waters of Lough Swilly. A longboat brought the captain and some of his crew each day to the sandy shore near MacSweeney Fanad's castle, Dundonald, in the northwest. Mountains, high and blue, stood in the distance beyond, but low hills of forest met the wide white strand onto which the boat was hauled. Not far away, the Carmelite Monastery, dedicated to the Blessed Virgin, hosted pilgrims, especially around feasts.

As it happened, no O'Donnells yet came to partake of the fine Spanish wines MacSweeney offered for Michaelmas festivities.

Ineen Dubh was at Donegal Castle overseeing care for her husband, which she did more and more of late. Seneschal

Donal enjoyed free reign to manage the Castle, which always involved defense of O'Donnell rights, and Tyrconnell itself. He observed a respectful deference when his stepmother was present. He knew better than his father how much it was spoken in Tyrconnell and beyond that all was not well with the aging man, and that the king's wife sat in his chair.

For her part, Ineen Dubh observed a courteous respect for Donal and his duties, though, as rarely as possible, not absenting herself when the Seneschal wished to speak with the O'Donnell. O'Donnell himself wanted them to work together, and so she was able to keep her hand in all O'Donnell affairs, political and financial.

Her longtime nursemaid, Annag, stayed at Ineen's side, overseeing the care of Ineen's wee daughters, Mairghead and Marie, as she once had of Ineen. Throughout her years with the O'Donnell, Ineen bore him four sons: Red Hugh, Rory, Manus, and Caffar; and three daughters: Nuala, Mairghead, and Marie.

Thousands of cattle, O'Donnell's true wealth, roamed the green fields while sheep grazed in autumnal hills. An abundance of trees boasted golden leaves as splotches of orange and red at harvest time. The O'Donnell, under the solicitous care of McDunlevy, his physician, waxed stronger with Ineen present.

"I too would prefer to be at Lough Swilly," Ineen told Nuala, who came to Donegal Castle at her mother's insistence.

Nuala, with eyes as blue and hair as black as her mother's, said, "I'm old enough to be at Rathmullen for festivities. I'm closest in age to Red. Closer than me brothers."

"Nuala," her mother raised her voice, "your sisters enjoy having you here, as does your father. There'll be another time to be at Rathmullen."

Ineen thought, *I myself want to be with Red, urge nobles that Red Hugh's name be put before them and gather after the feast at Kilmacrennan. But that must wait.* For that she needed to keep her husband alive.

Nuala turned, gave her mother an angry look, and stamped her eleven-year-old feet up the stone steps.

Ineen left the warmth of the turf fire radiating the great hall, walked up the cold steps to the little chapel in its corner of an upper room, and knelt on the oak *prie-dieu*. She looked up at the gold-framed Blessed Mother, cloaked in blue, holding her Child. *I offer up missing the festivities, Lord,* Ineen prayed, *that Red Hugh be named. That his father be well enough to gather the nobles . . . For this and so much more.*

Meanwhile, up at Rathmullen, Red Hugh and his friends were indeed celebrating Michaelmas, though not with wines offered on the strand near Castle Dundonald itself. With libations that quenched their thirst, they were out in the meadows and forests, falconing.

It was not until the last of the ships visiting Lough Swilly to vend holiday comestibles prepared to weigh anchor that the falconing party descended from the woods above Castle Dundonald. Red Hugh, sitting high on his black stallion, rode alongside his foster father, MacSweeney Doe. Behind them came the harpers, huntsmen, bards, and Redshanks and kerne. Hawkers also accompanied the nobles, as did all sorts of gillies and horse-boys.

"A grand hunt," Red beamed, his green mantle fastened at the shoulder by a gold brooch in accordance with his role as son of a king.

"And me foster son, you being the finest falconer of all! I'd be no truth teller if I didn't say that I've never see you let fly your falcon and the bird return so often with prey," MacSweeney Doe said.

"Aye, I do love falconing, though many here are fine hunters."

"A new round of Spanish wine to celebrate the Feast!" ordered MacSweeney Fanad, proud host of Dundonald, as soon as the falconers arrived to Fanad's castle.

Red and the lads responded with a boisterous cheer.

"Cupbearers to the strand! Bring only the finest for these merrymakers!"

"Little enough remaining," more than one gillie reported.

"Hasten, hasten! The last wine ship will sail before you get there!"

Even before Red and his cohorts reached the white sands of the beach, the cupbearers saw the Spanish hat of the merchant and his crew rowing back toward the remaining ship. They yelled for the boat to come back. The sailor in the Spanish hat looked round but did not halt the rowers.

"New guests are here!" the cupbearers called. "MacSweeney Doe! MacSweeney Banagh! Red Hugh O'Donnell!"

The boat was not so far out; the captain of the merchantman held his hand to his ear. "Who, you say?" he cried back in Irish.

The cupbearers cried the names out again, adding more, then cheered to see the merchant wave his rowers to turn back, and as they turned round, he waved his big, floppy hat with red and yellow plumes to the lads on the shore. In moments, the boat beached again and the captain himself swung his big boots and splashed onto the sand. He seemed a surprisingly short man for a ship's captain, with shrewd but merry eyes beneath a thick black brow, a red bulb of a nose, and a red mouth that seemed never to cease smiling, though a goiter swelled his neck on one side. It was wondered after these days if he was a full Spaniard; he spoke Irish with a Dublin accent he did nothing to hide, though he flaunted Spanish leather, gold silk, and sword, and called himself "Skipper of the Seven Seas."

He bid the cupbearers to tell him more about these late-come nobles. He did not wish to offend them but, pointing to the late-afternoon sky, and the men unfurling the sails on the yards and riggings of the ship, called the *Mateo*, said little enough wine remained in the hold.

Anxious not to disappoint their master, MacSweeney Fanad, the cupbearers begged the merchant to bring the last casks ashore for a handsome fee. The merchant recited all the trouble and inconvenience of reloading and lowering the cargo boats again. At last, scratching his goiter, he suggested a halfway measure.

"A few nobles, two or three or possibly a few more only, are welcome, if they will, to come to the ship in this longboat and enjoy the last of the best vintage and, perhaps, yes, say a little banquet of roast goose! But only for an hour. The ship sails before nightfall."

The cupbearers eagerly reported the captain's invitation, and before a quarter hour passed the three MacSweeneys, Red Hugh, and some of his friends were on the strand. Somewhat to their surprise, given the captain's statements, a second longboat was already arriving from the ship. There was room in each boat for only two, and soon enough MacSweeney Doe and Red Hugh stepped into one and MacSweeney Fanad and, at Red's urging, Owny O'Gallagher in the other, MacSweeney Banagh graciously making way for him. Just before shoving off, Red Hugh insisted MacSweeney Fanad's harper squeeze in with his master to further sweeten the final revels of the day. The captain laughed and waved him on, exclaiming the Crown's ban on harping was neither here nor there west of the Pale.

It was late afternoon. The sky, still a deep blue in the early autumn sunshine, stirred with clouds moving east like white mountains, rendering the dark colors of Lough Swilly,

Lake of Shadows, darker yet. As Rathmullen strand fell behind the two boats, whose oarsmen pulled to race each other to the ship, the woodsy hump of an island rose just behind the merchantman's stern to the south of the low bald Gollan Hill on Inishowen. Dropping for a moment from the high spirits of the party, Red stared at brown fields invaded by green forest on the slopes rising from the thin strand.

"Something troubling you, son?" asked MacSweeney Doe, his face as flushed with the adventure.

"Inch."

"Ach! Inch it is," his foster father said as he bowed his head.

"I must sail to it tomorrow. My wish is to pray where Alex McSorley was so treacherously slain," Red pledged.

"Aye, the 'treacherous grave,' the Saxons call it," MacSweeney whispered.

"'Twas their treachery that . . ." Red could say no more.

Their conversation fell still a moment, as the oars splashed them swiftly toward the rope ladder dangling against the hull of the ship.

"*Requiescat in pacem,*" breathed Red to himself. *Rest in peace, dear Alex.*

"Time enough for the grave tomorrow!" The sub-chieftain reminded him. "Today we squeeze the last of the finest grapes of Spain the last boat offers!"

Red Hugh suddenly grasped and kissed his foster father on both bearded cheeks. "Grateful I am for you."

At shipside the guests were somewhat surprised to see the crewmen scramble first up the ladder.

"Look alive, me lads!" the captain called after them. "Much to be done before we weigh anchor!" He turned his smile on the noble guests. "My apologies, sirs, for this wee breach of protocol, but our little compotation, as 'twas not on the schedule, but no mind, no mind." He did call to two of the seamen to assist the guests.

Once they were all aboard, the captain exclaimed in exuberant Irish, "How delighted I am to be honored by the greatest of Tyrconnell. And the *king's* son!"

He ushered the party into a snug captain's cabin and, having one of the young cabin-boys clear the captain's table, bid his guests to take their places on one of the two short benches on either side. The cabin reeked of damp saltwater, and the lantern swinging above the table was a bit dim, leaving all in shadow. Even two to a bench—MacSweeney Fanad and Owny O'Gallagher on the one, MacSweeney Doe and Red on the other—the fit was tight. The harper was relegated to what little space he could hunch into on the floor behind one bench. The captain himself remained standing. Presently a cabin-boy reappeared and placed a gleaming pewter goblet before each guest.

"May I suggest, gentlemen," said the captain, "it may be more comfortable without mantles?"

The mantles were tugged and twirled off and he lay them on the nearby bunk beside the hats they had all removed.

"And now gentlemen, the heartiest and tastiest sack of the wine stock for which you have honored me as my guests."

There proved to be considerably more than a little of that sweetish white wine still aboard. Bottles came up to fill the goblets and the captain called for more. Cramped in his tiny space, the harper, himself helped to goblet after gobletful, strummed his harp with airs as sweet as the wine on his tongue. A little bread and even less goose were served as well, but sack ruled, and the company laughed and sang and roared the splendors and greatness of Spain.

They toasted also their women—those remembered, those imagined.

"To Rose O'Neill," shouted Red Hugh, "my own dear Rosaleen."

"To Mairead McGroarty!" Owny pounded the table.

"To all the wives I never had," roared MacSweeney Fanad, "and all the wives I do!"

The captain, laughing with them, excused himself a moment. "A matter needing attending."

How many of the guests recognized the sound of bolts driven home on the cabin doors is not recounted. But they were startled to attention when the captain re-entered. Not only was the Spanish hat gone, so was the man's goiter, also the merry twinkle from his eyes. Now he was wearing an iron Saxon helmet and on his chest a breastplate that winked in the swinging lamplight. Not to mention, pressing quickly into the cabin, six soldiers also in Saxon helmet and breastplate, brandishing muskets and pistols.

"My good nobles!" the captain announced in a voice loud, clear, commanding, unsmiling, yet not without mockery. "As you may now surmise, you are on an English merchantman, and I am no Spaniard. I speak to you on behalf of Her Majesty, Queen of England and Ireland. Time after time, Lords Deputy have demanded pledges of Tyrconnell. You have all refused. Now Her Majesty's kingdoms lie in peril of Scotland and Spain. The mother of one Red Hugh O'Donnell here is a Scot and himself a half-breed. Also, the lad is Godson of Spain, so he is. Many they be on this accursed isle that look to Spain for aid in treacherous rebellion against Her Majesty."

He had not finished speaking when Red Hugh hurled his wine goblet at him but, bouncing against the wall, it merely splashed the man. One of the soldiers swung his pistol and the lad's head fell on the table, bloody. MacSweeney Doe roared to his feet, but the sack was as effective as a pistol-whip; he dropped to the deck. Clasping harp to breast, the harper shrank in the shadows. Owny O'Gallagher and MacSweeney Fanad alone remained seated, staring groggy and stupefied.

The Saxon, who in truth was not captain of the merchantman, ordered a poultice brought for Red Hugh's head.

"Most fortunate," the captain said to MacSweeney Fanad, "you brought Red Hugh along. Now there's no need to barter for him. Fortunate also a son of Owen O'Toole O'Gallagher is gracing us with his presence. All that is needed is a son of," again he nodded, "MacSweeney Doe."

"'Tis me foster son you have here," spat MacSweeney Doe.

"Your foster son indeed!" rejoined the Saxon. "You savage Irish care more for a son you buy with cattle than for the seed of your own loins! Very well, then. If this boy binds you faster than your own flesh and blood, so be it. But I mean to take a MacSweeney for the Crown's pleasure—yourself or another. This ship shall set sail within the hour."

"I shall supply a pledge," said MacSweeney Fanad, fat and miserable. "Host of Castle Dundonald I am. My duty under Brehon law is to provide for my lords and my guests." Still in a stupor of wine, he struggled with his corpulent body to remain on the bench, but upon delivering his words he burst into furious tears.

MacSweeney Doe regarded him with a less drunken eye, then ordered the harper ashore to fetch the boy his kinsman named.

As the harper was rowed to shore, the hostages aboard ship heard an unsteady strumming of a melancholy air that suddenly stopped, but not long afterwards a keening started up on the sand and in the distance and growing.

MacSweeney Fanad sent his ten-year-old son, Donald Gorm. When the small lad was brought aboard and ushered into the cramped cabin stale with smells of wine, sweat, and vomit, his father lurched to his feet and gripped his son in a hug that lost his footing and all but crushed him against a bulkhead.

Eyes wide, the young lad looked about at the armed Saxons and their cold eyes.

"A manly obligation I settle upon ye, lad!" Fanad wiped his eyes and nose. "Ye must stand for the clan for a while now. Ye'll be home again in six months. And ye shall be treated well for ye are a MacSweeney pledge."

"Father!" But bursting into tears, his son could say no more.

Red Hugh's wound was roughly dressed before a shot of whiskey emboldened him, and with a clumsy lunge he nearly earned a second blow on the head. The Saxon ordered him taken to the hold. And the fifty soldiers hidden there for days went double-time on deck to show their helmets and their firearms.

Hastily the longboat pushed out again from the ship with the two MacSweeney sub-chieftains in the stern, forlorn and riding to shore without cheer, without choice, without honor. The keening which greeted them on the beach, Fanad was to say again and again, was hard to bear as the wailing of banshees.

The merchantman wasted no time turning its sails to fill with wind and leaving those ashore, with a clear view of the taffrail, bristling helmets, for sure, and muskets mounted and aimed.

In the hold, Red Hugh was thrown to the deck in a tiny compartment without a lantern or any other light. Thrashing in pitch-dark against boxes and bulkhead and anything else Red's feet could reach, the lad cursed in Irish, Latin, Spanish, and Greek. Yet not even an hour had gone when the rolling and heaving of the cramped darkness made the worst of the wine in his belly, and his outrage fell aside as he wrenched to avoid vomiting on himself. Soon enough, nausea spent, his head cleared a bit.

There were more immediate hazards to face. Red managed to brace his back against a hard, smooth surface, but through the smell, he began to know the first sensations of something he had never known before and so could not name—*terror*.

Images came back from all his mother told him about English cruelty, true tales pressed so firmly into his mind he could almost hear the screams of the women and children butchered in caves of Rathlin Island. He could almost see the thousands of bodies of Scots slaughtered at Ardnarea, and the drawn-and-quartered body parts of priests dangling from belfries. And through the darkness came the severed head of Alex McSorley, which he might soon see directly spiked on the gate of Dublin Castle.

Still, Red himself was alive. "Pledge" be damned! Yet alive he was, as the grand St. Patrick himself was kept alive when he was kidnapped by Niall of the Nine Hostages. Surely, the Saint would intercede for him now.

Were these enemies taking him to England itself? To be imprisoned in the dread Tower of London—beheadings, tortures . . . the rack. Or to somewhere in the Pale; Dublin, he wondered?

The muffled knock of waves against the hull forced the captive to lie back, exhausted. He pictured his mother's face, the beauty and fire of her blue eyes. She would bring in more Scots than ever. She and his father would see that not a single Saxon in or near Tyrconnell would live to see the sunrise. They would not let the English touch one more hair of his head. They would avenge him and rescue him. He had a prophecy to fulfill!

He heard his mother's lilting voice recite the prophecy: *When Hugh is fathered by Hugh . . . and drive out the Gall.* But an image kept growing against the dark—the valiant, betrayed head of Alex McSorley howling in silence forever. His mother would think of Alex, too, and fear there might be more than one family head spiked on Dublin Castle gate.

XIII

Donegal Friary
Michaelmas 1587

*T*he bells rang somber along the River Eske to Donegal Castle as early morning chants rose up from the Friary to a pale sky. Ineen, who had not slept, and who at the tolling bells again picked up her missal and rosary, knelt in the castle chapel a fourth time since midnight. It seemed all the kingdom held its breath with her in wild hope Red Hugh O'Donnell was still alive.

When, the night before, MacSweeney Doe's messenger had brought the horrific news, Ineen sent immediately for Father Conan from the Friary to come pray with her and the O'Donnell. Then she draped herself in her blackest wool mantle and went to further ask the Franciscan to sleep in a guest chamber on the highest floor the three hours between each canonical hour.

Another thing she did clearheadedly was to make sure that the physician also stayed at the castle so that O'Donnell would take medicinal whiskey, enough to fall deep into sleep, yet not so much to worsen him. Though shocked, he kept saying, over and over, that the English queen wanted a pledge from him. But in her bones, Ineen knew this snatching of Red Hugh meant much more.

She herself, who could not sleep, knelt and paced. Infuriated. England wanted a pledge from the O'Donnell and those in London or Dublin would relish a Papist. But it was *not* all about Papistry for her relative Mary, Queen of Scots, though a Papist herself, had permitted Protestants and Catholics alike to practice their religion in Scotland. Why, one Earl of Argyll was known to be Protestant and then his successor Catholic, and Ineen respected each. No! It was about freedom. Free to be their own people, whether in Scotland or Ireland, as they had for thousands of years.

If she dozed at all, Ineen saw herself kneeling before a cross, reading the missal, ripping out its pages, banging it against the floor until she shook her head awake to find the book intact.

Then the bells began to ring for Terce, the third canonical hour of prayer, six hours after midnight. Daylight snuck in through the castle's slit windows as she let tears fall. *How could God let this happen?*

A cry came down from the watch atop the castle. "Horse from the north! MacSweeney colors!"

Without seeing if O'Donnell stirred, trusting his physician, Ineen dropped the missal and headed down the steps to the great hall, where more guards than usual stood, some before the turf fire. She flung the great hall's front door open. More than the usual number of Ineen's and O'Donnell's own Redshanks and kerne were already surrounding the castle. She saw in the torchlight MacSweeney Doe and others behind him on the bawn. She raced down the stone steps into the misty cold. Two campfires were still lit. By the time she reached one, two of her other sons had run from behind MacSweeney to meet her.

"Rory! Manus! Ye're safe, thank God!"

"Mother," Rory cried, "they captured Red Hugh!"

His younger brother cried, "And we're going to capture him back!"

The lads, their bright mantles and trews all muddy, rubbed up against the wool of their mother's mantle as she hugged them so tight, they almost screamed for breath. With sharp barks and wet tongue, a fourth face intruded. Red's wolfhound, Scotty, bounded up from somewhere in the grounds then stood back, looking here and there for his master. Ineen reached a hand to rub his wooly head, but he took off toward MacSweeney, barking sharper.

At the face of one lad then the other Ineen stared, her hair in her face, wet from tears. "Safe," she breathed. "You are safe. And Nuala and Caffar are here, and your wee sisters already sent to Scotland."

Then Ineen looked up at MacSweeney Doe, standing shame-faced behind her sons, his own festive mantle muddied, long beard drenched with mist or tears. Good breeding held her tongue to avoid berating a noble sub-chieftain, MacSweeney of the Battle Axes, before other men, but she glared at him.

"Jesus, Mary, and Joseph!" Ineen let explode at him, once inside the castle, then held her tongue. "What must we do," she cried, "to stop these accursed Saxons from killing us!"

She found Annag and Nuala there, looking over at her in terror, Caffar bawling and struggling in Nuala's arms. Ineen told her daughter and her servant to take the lads up to their bedchamber and clean and change them for chapel, as they would all go to the Friary for a Mass she had already requested. The guards she ordered to keep watch there and increase the watch on the bawn.

MacSweeney Doe was told to remain with her. "How could you let this happen to your own foster son?" she said, as she pointed her delicate finger straight at Red's foster father.

"I make no defense of myself, my lady," he replied, in tears.

"And in the very waters where Alex McSorley was treacherously butchered!"

MacSweeney tried to speak but bit his lip.

"Tell me everything!" said Ineen. She motioned him to dry himself before the turf burning in the fireplace—his mantle was dripping on the rushes—and called down the indoor stairs for a gillie to bring up hot mead.

"No, me lady. If there is a Mass, I will wait until after that."

"Aye. Sure enough you must go to the Mass and much you have to pray about in letting the English snatch my son. But you must tell me now!"

Saying not one word that might spare him the least responsibility for Red Hugh's fate, MacSweeney told her what happened. She listened, snapping out a word of her own only when the tale so overcame him the MacSweeney fell silent again.

"And they let you send pledges for yourselves," she said, "but you did nothing to find a pledge for your foster son?"

"They would not free Red Hugh. 'Tis him they wanted most."

"Of course, of course!" she said. "And has no one heard where the lads were taken?"

"Northeast the ship sailed," he said. "I know not where it is going to dock."

Ineen wanted to scream. "That could mean London. The Tower!"

MacSweeney shrugged. "I have dispatched spies to Inishowen and Tyrone and sent messengers. All of the Kingdom has heard, and down to Maguire of Enniskillen, and surely the English in Connaught if not the whole Pale."

Ineen dropped her face into her hands but did not halt. She seemed to have cried herself out all down the sleepless night. If even the valiant, stalwart MacSweeney Doe could be such a fool for wine, who could be proof against it? Hugh Roe O'Donnell was not! Nor did it escape her, despite her rage, that she still needed MacSweeney Doe to keep Red's rivals at bay. Doe's very territory, to the far northwest, served as watchtower on Glencolumbcille and Donal.

"Him you must tell," Ineen said at last with a nod at the ceiling.

"Me lady," MacSweeney said, nodding and wiping his face again.

"Know that I do give thanks, MacSweeney. You brought us Rory and Manus.

"Annag!" Ineen shouted up the spiral stairs. "Bring the children! We're off to chapel. Don't go up," she added to MacSweeney, "till the children are down."

When the children reached the great hall, Nuala still holding Caffar, MacSweeney commenced his trudge up to O'Donnell's bedchamber. Ineen called her children to her arms and held them in a restless embrace, Annag shifting foot to foot behind them.

"Your brother," Ineen made herself say, breathing past tears, "shall return. We shall bring him back."

They looked at her with tears streaming down their faces. And young Caffar, watching his brothers cry, cried loudest of all.

"Children!" Their mother looked each one in the eyes.

"Right now, we all go to chapel, and no tears when we reach there. All in that chapel will look upon us so we must remain dignified."

"I wanted to go to the ship," muttered Rory, "but Red wouldn't let me."

"He knew something was up?" Ineen stared at him.

"Na." Rory gave a little laugh. "Too young I am, he said, to taste the best wines."

"Children!" They fell quiet. "We will go through the tunnel to the Friary!"

"Lord be thanked we don't still have the wee girls here," said Annag.

"Aye," Ineen whispered. "Mairghead and Maire, their nursemaids, and Redshank guards may already be near Inveraray, on their way to the Earl of Argyll, thanks be to God."

Ineen moved to one side of the great hall where stood the massive fireplace, and there on the right of it, cunningly faced with rock, was a small door leading down to a secret tunnel beneath the castle. The tunnel door could be pried open with a small, dark stone kept behind a carved oak statue of Mary, once deemed *Our Lady Star of Dublin*. A fleeing friar had rescued the statue from the ashes of a monastery in the Pale, dissolved on orders of the English queen's father, Henry VIII.

Ineen, looking upon Our Lady, reached for the stone on the mantel. *Let Red at least sail to Dublin,* she prayed as a pain struck her heart. *Most of all let him come safe home.*

She felt her grief harden and sink in her like the stone. She heaved a deep breath, then another, and as she did, turned the statue to face the wall.

"What you do that for?" asked Rory.

His mother answered, "When Our Lady brings your brother safe home, she'll be turned around again to reign in this house.

"Rory," Ineen commanded, handing him the fire shovel and the stone. "Clear the way and pry open the tunnel door."

The sweet burning turf was burning low and was easily raked aside.

"Manus, gather rushes from the floor," she ordered.

Rory knew just how to insert the stone to pry open the creaky, secret door. After the entrance to the tunnel was open, he handed the stone back to his mother so she could replace it behind the turned statue.

Once Manus gathered enough rushes, he and Rory quickly wrapped them in clods of turf from the fireplace, whose flames had burned out. Everyone but Annag would carry two of these improvised torches, one to light now and one to light in a little while from the last flickers of the first. Annag would have her hands full carrying Caffar and a bit of linen dipped in honey for the little one, who hated the tunnel, to suck on.

Ineen told Rory, "You go first, then Nuala, then Manus, followed by Annag with Caffar. Do what I say. Now go!"

"Shouldn't we wait for Father?" Nuala asked.

"He'll come with his Brehons, O'Clery, and MacSweeney Doe," Ineen answered, wondering, *Will I ever begin to forgive MacSweeney?*

The secret stairway spiraled down and down until, beneath the bottom castle floor, they stepped one-by-one into the dank, cold tunnel along which they hurried with bent shoulders and flaming rush-torches. Braced with supports of oak and stone, the tunnel ran along the river and bent with it toward the Friary, where it ended beneath the kitchen and steps led up to the cloister walk. Caffar squirmed in Annag's arms but never stopped sucking the honey-cloth.

Ineen thought that it seemed a miracle that the rest of her children had been delivered to her safely. The children. *Hidden they must be kept, yes; driven far away to some ring fort no foreigner could ever find. Or to a monastery. Monasteries in Ulster thrive still. But where best to go? To Scotland?* She pushed her children on and drove them toward the Friary.

The exit from the tunnel stood beside the Friary kitchen. Rory, on the highest steps up from the tunnel floor, unlocked the door and gave it the three pounds that told who was trying to enter. Shortly the door was opened by the burly friar cook. The door was locked on both sides to secure the Friary from any invaders who might find their way into the tunnel from the castle, and to close the tunnel to any invaders who would find their way to the castle through the Friary. Patterns of knocks on either side of the door served as sign and countersign.

The children and their mother, with Annag, huddled inside the kitchen while the cook made sure the cloister alley to the chapel was clear though already the Friary grounds were surrounded by more Redshanks than usual.

"Hold your heads high," Ineen admonished her children. "I remind you again that all inside will have their eyes upon us."

The candlelit dusk of the chapel was charged with anxious murmurs, which dropped at the entry of Ineen and family. A burst of keening greeted the mother of Red Hugh. With a nod only to nobles who caught her eye, it was all Ineen could do not to add her own keening to the crows. Her children stared at her, but a resolute headshake, head raised, served to quiet them a little longer.

She kept them moving, first to the side altar of the Blessed Mother, where each genuflected, then to their places beside their father's chair before the main altar. The usual chill of the chancel was stuffy from crowding bodies and mantles strong with the smell of wet wool. Ineen inhaled slowly the honeycomb fragrance of the beeswax melting in the altar candles, mingled with traces of incense from the last canonical hour. The harper's strings struck up a melody solemn but sweet as the friars filed into their choir behind the screen. Voices at the rear again fell silent, which meant the O'Donnell had arrived.

Ineen did not look round at first but felt the parting of the crowd for the painful steps of their king. Presently he halted beside her, not taking his chair. When she felt his arm slide under hers, she forced herself to hold in her sobs. Caffar began to cry in Nuala's arms and Nuala with him. Ineen patted the child's head, managed to swallow her grief again, and whispered to Nuala, "No tears!"

But when Ineen looked up to her husband, she was shocked to see his hair so whitened since he took to bed last night. His beard was totally white, it seemed, in the poor light. He, who had been victorious overthrowing her own father's killer at Farsetmore, did not return her glance but stood, face to the altar, with a *kingly* spine no longer held quite as straight. With another quick, close glance she realized his eyes gazing forward as though all strength was gone. Old. Very old.

Then, without breaking the forward gaze, he whispered, "Tyrone has come."

"Hugh O'Neill's here?" She looked round. "At Mass?"

O'Donnell moved his head, "Yes."

She caught her breath. "He has news of Red?"

"After," O'Donnell said.

Ineen wanted to rush to Hugh O'Neill. She craned and strained to see him but, in the crowd, caught herself looking instead straight into the face of Donal. Her stepson, staring as though he had been staring at her all along, nodded. Donal had lost no time to ride to O'Donnell's side. *Does he think the way is now open for him if Red does not return?*

Niall Garbh, his brothers, and their leader Hugh McDean were there, too, to win the old king's favor with an exhibition of support—each and every man eager to prove his might with Red Hugh taken by the English.

Guardian of the Friary, Abbot Thady O'Boyle, processioned into the chapel, accompanied by a friar acolyte. Blessing his king and all present, who crossed themselves, he commenced the *Introit* of the Mass.

"Kyrie Eleison," the Abbot chanted. Lord have mercy. *"Mercy!"* Ineen joined, as all the voices echoed *"Eleison,"* but she could not help think, *And where was Your mercy, O Lord, when my son rowed out to the false merchantman? Is it not enough that we keep true faith?*

The incense from the altar mingled with the stink of wet wool. Usually sweet and exalting, now incense only irritated nose and throat. Ineen coughed into her dark mantle, so like mourning clothes for her captured son. She recalled herself, praying the Lord accept her resolute presence as penance to merit deliverance of her son from captivity, from torment, from death. *Red! Red!* All she could think of was her Red. Was he being taken to that Tower in London? Were they strapping him to hellish racks to break him?

"Have mercy on *him,* my Lord," she prayed under her breath.

"Are you well?" the O'Donnell whispered, interrupting the swirl of her thoughts.

"How can I be well?" she whispered back. "My son is stolen! They have taken my son. Our Red is kidnapped."

"The Lord will deliver him. The prophecy, Wife. The prophecy," O'Donnell whispered and peered at her from the corner of his eye.

She reached her free hand across to squeeze his arm. But as she answered his gaze, she could not help notice how his face sagged beneath his eyes, and how his deep green eyes, which then turned forward to follow the priest, looked wearier than hers.

At Communion, it was all her parched throat could do to swallow the Host. *If Red is alive!* And she felt with a mother's heart he must be. *Every day, every hour—you must never, my Red, forget the prophecy.*

To keep herself in place through the last of the Mass, Ineen reached inside a pouch in her mantle for the gold medallion Alex had given her. It read *In Deo Nostra Spes*: In God Our Hope. She wanted to cry out to God, as His Own Son had cried out, *My God, why have You forsaken me!* O'Donnell spoke true; it was too soon for that. She squeezed the raised letters of the medallion till they bit into the flesh of her hand and she felt the blood.

When the Abbot gave the final blessing and the chapel bells pealed, Ineen clutched her husband's arm and pulled him as swiftly as she could through the parting crowd, looking right and left for Hugh O'Neill, whom she could not see. When they reached the arched doorway, she saw him standing in the drizzle with his retinue. Covered in a long mantle, head couched in a great fur collar, despite a beard as sharp as any Saxon, he looked more Irish like the Ulster man

150

he really was. She made for him, but he moved first to the O'Donnell and gripped the arms of the aging king.

"My dear father-in-law," said Tyrone, "I rode here as soon as I heard of this foul ruse that took Red Hugh from your kingdom."

O'Donnell greeted him. "'Tis most grand of you to come."

"'Twas my good fortune to be at Strabane, conferring with my cousin Turlough O'Neill." He turned to Ineen, with a bow and lifting his knee, in Irish fashion. "And with the strong prayers of your mother, Agnes, for her grandson Red that I come from there."

"All of Ulster must know this crime by now," Ineen managed to say. "'Tis grateful I am to have news of prayers, even my mother's."

Tyrone bowed again.

"Come to the castle with us," O'Donnell said, "that we might talk."

O'Neill responded with his voice lowered, "Another reason that I have come."

Then Ineen instructed, "Annag," who was standing by the church, "take the children straight on to the castle. I will command a bodyguard of Redshanks to escort you."

Manus darted ahead, racing to be first to reach the castle. Annag shouted to him, and Rory darted after. Ineen noticed but said nothing, so intent she was about O'Neill's presence.

"I thank you, Hugh O'Neill, for attending this Mass." She was startled to hear herself thank Hugh O'Neill for anything.

"That and more that I have waited for you, my lady," he nodded.

"Tell me where my son Red Hugh is!" she raised her voice.

"My dearest Ineen, I do not yet know." He reached over as they walked, touching her elbow to assure her. "I rode here too soon to hear where he might be taken. But I sent a man to Dublin to find out."

She did not challenge his use of "Ineen" as she often did. It sank in upon her that instant that all had changed. She fixed her eyes upon him. It shocked her to see his eyes wet, and not from the drizzle; it was well known how strong emotion brought tears to his eyes.

"Hugh O'Neill," she still could not call him by his Saxon title, Earl of Tyrone. "Find Red Hugh!"

Bowing, he said, "*Misneach!*"

"Courage we all need. You, who sit in Dublin's Parliament, can do something. Help me find a way to rescue our son and your kidnapped son-in-law."

O'Neill, though looking thoughtful, said nothing.

Ineen leaned close to him and whispered, "Help us bring Red Hugh safe home from . . . from your English *friends.*"

XIV

Dublin Castle
The Pale, 25 September 1587

*I*n front of Red Hugh spread a castle yard wide and broad, paved with stones and a wooden drawbridge. The walls looked higher and more massive than Irish castle walls, weather-grimed, and at the corners fortified with stout crenellated towers that he knew were built four hundred years earlier by Normans. Red breathed a sigh of hope that he was in Dublin and not London. Even the gray morn and its dreariness did not dampen his determination, for at least he was still in Ireland. He moved his shackled ankles forward with resolve.

He saw the other captives for the first time since being snatched at Lough Swilly. They had been packed close together in the ship's hold, though in separate compartments. In the gray wet air, Donny's young face turned every which way, looking red-eyed and muttering that they were going to be killed.

Donny was youngest, so Red said, "Nay, lad, they would have thrown us in the sea if—" but a Saxon soldier slapped him and told him to keep his tongue.

Keeping his tongue was what Owny seemed to be doing, as if they had torn it out; he stumbled forward, shivering, eyes staring wide.

"Do ye hear him?" laughed the English captain in bad Irish amid the jeers surrounding them, pointing at one of the crude balls of tar spiked at the castle gate.

At first Red Hugh thought the ghastly tar balls one more demonic decoration.

"'Tis your kinsman, Alexander McSorley, calling, 'Welcome! Been too long! I been countin' the days till you join me in hell!'" The captain continued.

Red looked up and bit his tongue so as not to ask, *Which one?* The tar heads took on shapes of eye hollows and fallen jaws. Not even the one the captain pointed at resembled the Alex McSorley he knew so well. Yet Alex's head must be there, for they heard that even from Hugh O'Neill. Red's fleeting gaze was caught by the third or fourth head from one end. At that moment, he shivered all over, struggling to hold onto hope. *Alex!* He breathed to himself. *Thank God Mother does not see you. I am trusting you to watch out for me and the lads.*

All this happened within seconds as the captain but paused in the march, taking Red Hugh and, behind him, Owny and Donny, all bound and dragging chains. They walked between files of sharp-helmeted guards onto the drawbridge to reach the royal stone of Dublin Castle.

Stay with us, Alex! Red garnered courage. *We will avenge you yet.*

The captain halted them, sweeping his hand with a smile at the walls and towers, then he shouted, and castle guards led them across the bridge. A castle official, Captain Wood, was standing there—tall, with deep eyes and a pointed beard the color of wet sand. He ordered the guards to take Owny and Donny Gorm into Bermingham Tower, named after a noble prisoner hanged there two hundred years earlier. Red Hugh he ordered detached and to come with him.

Captain Wood waited till the other lads were taken away, told the guardsmen to follow, and, crossing to Red's right side, seemed to lose a step and tripped the lad. The guardsman laughed, but given an instruction, he shut up. Red's chains made it difficult for him to stand up again. With a sharp tug at his arm, Captain Wood steadied him upright, breathing in Irish, "Your father-in-law, the Earl of Tyrone, sends his assurances."

Snapping his arm out of the English captain's light grip, Red glared at him but could not help ask, "Hugh O'Neill?"

"Take heed, lad," this official answered in English; then harshly in Irish, "Yes. You are under his protection here."

Red kept glaring. The official gestured forward, and they resumed their march toward the tower opposite Bermingham in the front wall. In Irish he continued his tone, "Mind my words, not my manner. Tyrone has many friends in Dublin. He is cordial with the Lord Deputy, who awaits us."

"Perrot!" Red Hugh snapped.

"Speak the Lord Deputy's name with due reverence!" Wood answered in English. And in Irish added, "Take heed, son. Beware; the Lord Deputy speaks Irish."

At the entrance to the tower the captain stepped aside, nodding the guardsman to open the heavy door. The captain ushered Red inside.

Within a second interior room to which another soldier escorted them, behind a large ornate desk with candelabra of a dozen flaming candles, smiled a large, fit-looking man with pointed reddish beard and dark, delighted eyes. A heavy gold chain of office reposed on his jerkin. He did not stand up.

"I deliver to you, sir," announced Captain Wood, "the hostage, Red Hugh O'Donnell."

"Thank you, Captain Wood," said the Lord Deputy, sucking a back tooth with his right finger with immense satisfaction. "Prince of Tyrconnell, Hugh Roe O'Donnell."

Though in pain in his chains, Red stood erect, glowered, and, as a point of pride, said nothing.

Remaining seated, Lord Deputy Perrot continued in Irish, "You are a guest of the Crown—a pledge of loyalty on behalf of your father and your mother."

Red could no longer hold his tongue. "The O'Donnell and my mother are loyal to Tyrconnell."

Perrot resumed in Irish, "Your father is in arrears in his cattle rent ever since he married your mother. He owes the Crown 200 beeves each year, for many years now. And your mother continues to bring in Redshanks. Most recalcitrant."

Red said nothing.

"But you are worth more than many cows, Prince Hugh Roe." The Lord Deputy pushed back his chair and stood up. "Captain Wood, have our guest's gyves removed."

Captain Wood, opening the office door, called the soldier sitting at a small desk in the anteroom, who entered promptly and removed the chains from Red's arms and legs. Much as he wished to stand firm as a pillar of defiance, Red could not help rub his freed wrists and arms and move his legs.

When the Lord Deputy stood up, he seemed two heads taller than Red Hugh. He said, "As much or more than your father, 'tis your mother who has brought you here."

"*You* brought me here!" Red said.

"Take it as tribute to your father's obstinacy and strength that the Crown was constrained to employ a ruse to deliver its invitation to you."

"You kidnapped me! You kidnapped all three from Tyrconnell."

Perrot suppressed a smile. "Red Hugh, your mother keeps bringing in Scots in flagrant and impudent violation of a royal decree."

"She is queen and has the right of it."

Perrot, looking Red Hugh eye to eye, made no immediate answer; then, "And she and your father continue to refuse submission to the New Religion, and continue to support and protect friars in defiance of the Crown's reform. To defy the English queen is to defy God. Have you no fear of that?"

"God, I fear—not an evil monarch."

"Ah! Best rid yourself of speech like that, Hugh O'Donnell, if you care to remain your father's pledge and not be declared *rebel*—like your kinsman Alex McSorley, whose head now adorns this Castle's gate."

It was all he could do for Red to hold his tongue, but he struggled to hold back tears.

"Alex is—*was*—a Scot, and your mother's a Scot, and you, Red Hugh O'Donnell, are a half-breed as London calls you. So," said Lord Deputy Perrot after a beat, "here you are in Dublin Castle."

Red only grimaced, not trusting his tongue.

The Lord Deputy returned beside his desk. "There is an additional consideration, young Master O'Donnell. The Queen of England and Ireland is not pleased to see another uniting of O'Donnells and O'Neills. No," Perrott shuffled his feet covered by golden buckled shoes, "the English queen does not want you to marry a daughter of the Earl of Tyrone. He is already married to your half-sister, Siobhan.

"In this, I do you a favor in warning you. This demonstrates to you that you are not a mere prisoner, Hugh Roe." He gestured generously. "You are my guest. And as my guest you shall take residence in a fine room, fit for becoming a gentleman. If you indeed become as proper a gentleman as the Earl of Tyrone, perhaps Her Majesty will be less displeased with another marriage between an O'Donnell and Tyrone."

Red, looking at the Lord Deputy, reminded him, "It is for my father and Tyrone to decide if such a marriage goes forward. I am already promised to Tyrone's Rose O'Neill."

The Lord Deputy sat down, sliding his chair in and picking up a quill. "You shall have time to think upon what I have said. Six months is the usual time a pledge is held in this castle," Perrot advised.

"Kindly escort Prince O'Donnell to his room in the state prisoner's section of Bermingham Tower." He nodded to Wood and gestured dismissal.

Captain Wood, pacing his charge, sent two guardsmen forward to open the tower door as they marched across the stones of the courtyard. "I must warn you to trust no castle Catholics hereabouts, but methinks you'll trust no one at all."

"And why should I trust one who kidnaps me?" Red asked.

"I carry out the Lord Deputy's orders," said Wood, "and Tyrone's wishes—not my own."

Soon Red wound round and round up the spiral staircase to the top of Bermingham Tower, glad his chains were gone; not that he felt any gratitude to Perrot for the relief. At the top, he leaned aside for Captain Wood, who reached over him to unlock and shove the door open. Wood nudged him forward.

Entering, the lad was astonished to see his two friends dressed in brown Saxon doublet and hose.

"Red!" cried Owny with a smile that was still a frown. "We were after thinking your head might be joining Alex's!"

"What have they done with your mantles?" was the best Red could manage.

"Mine they took away!" Donny Gorm said.

"They burned mine a bit," said Owny, "to make the damn point, then took it away—into a cesspool, they'd toss them."

Red looked at Wood. "So, that's the way of it for my mantle, too?"

"With theirs I had nothing to do," said Wood mildly. "Your own shan't go in a cesspool."

"And 'tis wearing these accursed Saxon togs I'm supposed to do that?"

But already Red was taking off his vomit-stained, ragged mantle, tossing it to Wood. He suddenly felt very tired. He looked about the room.

The cell, though circular, was not much different from a chamber atop a castle in many parts of Ulster. But logs instead of turf burned in the fireplace, compliments of Saxon axes chopping Ireland's trees. There were stools at the hearth, four chairs around a small wooden table mid-cell, and behind a door a wooden bucket with wooden lid that obviously served as chamber pot. The stone floor was covered on one side with a dark wool ruglet. At places along the curving wall lay three low cots with coverlets. On one bed was Red Hugh's set of English clothing—black doublet, ruffled shirt, hose, and buckled shoes.

Noticing Red's stare at them, Captain Wood said, "They are clean."

"I'll not be after wearing any of those," Red shot back.

"My orders are to put your gyves on again if you do not take the togs. And no food till you do."

"No food!" cried Donny.

Red looked at the youngest lad's face.

After Red changed clothes, almost tearing at the Saxon fabrics while tugging them on, Wood nodded, promising food, and left, locking the door behind him. Red flung himself on the cot. He did not want to trust this Captain Wood. Wood needed to earn his trust.

Lying without chains, Red tried to keep his eyes open. He could almost hear the harper strumming an air, harp strings being the last sounds of Tyrconnell he heard as the small boat with the harper rowed away from that treacherous merchantman in Lough Swilly. That harper was most fortunate they had not murdered him, given harpers were outlawed by English law. How long would it be before he heard the strings of a harp again?

In God our hope! he prayed, recalling the words on the MacDonnell medal Alex had given his mother. But then, there was Alex's head somewhere behind the small, barred window below him.

He grasped one of the jerkin buttons, ripped it off, and tossed it toward the nearby window. It hit the wall and fell on the floor.

Donny, who kept jumping, declared, "I want me own togs back!"

"Nay," said Red. "Not now. Not yet." He sat up suddenly. "Lads, we will escape! And we'll need these togs to get out of here and out of the Pale."

"How?" asked Owny.

"Tomorrow!" said Donny.

"As soon as we find a way," Red answered. "'Twas never a castle I have ever been in that doesn't have a way to escape."

XV

Bermingham Tower
October 1587

*S*eizing the sides of the barred window as though he could tear it apart, Red saw a darkening sky and menacing clouds that flung sleet upon the tar heads spiked on Dublin Castle gate. He imagined Alex's head turned around to gaze up at him.

"Curse the Saxon headsmen! Oh, what I'd give to be Sweeney Mad and fly from tree to tree. Be over Wicklow Mountains for sunset," Red shouted to Owny and Donny, banging his body against the stone wall and dropping to the floor.

Owny responded, "If I were free, I'd find a tavern. I'm thirsty."

"Me too," said Donny, "weary I am of Saxon wheat bread." He slumped beside the hearth and scratched madly at his scalp, his carrot curls plagued by lice.

"The blood of Milesius cries out from the spikes!" Red brandished his fists. "Cries out for justice!"

The other two agreed and scratched their heads furiously.

Days, weeks had passed as weary routine marked them. Counting down the months, they had five more months, with six being the term for hostages. Despite the occasional cold, they had escaped the typhus and smallpox and no word of plague reached their ears.

Just then, the locks on their door rattled and in swept their assigned tutor, Master Buckley; hale, hearty, and the better for a mug or two.

"Top of the morning, gentlemen, you sons of Niall of the Nine Hostages!"

A grunt managed to arise from one or other of the lads.

The tutor grinned with a rosy face, red as a new berry, and the lads could expect his breath to be ripened by English ale. His doublet bulged. He took pride in repeating, every day, his opinion that all that they learned about the English would be to their advantage, and so he taught English language, English history, mathematics, and logic—subjects most suitable to reform wild Irish minds.

It had not taken Red Hugh long to realize Master Buckley had mastered only a smattering of Irish and remembered but a few words of Latin, knew no Greek, and no Spanish. This proved helpful to Red and the lads. Red himself knew Irish as well as Latin, Greek, and Spanish, thanks to the holy friars. The little English he knew he was determined to speak but rarely. So, he would answer the tutor's English pointedly in Latin, the language of the Roman Church, or in Irish, and Owny and Donny followed his example. As a result, the three hostages learned a little more English and the tutor a lot more Latin and Irish.

But this day happened to be 30 October, the day before the Eve of All Hallows, and indeed Red Hugh's fifteenth birthday, of which the hostage was well aware. And there was Master Buckley not with his usual books.

He lifted a pile of small, thick books, which he passed to the boys. "The *Book of Common Prayer*," Master Buckley urged.

"Heretics' prayers," Red said in Irish to his friends, who froze while holding theirs, uncertain what to do with them.

"Now, now, Master O'Donnell, I understood that. Similar prayers the Papists pray, only in English."

"Prayer is said in Latin," said Red.

Owny and Donny stared at Red.

"I believe I should know how Papists pray." More than once Buckley told them he was raised Papist but was happy to be Church of Ireland, purged of religious corruptions. "'Tis a blessed day, indeed. Your progress is such that we shall attend chapel midday to pray psalms together. Hence these books."

Red grabbed the book from Buckley's hands, struggling not to hit the man with it. After hesitating, he slammed it hard on the table. From the first, when Master Buckley had introduced himself, Red remembered Captain Wood's warning, "Beware Castle Catholics."

Master Buckley's face lost its smiling mildness. "Now, gentlemen," he pronounced incisively in English, "—and I shall call you that for you shall become gentlemen—going to chapel is not an option." He stared at all three of them in turn.

"I will take no part in such services," Red spat out the words.

Master Buckley straightened his back and looked down sternly at the lad. "I am commanded to take you," he recited in poor Irish, "or you shall be removed from this state prison cell to another . . ." he lapsed into English, "a less congenial place," then climbed back shakily into Irish: "*never* to return here."

"I prefer the dungeon . . ." Red began in Irish before seeing the startled faces of his fellow hostages.

For answer, Master Buckley tugged open the door, called the guards, and without closing the door, took his leave. In moments, the lads heard the guards' shoes racing up to squeeze past Buckley, and soon two guards entered. One by one they tugged Donny and Owny to the stairs, and then two more squeezed in to seize Red's arms till he stumbled onto the stairs. With a guard in front and one behind, Red wondered in outrage, *Where are you, O Friend Captain Wood, who wants me to trust you!*

They were soon met by Captain Wood himself at the base of Bermingham Tower stairs, who pointed them across the castle yard toward the corner tower where they were taken. The chapel in the Cork Tower had ample space and windows fitted with glass, dull without the light of the sun, which was hidden behind Dublin's dark clouds. At the entrance, Red balked. His first view of a reformed chapel was of darkness. *Dark pool*, he thought, the name of Dublin itself.

For centuries this had been a Papist chapel, but now reformed. It lacked a tabernacle, tapers, statues, even portraits of the Blessed Mother. Behind a long table stood a high, stern, empty cross—not a Crucifix that displayed the crucified Christ.

As the darkness lightened to dimness, Red made out the figures of men and a few women in the pews, finely dressed in English fashion. They sat waiting for someone.

Presently, a tall man robed in black stood up in assembly, opened and closed his hands in a priest-like arc, and began to pray in English.

Red blurted, loud and clear in Latin, *"Pater Noster."* Our Father.

The minister pretended not to acknowledge this disturbance, and only a head or two turned to glare at the lads. But when the minister raised his voice to announce, "To be a Papist is to be an idolater!" Red shouted in Latin, then in English, "He preaches no true faith. *Ave Maria, gratia plena, Hail Mary full of grace."*

Suddenly the voices of Owny and Donny chimed in, *"Dominus tecum, The Lord is with you!"*

The three were seized by the guards and an uproar of gentlemanly shouts and womanly shrieks cut off the minister. They were being dragged out of the chapel and Captain Wood clapped a hand on Red's mouth.

The lads struggled with their captors into the castle yard till Captain Wood released Red, and with a gesture he ordered the other two freed. They instantly stopped struggling and walked, almost gaily, back toward Bermingham Tower.

"Terrible! Terrible!" wailed Master Buckley, hastening after them, waving hands clutching prayer books in distress. "You blaspheme the Holy Church of the Queen—"

"That is all, Master Buckley." Captain Wood halted the tutor. "You are dismissed for the day." Seeing the horror on Buckley's face, Wood continued, "'Tis a punishment for your students here."

Uncertain at this, but endeavoring to collect himself, Buckley swelled his lungs, then expelled, "They are foul, foul, incorrigible heathens!" And on that note, he spun dramatically to show them all his back, nearly stumbling. But recovering himself, Master Buckley marched gravely and haughtily back to the chapel.

"You must truly want the dungeon, Hugh Roe O'Donnell!" Captain Wood said to his charge, with barely controlled anger, waving the other guards to hasten Owny and Donny into Bermingham Tower.

"That service insulted the true faith," said Red.

"You will never leave here alive if your behavior ends you up in the dungeon."

"Better the dungeon than a pit of heretics!"

"You insult me, you know. I'm Church of England." Wood tugged him to a halt. "Tyrone's warning I give you, not mine."

"You keep saying that, but how can I trust you?"

"You've been here less than two months—and arrangements to free you take time."

"Yeah, yeah!" Red blurted out.

Captain Wood turned Red to look him in the eye. "'Tis no one else as close to Bermingham Tower to do as I'm doing for you."

Red snorted a laugh.

"So as not to be removed from your keep," Wood continued, "I must administer a chastisement."

"What—"

But before Red could finish speaking, he was on the stones of the castle yard, hands on his throbbing ear, and trying to reel back the howl that turned the heads of his companions and their guards, who cheered Captain Wood.

"You shall have to stand up on your own this time," said Wood, once again in harsh Irish. "Your big mouth I should bloody, but I am sworn to observe limits."

Red staggered to his feet, stepping away from Wood, rubbing his ear.

"Know who your friends are," said the captain, taking hold of Red's arm again, "and consider what they risk for you."

Red said nothing. He kept his mouth pinned as he climbed to his room until, in a voice that rasped his throat, he whispered fiercely to Wood behind him, "I won't pray in English or with reformers or in their chapel."

In a mutter of his own, Captain Wood responded, "I suspect you shan't be welcome in the chapel again. Now tuck in your shirt and stop playing the wild Irish."

Red snapped round at Wood and was surprised to see his antagonist's smile more amused than harsh. He tucked in the shirt, smoothed the doublet, and climbed. But when he reached the room, expecting Captain Wood to follow in and deliver a new lecture, Captain Wood kept by the door, hand on lock. Before he closed and locked the cell door behind him, he said merely, "'Tis gruel you eat this night."

And so they did.

But later in the evening, the cell door swung suddenly open and Captain Wood entered carrying a basket.

"Compliments of your mother, Red Hugh." He placed the basket on the table.

The lads swarmed over it, but Red slapped away their hands and snatched off the covering cloth. In the basket were oatcakes, honey, butter, apples, and jugs of mead.

Red stared at Captain Wood.

"And how are we to trust no poison in these?" He referred to Bottle Smythe, the notorious poisoner at Dublin Castle.

"You don't. But you might break open the largest oatcake on top."

The lads gave him alarmed and questioning looks.

"You needn't eat," Wood continued laconically, "if you do not care to."

Red picked up the large oatcake and noticed as he did a shred of parchment underneath. He grabbed it up and read, *In Deo Nostra Spes.*

"*In God Our Hope,*" he said in Irish. "Words from Alex's Medallion." *The Medallion given to my mother.* He read the words beneath the proverb: "Love, Mother." His breath caught a cough. Tears burst from his eyes.

He waved to the others, "Eat." He moved over to the slit-window and read the parchment again, several times, then stuffed it into his doublet, over his heart. His mother's love reached him. And on his birthday. And likely with the help of Hugh O'Neill.

Meanwhile, Owny and Donny dived into the oat cakes and slurped the mead.

Captain Wood said, "I'll be taking my leave now."

Red turned. They looked at each other, Captain Wood not yet moving. Red swallowed and strode to the table, picked up and stared at the pewter cup of mead Owny had poured for him. Then he looked at Wood, and lip trembling a little, raised the cup. "*Sláinte!*"

"*Sláinte!* Happy Birthday, Red Hugh!" chimed the other two lads.

Captain Wood nodded, "*Sláinte* and birthday greetings." He added, "'Tis my understanding these are not the last of gifts from your mother."

Then Captain Wood closed and locked the cell door behind him.

Red let the mead swirl about his tongue, unable to swallow it just yet. Although he did not want to say he trusted Wood—not aloud, lest the guard turn fool. But the long arms of his mother—and of Tyrone's English friends— did indeed reach into Dublin Castle.

The days ahead appeared shorter.

XVI

Armagh
Ninth Day of Christmas 1588

T he clouds brooding in the morn over Castle Dungannon lit up outside the glass windows with a great roll of thunder. "Welcome you always are, dear Ineen," said O'Neill, "and I've grand hopes your gold will bring back your son."

Ineen felt hope and yet a heavy omen, as with one hand she set a bag of gold on Hugh O'Neill's desk. The writing desk was carved with whorls and swirls and impudent faces in a chamber of Hugh O'Neill's off the great hall. With the other hand, she shook a parchment.

O'Neill noted, with a smile, that grief did not disarrange the care Red's mother took with her appearance. Even in a long, dark mantle and simple léine she stood strong, her hair tumbled to her shoulders, raven-black and aglow, illuminated from the nearby candelabra.

"Do you have later news than this?" she asked O'Neill as he took the parchment and swung out an ornate chair for her.

"Please sit, Ineen." He glanced at the parchment, written by O'Clery, the O'Donnell scribe. No doubt it was behindhand.

Fire crackled in the blazing logs of the immense fireplace as he scanned the scholar's words.

The English did not even pretend hospitality in seizing Red Hugh O'Donnell. Yet, they summoned him to them without delay so that he might meet face to face with them, and they proceeded to converse with him and ask information of him and in their way to observe and search into the nature of his qualities. In the end they ordered him to be put in a strong stone castle where the noble descendants of the sons of Milesius were in chains and captivity, expecting slaughter and death.

Setting the parchment on the table, he said, "Happily, Red Hugh does not lie in the dungeon, 'expecting slaughter and death.' And he has only two months left of a hostage's six months."

"Two months too many!" Ineen answered.

"Aye." He paced before the fire. "But Red fares well."

"You have seen him?" Ineen asked.

"Not yet, but I have spies who have."

Ineen said, "That I count on!"

"I have made arrangements," O'Neill added, with a sudden air of authority, "and a connection with the English today—beyond what you requested. You must give me your trust, Ineen Dubh, if I bring you with me so that you are assured that your gold is accepted by the English."

Trust was not something Ineen wished to give any Irishman who trafficked, as Hugh O'Neill did, with Dublin and the Crown, but he did dress differently in his castle than when riding about Tyrone or Tyrconnell in the fashions of the Saxon court. His beard was no longer trimly pointed but growing bushy, and his hair lay shaggy on his neck, reaching into the fur of a large velvet mantle that whirled as he turned sharply this way and that.

"I have spies, knew it would take gold," O'Neill sighed. "But I did think events would move more swiftly. I know every man in Dublin, in the Council and out, whom to approach, whom to avoid, and I have done it all. I cannot say 'tis Perrot who obstructs me. Perrot is not above taking a bribe, but to his credit his word, though bought, is good."

"Do I understand you to mean that when Perrot takes my gold, he will free Red?"

O'Neill hesitated only a moment. "Aye."

Ineen gave a grateful smile. "What devils we must pay to free my son!"

O'Neill regarded her but said nothing. Then, "'Tis time!"

"One thing more," Ineen said and stood up. "There's a letter I wish you to send your friend Walsingham."

"Walsingham!" O'Neill said. "He is a tricky one, a spymaster. May not be best for you to deal with him."

"I do not intend to. I plan to reach him through you. I will dictate the letter and have you sign it. 'Twill be brief and to the point. And you will know best how to get it into your friend's hands."

"I don't know what you know about Sir Francis," O'Neill wondered.

"I know you, Hugh. And if this gold buys my son's release, no letter will be necessary. If not . . . yet another offer to the Crown," Ineen informed him.

Without another word, but with no display of eagerness for all Ineen's demands, O'Neill retrieved parchment, quill, and black ink bottle from a cabinet. He sat then at his desk, dipped the quill in the ink, and looked at Ineen. "Begin . . ."

Rising from her chair, she raised her voice and spoke firmly. *"Your honor,"* she recited, pacing, *"is the only man next until the Earl of Leicester on whom I rely, and O'Donnell hath no friends but mine."*

O'Neill nodded for her to continue.

"I therefore and for that O'Donnell," she said, with a catch in her throat, *"will deliver unto the Lord Deputy of Ireland the said Red Hugh's second brother, by that same father and mother as a hostage—"* she expelled a breath.

O'Neill looked up sharply. "You and O'Donnell both pledge this?"

She nodded unhappily. "Not a new thought. One we discussed some time ago."

O'Neill said, "Please continue."

She resumed pacing. *"And deliver,"* she sighed, *"any other pledges in Tyrconnell that his Lordship will choose."* She heaved another breath. *"I beseech your honor, as ever you will have O'Donnell and me to depend upon you during our lives, to plead this exchange with Her Highness."*

At the cessation of her voice O'Neill looked up again. "That is all?"

"Aye."

O'Neill gave a small sigh of his own. "Nonetheless, 'tis quite a lot."

She nodded. "Aye. It pains O'Donnell. His failing health kept him at Donegal. But if, as you say, the Saxons have treated Red Hugh well . . . Please, Hugh, sign your name to it and let's be going." She pulled her warm mantle from the chair, and he stood and wrapped it around her.

"Only if the gold fails," she reminded him, hugging herself as she shivered despite the warm mantle.

"I'll sign it now. And order us hot mead," he said, putting aside the quill and parchment after signing the missive.

"Not necessary, Hugh."

"'Tis for me, too!" he laughed, rubbing his arms. "This letter blows ice and snow through me."

"Only if—"

"The gold fails, aye." He stuck the folded parchment in a deep pocket inside his doublet.

"I must freshen up before we leave, as I am to go on to Newry this night, for the envoy to the English queen will be

177

there." O'Neill strode quickly to the spiral staircase and called down for two pewter mugs and a jug of mead.

When they proceeded to the entourage awaiting them, Hugh walked alongside Ineen. Outside, the cold rain gave way, and the lowering clouds sifted fresh snow upon the hardened snow in the bawn and the winter pastures sloping down toward Lough Neagh in the distance.

Ineen gave O'Neill a strange look yet said nothing. She planned to return to Mongavlin from wherever they were heading.

Only O'Neill and his trusted horse-boy knew where they would be going, and the horse-boy had been told too late to fetch even a shilling for this tantalizing bit of intelligence.

In her dark mantle, a fur-trimmed hood pulled over her black hair, Ineen hoped that O'Neill, traveling with yet another woman not his wife, would not attract special attention. Mounting her white stallion, she placed one leg over the bow to ride in the most proper Saxon fashion, as O'Neill urged.

Were she not so desperate to do whatever it took to rescue her son, she would have trusted O'Neill's assurances less—that his steel-helmeted Saxon pikemen and musketeers would provoke no trouble with her Redshanks. But O'Neill allowed the Redshanks only upon Ineen's agreement to keep them as a rearguard and hide them in the forest before he approached the English contact, who he felt sure would take the gold. O'Neill himself employed Redshanks but left his in Dungannon.

O'Neill's banner waved in the snowy wind. The contingent marched down the hill of Dungannon toward the forest of whitened oaks and evergreens, just off the rutted road and across the frozen grasses till they reached the woods.

"Hugh, do you ever think upon all the dead?" Ineen asked. "I see them at night, on foggy days . . . my father, my brothers, Alex, even the Queen of Scots."

"Ineen, milady—"

"So many killed in so few years—" she continued.

"'Tis not the time to speak of this," O'Neill blurted, in a tone to halt further talk.

But Ineen said all she meant to say, for the moment.

Above the conifers and through the naked branches of oak and ash, the sky toward Armagh stayed white. Shortly they reached the Blackwater, *An Abhainn Mhor, the Great River*, leading into the heart of Ulster. It was the northernmost of two fords, at the hamlet of Moy. Running shallow here, the dark water raced north and east over stony bottom, too swift for ice to form except along the embankments, swallowing dollops of snow fallen from tree branches.

Riding close to Tyrone, near enough for his horse-boy to see and hear, Ineen rose in her saddle and craned to peer south, upstream.

"Where is Portmore, Hugh?"

"Further up, above Blackwater town. Why?"

"You built the fort for the Saxons."

"The Crown built it, I merely gave my leave," the earl corrected her.

"In return for a golden chain," she said.

"To be an Earl of Tyrone, as your own husband, I remind you, accepted a golden chain to become Earl of Tyrconnell."

"O'Donnell's chain is put away; he pays no tribute to the Crown."

"And so, your lad's in Bermingham Tower."

Ineen held her tongue for a breath. She rode a little further before answering, "When Red Hugh succeeds his father, he shall repay the Saxons a hundred thousand times."

"Milady—Ineen—talk like this will get your Red shipped from Bermingham Tower to the Tower of London! So, I ask you, Ineen, before your answers drive my horse to run ahead from your mouth, say no more."

Her look turned angry, but she held her tongue.

"And in Armagh, best to let me do all, including giving your gold for the release of your son. For what I have not told you, till now, is that the meeting I have arranged is with the Lord Deputy himself."

Ineen gasped. "Perrot!"

"Aye, the kidnapper himself. He who awaits your ransom."

"Hugh, how could you—"

"How could I?" O'Neill raised his voice, flushing with color, eyes starting with his famously sudden tears. "How could I not, if I must keep ways open to and from Dublin! The Lord Deputy planned to be in Newry. 'Twas easy enough to ask him to meet with me in Armagh in order to share information about Ulster. And you will know when he takes your gold."

This silenced Ineen till the forest thinned and thatched roofs appeared, and the spires and tower of St. Patrick's Cathedral loomed against the sky.

As agreed, Ineen and her Redshanks remained in the forest, though in vigilant formations, while the rest of the contingent advanced onto the Cathedral path.

Ineen asked, "Can Perrot have Red released by Christmas of the Stars?"

"That we shall see," O'Neill answered. "The English call it Twelfth Night."

"Aye, I know."

"He also knows you have an agent of your own named MacCleary in Scotland, who helps you bring in your Redshanks. He knows your brother is Lord of the Isles—the brother who knew enough *not* to go to Ardnarea. He knows Owen O'Toole O'Gallagher, whose son is captive with your Red, is your Chief Counselor. And what he knows the English queen knows."

"And does she know I'm here to bribe her Deputy today?"

"That," said O'Neill, "I doubt."

Only a few steps later Ineen said, gazing toward St. Patrick's Cathedral, "I should like to visit my father's grave where he was buried after his murderous death."

"You shall. But first you must wait. If you look toward the hillock opposite, you will see the Lord Deputy is waiting and English troops surrounding him. He may or may not know you are here. 'Tis best if you not come with me and delay going to the grave until he leaves."

Ineen looked sharply to the left, and there against a rise of trampled snow stood a formation of unnatural blues and browns and sharp steel helmets gleaming dull in the afternoon light, topped by long pikes, halberds, shouldered calivers, and banners with lions rampant snapping in the winter breeze. In number the force appeared no larger than the number of O'Neill's troops. But in front alone, clean-shaven horseman descended the hill at an ambling pace on a black horse, suited not in armor but in silken black, setting off the large gold chain of office on his chest.

Ordering his own contingent to stand fast, O'Neill trotted toward the English horseman, remembering well the rumors that Perrot was a bastard of Henry VIII, and the auburn locks protruding beneath the tall-crowned black hat he sported were the color of Henry's famous hair.

When the Lord Deputy dismounted, O'Neill did the same.

The two walked into St. Patrick's Cathedral, O'Neill gripping the bag of Ineen's gold in his left hand. The

Cathedral was now in Protestant hands, Armagh's bishop exiled on the continent.

Inside the Cathedral, Perrot said, "What's so important that I meet you here before we are together in Newry?"

O'Neill answered, "My Grace, Fionnuala, the wife of Sir Hugh O'Donnell and mother of your hostage, Red Hugh, brought this gold for me to give you in the spirit of this goodly season. I did not wish to give it to you at Newry. She hopes Red Hugh might be released before Twelfth Night."

Perrot responded as if he were on a throne and not standing in a snow-covered Cathedral in Armagh.

"Lord Deputy," O'Neill said like good wine gone bad, "Lord Deputy," he repeated, "I offer you Ineen's two thousand pounds of gold for the immediate release of her son, who is also my wife's half-brother and my daughter's betrothed."

It was a plea, more than an offer.

Perrot said, "Ah, that release is surely to come. Her son is simply a guest of the Crown. He is offered the surroundings of civility that he becomes like you, Hugh O'Neill, our Earl of Tyrone. Tell her hold onto the gold. Her husband, our Earl of Tyrconnell, must convince Her Majesty that the O'Donnell cattle rent is paid, the rent that is much in arrears. And that his Scotswoman must bring not one more Redshank into Ireland."

"I'm sure that O'Donnell's wife means that this is *in addition to* any cattle rent," O'Neill quickly added. "And the O'Donnell has enough Redshanks so that his wife has no need to recruit more. Can this gold be a goodly offer this Christmastide—for Twelfth Night?"

"I shall think upon this offer when the cattle rent is paid. And there are no more Redshanks recruited," Perrot scoffed.

O'Neill stifled disappointment. "I too offer you gold for the release of my daughter's betrothed."

Perrot stared at O'Neill, speaking in a harsher tone, "Do you not realize that Red Hugh is held as much to curtail his Scots mother? For any consideration at all, even for your gold, Tyrone, tell the O'Donnell to see that his wife stops bringing in Redshanks! That is not only my command, it is Queen Elizabeth's."

O'Neill assured him, "The O'Donnell will do his duty. Give the Crown the cattle due," he said, knowing that was unlikely. Cattle, an Irishman's wealth, rankled when ordered to give them over to the Queen of England, even more so since O'Donnell's wife first came from Scotland.

"Ah, now we must proceed to Bagenal's," Perrot said, giving O'Neill an order.

O'Neill dreaded the stop yet knew he had no choice. He tossed his rich velvet cloak over one shoulder, revealing a black doublet with strands of gold.

Ineen waited behind a large tree dripping with snow, where she could best look out for the signal that she and O'Neill arranged to communicate whether her bribe was taken. She could see that at the bottom of the hill O'Neill and Perrot were leaving. She would have her answer. She took a deep breath. *Lord,* she begged . . . before she saw O'Neill raise his hand enough to show he held her bag of gold. Her tears froze as they fell.

The bells of evening tolled for the Angelus, and Ineen answered in anguish, *Angelus Domini nunavit, Maria,* before the toll. *The angel of the Lord declared unto Mary* reminded her that it was bells of the Church of England ringing where once they rang for the very church St. Patrick had built.

Several of Ineen's Redshanks, seeing that O'Neill, his entourage, and Perrot's troops had left, trudged up the hill with Ineen, kneeling at St. Patrick's grave for a prayer. As they passed by Brian Boru's burial, Ineen knelt once more, praying that the High King rest in peace.

When she reached her father's grave, she knelt on the frigid stone where some good soul wrote, *Here Lies the Lord of the Isles, James MacDonnell, 6th Chief of Dunnyveg who died in 1566.*

Ineen kissed the frigid ground. Her lips stung with the cold, though she remained kneeling. She lifted her head but her right hand, empty of the gold, commanded that her first prayer be that O'Neill would put the gold to abundant use on Red's behalf. She bent over the icy stone.

Requiest in pace, Father. My blood comes from you and runs from me to Red Hugh, your grandson.

Father, much happened only months before your grandson's kidnapping. The English beheaded dear Alex, your foster son. Even now Alex's tarred head, spiked on a castle gate, looks up at Red Hugh. And your dear brother,

185

Sorley Boy, broken with grief, passed by his son's blackened head and knelt in Dublin Castle before a portrait of the English queen and submitted. Pray God that Red returns safe home to keep faith with his destiny.

Again, her tears froze on her cheeks. She rose. The snow moved in a mournful dance against the blackening sky.

She forced herself to hurry away and down the hill, surrounded by her bodyguard of Redshanks. Another Redshank waited below with her horse. She mounted.

"We return to Mongavlin," she commanded.

XVII

Manor House at Newry
Ninth Day of Christmas, Ulster 1588

As he rode with the Lord Deputy toward Newry, O'Neill checked to be sure the letter to Walsingham remained secure in his doublet; Ineen's gold he carried in a saddlebag. He knew Perrot well enough to keep up canter and trot to beat the deeper dark. So thoroughly an English town, Newry stood a little north of the Pale of an English settlement. There was a broad ditch bristling a double palisade of ancient trees, stripped and hewn; one rank of stakes pointing out against any attacking horsemen, with the rank behind it a high stockade wall. The Pale wound in a serpentine line of garrisoned entry points from Dundalk in the north down through parts of Meath, Kildare, and Louth, then east again to the sea below Dublin at Dalkey.

Upon passing into Newry proper, Tyrone and the Lord Deputy reached Marshall Bagenal's Green Castle, more manor house than castle. It was beyond a little surprising to

Tyrone that Perrot was going to Bagenal's, as he recently, in self-defense of course, threw old Sir Nicholas Bagenal, Marshal of the Army, onto the Dublin Council Chamber floor in a spirited debate. For reasons of state, the Lord Deputy and the Marshal of the Army had made a show of reconciliation.

As for the Bagenals and O'Neill, they had known each other a long time, never with admiration, but at an invoking of the Crown they could coordinate their separate activities—always with an eye to gaining advantage over the other.

Cool to the point of grudging, however, was the reception the old Marshal and his son gave Perrot and O'Neill in the foyer where they received guests. That they agreed to this hosting of adversaries at all was explained clearly enough by the presence beside them of Sir Henry Sayer, the queen's envoy, attired in a gold fringed doublet.

Old Sir Nicholas Bagenal, whose white hair hung from a bare pate like listless wings, stuck out his jaw in a jagged smile that threatened a bulldog's bite; though, in O'Neill's experience, it usually bit more air than otherwise. His old man's pallor was chafed in the cheeks more by rouge than drink, though drink was not needed to addle his judgment.

It was expected his rank as Marshal of the Army in Ireland would soon pass to his son, Sir Henry Bagenal, who in O'Neill's view did not exceed his father in either bulldog valor or blockhead judgment. Sir Henry, with brown hair, more teeth, and less rouge than whiskey in his cheeks, looked like Sir Nicholas's twin a generation younger.

Ignoring their frowns, O'Neill greeted Marshal and son with an easy geniality after the Lord Deputy.

As they entered the parlor, with an almost feverish cheer, Perrot swept Henry Sayer to join him behind the nearest door. But before O'Neill could take more than a couple sips of brandy or appreciate the large silver chandelier and the Venetian goblets catching its light, Perrot issued Sayer back into the parlor and beckoned O'Neill to join him behind the door.

"I am pleased to tell you, Earl of Tyrone," said Perrot, clapping his hands, "Her Majesty has graciously accepted my resignation as Lord Deputy. Sir Henry has just confirmed it. I shall soon depart this accursed isle which you love so dearly."

With the briefest hesitation O'Neill responded, "Do I congratulate you, or commiserate?"

"To leave Ireland in my dust!"

"You tendered your resignation?" Tyrone said.

"I know all the rumors, my dear man. Do you think I'd be so elated if I were walking someone's plank?"

"Then you have my congratulations," Hugh O'Neill said.

"'Tis pleased I am to hear the despondent note in these congratulations, Tyrone, and I shall never forget your assistance in many touchy matters."

O'Neill felt a sudden access of emotion at his next thought. "In view of your gratitude, and as, shall I say, a celebration of your magnanimity," but already his heart sank at the sharp smile growing in the other's lips, "I request amnesty for Red Hugh O'Donnell."

"But, my good man, Red Hugh O'Donnell is my warrant to return home to Pembrokeshire!"

Except for tears starting to his eyes, Hugh O'Neill made no immediate response.

"No achievement in the south is as dear to me as the immense stroke of securing peace in the north of Ireland. By holding young O'Donnell pledge, his mother may desist from fetching savage Scots to infest the wilds of Ulster. Sorley Boy MacDonnell came to terms and his Scots niece shall come to terms in her part of Ulster, too."

"I can give no assurance," O'Neill brought himself to speak, "that such a policy will succeed."

"My policy has succeeded. The valor of your attempt— on behalf of amnesty—becomes you well, Hugh O'Neill." Perrot clapped him on the arm. "I shall toast your effort with Bagenal's best brandy, as you shall toast my Godspeed home to Wales."

"I bring you all news to celebrate, my good Marshall Bagenal!" cried Perrot, as he reentered the parlor.

At the news of Perrot's imminent departure, both Bagenals found cause to lighten their spirits.

The one spectacular virtue both Bagenals did share, to O'Neill's eye, was their daughter and sister Mabel. He had certainly noticed her from time to time, as the girl grew toward womanliness in lovely little spurts. With chestnut curls and wide brown eyes, this evening she gave O'Neill a glad smile. In a neatly fitted gown of black velvet with puffed sleeves, she held out her hand for him to kiss. A large ruby hung by a wide gold chain upon her delightful bosom. *What a beauty!*

"A pleasure, Mistress Bagenal. I scarcely recognize you, my dear, though we have met many times in your life." O'Neill spoke with all the charm for which he was known.

"The pleasure is all mine," she replied, lowering her eyes but not withdrawing her hand from his warm, vigorous yet gentle touch.

Her brother stepped out of banter with Perrot. "Mabel is just come from being in Dublin." His hot manner did not hide irritation. "She's yet tired from her journey."

"I came from Dublin two days ago, Henry!"

"At any rate, you won't be going with us back to Dublin."

"Henry!" She stared at him, shocked.

"Or to Munster to visit Spenser and Raleigh in their Irish castles," her brother stated.

"My dear!" her father barked, with a sharp headshake. "Do rest. And return at dinner."

She clearly had much to say, but with a heaving sigh— the vision of which was not lost on the Earl O'Neill—she made a show of composing herself and, with glaring

191

obedience, left the room. But she gave a soft backward glance to O'Neill.

Ahh! O'Neill thought. But he also had urgent business with the Queen's envoy. "Are you leaving for England soon, Sir Henry?"

"Presently. As soon as weather permits a voyage on the Irish Sea," Sayer replied.

"May I press a favor upon you?" O'Neill asked.

"What sort of favor?"

O'Neill gestured him to withdraw to the side room, where he shut the door, and held it shut. "My good friend, Sir Francis Walsingham, is ailing, I've heard. I have a letter for him."

"He ages. He's less often seen," Sayer noted.

"Whatever expense it will take to deliver him this letter I shall gladly undertake."

"Well, perhaps it can be arranged. You have it here?"

O'Neill removed the letter from a pocket in his doublet but, not handing it over immediately, beckoned the envoy a step closer and dropped his voice. "No light greetings, this letter. It concerns a matter of grave urgency."

"I'll make sure it is delivered."

"'Tis not to be mentioned to the Lord Deputy."

"An exceptionally close matter?" Sayer asked.

"As you well know, Red Hugh O'Donnell is my wife's half-brother and, by virtue of betrothal to my daughter Rose, my future son-in-law."

"Yes?"

"I do not approve his imprisonment, especially the kidnapping, but I do respect the Lord Deputy's motive—securing peace in Ulster."

Sayer blinked, awaiting O'Neill's next words.

"But a pledge's term is six months," O'Neill continued, "and for the peace of Ulster, Red Hugh must be released when his term ends, if not before."

"That is up to the Crown," Sayer started to reply, but O'Neill held up his hand.

He did not for a moment trust Sayer. O'Neill had been a diplomat too long himself but had no other recourse. Sayer would take this letter directly to the queen.

"This missive bears three seals," Sir Henry observed, "in three different waxes."

"Yes. 'Tis critical in the extreme that only Sir Francis receive it. Forthwith."

Both of them knew Walsingham's skill at detecting even the subtlest breaking of one seal, let alone three.

"And certainly, for perils involved in its transmission, I have in my possession five hundred in gold to guarantee swift and secure delivery to Sir Francis."

"Oh!" Henry Sayer coughed. "A mission of this delicacy and—"

"Swiftness."

"Swiftness!" Sayer repeated. "But for the sake of the Crown, and the peace of the North of Ireland, I shall see the letter is delivered in the swiftest time possible. All the same, by the time Sir Francis Walsingham responds, your son-in-law may well be released."

"God willing!" O'Neill sighed. He was certain everything, except the payment in gold, would be relayed to the Queen.

"We plan to go to Dublin on the morrow," Sayer smiled. "Then take the first boat that sails to England."

"I stress again," O'Neill reminded him, "if Red Hugh O'Donnell remains in Dublin Castle more than a pledge's customary six months, I fear for what might happen."

The two made arrangements for the transfer of gold, and Sir Henry Sayer bowed out to the adjoining parlor. O'Neill paused, remaining alone a moment. He was surprised to feel the whole business plunge him into melancholy. The entire circumstance, first at Armagh, now here, made him realize that something was changing in Dublin.

Then he heard a musical voice in the parlor. Mabel! What medicine for melancholy!

O'Neill did not have to force the smile that broke out in his red beard. Reentering the parlor, he said, "My, my, my dear. May I ask you to indulge us with another song?"

XVIII

A New Lord Deputy
Dublin Castle, June 1588

A whirlwind of sleet and snow blew through Ulster past St. Bridget's Day, when spring winds came but brought no hopeful news about Red Hugh. So, this June day, between the O'Donnell and Hugh O'Neill, Ineen rode toward the iron gate of Dublin Castle with more gold in a velvet bag inside her mantle. Earlier rain was gone with black clouds now fleeing overhead toward Dublin Bay. As they moved up the muddy street Ineen gazed at festoons of gay bunting athwart the street. She wore a silk mantle the color of the lightest summer raspberries, and O'Neill noted she had an ample hood upon her shoulders, which could be pulled up easily to obscure her face.

Ten long months had passed since the kidnapping, and her son still remained a hostage—four months longer than the usual hostage term. Owny and Donny were still there, too. Ineen intended to convince Perrot to free Red Hugh with gold before the Lord Deputy relinquished his office to Sir William Fitzwilliam that very day and went home to Wales. This, despite Perrot's not yet taking any of her gold. Ineen insisted on accompanying O'Donnell to the installation. The O'Donnell and Hugh O'Neill were *not* pleased.

"If you wish Red Hugh to remain alive, and yourself not to be taken hostage, you must heed me," O'Neill warned Ineen.

"I shall, Hugh," Ineen said, for she knew much depended on it.

"Sure, and I'll be keeping her in line, too." O'Donnell winked.

As they reached the castle, white garlanding decorated the walls and there were baskets of bright flowers posted up to the drawbridge. But for all that, the great granite mass of the thirteenth century edifice and the helmeted archers visible on the crenellated towers seemed to overbear any festivity. O'Neill was decked out in short cape and crimson doublet with golden threads that swirled along his sleeves, while O'Donnell wore a festive mantle of burgundy with dark stripes along the edges.

Ineen looked over the narrow moat where hung the portcullis of the gate, and jutting on stakes from atop the bridge tower were tarred heads. A castle guardsman ordered the company to halt. Summoning fierce resolve, Ineen looked from one tar-gob to the next, ready to fix her gaze on

196

the one whose lines she could not mistake as Alex McSorley's. But each looked like the other. For a wild instant, she thought perhaps Alex was not there after all. Then a pale strip of light shone behind one of the tar heads.

She sighed and ground her teeth. In her mind's eye, she tried to see a fair face with a head of hair. She made herself think his head *was* this one. *Those we love in this life, care even more for us after crossing into eternity* . . . Alex, surely, dying a martyr's death, holding to the true faith, must have heard her. She closed her eyes. *Above all*, she prayed, *I come to bring Red safe home from this hell—to make sure his head does not join yours, my Alex!*

To the castle guardsman in charge, O'Neill produced his warrant. The officer signaled satisfaction, ordered O'Neill's troops to remain in the street and the banner of the red hand of O'Neill to be lowered. O'Neill commanded his men to comply. The visitors dismounted, tugging their horses aside, though Ineen made sure she still held the gold within her mantle. At the head guardsman's instruction, their horse-train of carts, laden with victuals for the three Tyrconnell hostages, were permitted to roll through the gate. Drums beat and trumpets blared into the warm castle air. A squad of pikemen stood at attention just inside the yard. Ineen noted the spikes and blades of their halberds and the long barrels of the arquebuses, their prized weapons.

"Orderly," O'Donnell observed.

Ominously orderly, Ineen thought.

O'Neill and O'Donnell walked beside her.

Glancing from one to the other, she said, "I'll give you no reason for concern as long as I see my son, offer my bribe, and remove Red from this evil place."

Tyrone put finger to lips. He said under his breath, "Nothing in Ireland, let alone the Pale, is totally safe, Ineen. But I have made the best arrangements possible."

Ineen stared from tower to tower around the castle walls. "Where is Red Hugh?"

"Bermingham Tower. For state prisoners and hostages." O'Neill pointed to its top, rising barely visible above the high-pitched roof of an enormous building in front of them.

Then they heard, by one of the doorways to the Queen's Hall, guardsmen yelling at a servant. One of them knocked the pleading man against a door with his sword, ripped his tunic and slashed his arm, shaking the blood onto the muddy stones.

"Think you can sneak to a Papist mass in the queen's town?" The Queen of England forbade the Roman Mass. The other guards jeered. "This will be brought to the attention of the jailor."

Ineen gasped; O'Neill grasped her shoulder. The guards looked over, raising their swords. O'Neill propelled his guests rapidly away.

O'Neill rubbed his beard, finger to lips again, and said in Irish, "So long as Red stays atop Bermingham Tower he'll have no harm like what we just saw."

O'Neill saluted two guards standing. They returned the salute and ushered him into the tower door. To all observers, these Irish nobles were officially in town as great northern lords to greet the new Lord Deputy. Inside, a guard opened a second door into a parlor.

"Wait here," O'Neill said. "I'll return shortly."

As Ineen looked round the dimly lit, opulently furnished room, her heart beat strangely, as though they had trespassed into a heathen temple. The room looked as though a great hall were compressed into a small room. There was a fireplace with a long burning hearth, though it was June, and an ornate clock. On a long table, a tray and a carafe and four crystal cups stood. Plump upholstered chairs were placed on the vine-patterned rug. Two small, mullioned windows faced a portion of the Yard and the Queen's Hall across the way.

The fire in the hearth was not out of place, yet it made the close room a little too warm, and the log flames, together with the flickers of thick candles on the table, reddened it.

On the wall facing the hearth hung a tall portrait of a woman dressed in a voluminous gown like a sunburst with red-gold filigree. The face was long, oval, pale, with eyes pointed at the beholder and a severe red line of mouth. A high white ruffled collar separated head from body, and the hair beneath a beaded crown was as red as the gown's bodice.

"Herself, no doubt," said O'Donnell.

Ineen thought instantly that this could be the very portrait that her Uncle Sorley Boy knelt and submitted to while his son Alex's head hung outside. She started to say something when the door reopened, and O'Neill swept in.

"Where is Red?" Ineen began, and a young man stepped in behind O'Neill.

"Red Hugh!" Ineen rushed toward and embraced him.

He repeated, "Mother! Mother!"

Then for the longest moment neither could speak.

O'Donnell burst into tears and gripped his son's shoulders. "Hugh Roe, Hugh Roe!"

O'Neill, standing by the portrait of the Queen, bit his tongue, but no moment of strong emotion could leave his own eyes dry.

"Take us home!" Red finally managed to say, a hand on his mother's shoulder.

"Ach, Red, Red." She rocked him; then, noticing a feathery touch against her cheek, she ran her fingertips along her son's jaw and over his lips. She held him back a little to peer into the flickering shadow of the room. "You're growing a beard!" She rubbed the red hair falling from head to neck.

The young man laughed in his tears. He was also wearing a plain black English doublet with ruffled shirt, hose, and buckled shoes.

"Ach, such hateful togs!" said his mother, holding him close again. "It's hiding you in my mantle if we can—"

With a forced laugh he said, "And how would I not be smothered before we reached Ulster?" He swallowed and closed his eyes to keep from weeping.

"'Tis a man's beard you wear now!" said his father with a short laugh, trying to ease his own emotion.

Ineen calmed but little. She held her son back to look him down and up, and let go his arms to pick up his hands. "You've kept your nails clean, Red Hugh, like a lord of our kingdom." She pulled his fingers closer to her eyes. "They could be a little rounder."

"Knives are not allowed us," the lad responded with a broken laugh, wiping his tears.

"You are the man, now, son," said his father, rubbing the bristles of his son's chin, "the man."

Red turned to Hugh O'Neill. "And how are you and my dear Rose—Father O'Neill?"

"Well, son, and Rose is eager to have you home. She sends her strongest love."

"So, will they amnesty us—today?" Red asked, looking into O'Neill's wet eyes.

"I tell you, Red, and your parents, once again: keep your hopes high, but your expectations modest. You are so valuable to the Crown."

"Hugh, Hugh!" Ineen broke in. "Are you telling us there's no hope for today?"

"I hope always. I promised you shall meet your son, and you have. I know these Lords Deputy too well to promise more. A chance there always is, hope there always is."

Silence fell in the room, and Ineen embraced her son again, squeezing him tight.

"I'm after appreciating what you have done, today, Hugh O'Neill," said Red after a moment, his eyes drying.

"I know better than to counsel patience, my son," said O'Neill. "I'm not a patient man myself. Yet I know what these matters require."

"What they require," Red echoed. "There have been rumors of names mentioned in exchange for we three hostages."

His mother all but gasped, realizing that is what she wanted.

"Not Rory, Mother," he peered at her resolutely. "Not Manus, not anybody for me."

"Red—" she began, but O'Neill cut her off, giving his head a shake.

But three of those present were sharply aware of the letter to Walsingham to exchange Rory for Red Hugh.

"Red!" his mother touched his arm; he did not shake it off.

"Nobody has been too rough with us, Mother," Red said softly. "Be assured of that. Still, I never want a brother of mine to be a guest of the English in this accursed castle."

"I've brought gold," Ineen whispered, touching the velvet purse secured beneath her mantle. "I hope . . ." She glanced at O'Neill, who frowned. "I *expect* Perrot to take this today and amnesty you, Red Hugh."

"That we shall see about," O'Neill broke in, "when Perrot himself comes."

"Aye," said Ineen, controlling her voice short of letting tears fall.

"Our moments here are brief," O'Neill went on. "Best visit while you can." He moved for the door.

"No need to leave, Hugh," said O'Donnell.

"I'm not. I man the gap!" With a smile he opened the door and disappeared.

Red answered his parents' questions about the food and other provisions they had sent him, his room in the Tower, how the other lads fared, the kind of instruction they were forced to endure, and exercise in the Castle Yard.

"God bless you and keep you!" his mother breathed.

"Brave lad!" his father echoed. "Strong lad!"

"Aye." To change the subject Red said, "I talk to Alex every day."

"Alex!" sighed his mother. She did not smile. "Which—?" she started to ask, but stopped.

"To keep courage. To return home strong." He understood her halted question.

"Enough about Alex," said his father.

"Only I remember all he taught me," Red assured his father.

"Good, good," said his mother hastily. "Pray for him . . ." She decided to say no more.

Looking round the dimly flickering parlor, Red noticed the table with four crystal cups grouped about the carafe. "I wouldn't drink from any cup a Saxon hasn't drunk from. There is a poisoner here."

He then looked at the portrait of the British queen. "'Tis said your Uncle Solley Boy submitted to the Crown here in this castle, Mother."

"True," his mother answered as a tear dropped down her cheek.

Red asked about his brothers and sisters, about Siobhan at Dungannon, more about Rose, and little about Donal. But the O'Donnell raised a sturdy finger to his lips, and said, in a surprisingly commanding tone that made Red glance at his mother, who lowered her eyes, "Our kingdom stands united. It shall always stand united, and Donal helps me see to that."

There came a sudden knock on the door and O'Neill reentered. Behind him was an English captain, who happened to be Captain Wood.

"I regret to say," said O'Neill, "the ceremony of the changing of the Lord Deputy is soon to begin. This parlor, and the other castle parlors, will be closed. Red Hugh, you must return above."

"A moment more," Ineen insisted, and hugged her son again, not holding back her tears. "And Perrot?" she asked, slapping her mantle against the hidden purse of gold.

"I can hold off guards no longer," said Captain Wood in English.

He and O'Neill stepped out again.

Ineen dug under her garment and brought out a loose package she put into her son's hands.

"Open! Quickly!"

Her son unwrapped the cloth and found lying in it the gold medallion embossed with *In Deo Nostra Spes.* Hand shaking, he turned it over. It showed a boat with a tall sail upon blue scrolls like sea waves. But only a year and a half ago he had watched Alex bestow it on his mother.

"Alex's medallion!" He kissed it. "But I cannot take it yet."

"Of course you can take it!" said his mother. "'Tis yours now."

"There's no place to keep it in the Tower."

"Under a stone in the floor?" Ineen pleaded. "A reminder of Alex's promise to you."

He shook his head. "The stones are too thick and heavy. No, they'd find this and throw it in the dung heap. Mother. Here—quickly." Eyeing the door, he tugged at the strong cord threaded through the medallion's eye.

O'Donnell pulled a small knife hidden in his mantle.

"Thank you, Father." Red cut the cord, kissed it, and stuffed it up his sleeve. "'Twill be a sacred reminder. When I am safe home, you may hang the medallion on it, Mother. I shall wear it, always!" He pressed the medallion into his mother's hands just as the door reopened.

O'Neill halted inside with Captain Wood and two guards behind him. "Young Mr. O'Donnell will say his farewell." He nodded to Red.

The lad seemed to droop and shrink, face flushing. He could barely open his lips. "Mother!"

His mother, who had adroitly returned the medallion into a pocket, kissed her son on the cheek. "'Twill not be long, my son. God is with you and the prophecy will be fulfilled. The prayers of the friars and their devotion to the Blessed Mother and those of the souls of our people continue for you, always."

"Such prayers you have," added his father, with one last clap of his son's shoulder.

Red looked long at each of his parents. In Irish, he whispered, "I will live. Live to fulfill the prophecy—*When Hugh is fathered by Hugh . . .*"

Unable to say more, Red Hugh turned for the door. But with one last glance at his mother, he adjusted his sleeve, patted where he placed the cord of the medallion, and winked, though with tears watering his eyes.

"We remain for Perrot," O'Neill said.

And within a few moments, whose delay caused Ineen to grasp her husband's arm, the dark Tudor eyes of Sir John Perrot appeared in the doorway. The surprise was the sharp beard his jaws and lips sported, very unlike the way that he presented at Armagh months before. His doublet shone festively with silver threads and jeweled buttons of gold. The cape thrown over one shoulder was a rich black that shone in the flickering firelight of the parlor. The heavy gold chain of office he still wore upon his chest, until it would soon be handed over to the new Lord Deputy.

"Welcome, O'Donnells!" he said in Irish with a flourish and a slight bow.

O'Donnell himself opened his mouth but found it speechless.

"Release our son!" Ineen all but cried after an instant of shock and pulled the gold out from her mantle.

Without missing a beat, Perrot accepted it from her and dropped it on the table with a dismissive gesture. "Lady Ineen, as you know from Armagh, gold means little if you continue to bring in Redshanks."

"Why, O why have you brought this man here!" Ineen demanded of O'Neill.

"You have seen your son," said O'Neill, "but at the Lord Deputy's request, Perrot means to deliver a message."

Unfazed, Perrot resumed, "You have just seen that young O'Donnell is well cared for. And I am sure his health and dress, not to mention his words, do not make a special demonstration to belie any actual mistreatment. All three lads are being schooled, and to encourage their studiousness, the master's rod, unlike in England, has indeed been spared."

"What assurance is there that such 'treatment,' pledged by a man who would kidnap my son, will continue?" asked Ineen.

"The Crown assures you," Perrot replied suavely, "that as long as you behave, the Crown shall treat your pledge in the same manner."

Ineen stood straight, looked into Perrot's Tudor eyes, and said, "We appreciate that Red Hugh is in the State Apartments in this Tower; but we all know that a pledge is not usually more than six months. It is now well past that time."

"Which means," Perrot went on, "no more Scots brought into Tyrconnell, and O'Donnell must pay the Crown's cattle rent and your son should be released.

"Does Lady O'Donnell give *her* pledge that no more Scots will be brought in?"

Ineen glared. She was not about to answer, but the door opened suddenly again, and into the room with guards near him, stumped a very wide man whose trimmed beard seemed stuck into a face of grossly thumbed clay.

"Sir John," the intruder boomed, "we must be about the changing."

Visibly annoyed, Perrot went on, again in Irish, "The pledge of no more Scots that I ask for, Lady MacDonnell, had best be given to the new Lord Deputy—Sir William Fitzwilliam."

Fitzwilliam stood in the flickering shadow, half slumped to one side as though leaning on a cane, though he had no cane. His tightly corseted girth bulged in various directions. An attempt to cloak it with a long cape and puffed sleeves of pure gold thread was hardly successful. His tight, dark silk doublet glittered with dark gold buttons like currants on an overlarge bun.

"And what pledge is that," Fitzwilliam ran his eager little eyes back and forth, and pointed with a finger whose flesh swelled about a ruby ring, "from these magnificent savages you entertain? Notice, all, Irish is not lost on me."

Perrot glared. "Lord Fitzwilliam," he said in emphatic English, "The Earl of Tyrconnell and his wife. And, of course, the Earl of Tyrone."

Hugh O'Neill spoke up diplomatically. "Greetings. How is your dear wife, Ann, whom I've long known through my dear friendship with her father, Henry Sydney?"

Fitzwilliam brushed the remark away. "Well enough." He looked at O'Donnell.

O'Donnell—officially present as the "Earl of Tyrconnell"—moved to flex his knee in the Irish custom. Fitzwilliam gestured dismissively.

"In Her Majesty's castle," he said in Irish, sliding his eyes at no one in particular, "one does not lift the knee in the native fashion. It requires a bit of a bow."

O'Donnell bowed his head, slightly.

"You may remember me, my Earl of Tyrconnell, from my previous service as Lord Deputy some years ago. My attentions at that time were very much on Munster—the Desmond rebellion, you know. You may recall I accepted the submission of Desmond to end the rebellion there, something my predecessor failed to do."

It was understood he meant to disparage Perrot, who had been President of Munster.

"For that service I was put in charge of Fotheringhay Castle, in Northhamptonshire, where one of my illustrious guests was Mary, Queen of Scots—to the end of her life! Silly Papist wench. I supervised her execution. Quite decorous, she was, I must say, under the ax."

As he went on, turning from O'Donnell to Perrot to Hugh O'Neill, he never once gave an eye to Ineen, so he did not catch her gasp.

"Let's on with it, Sir John." He turned to heave himself toward the door.

"Oh!" He half-turned back, again directing words to no one in particular, "O'Donnell must pay his cattle rent. His wife must bring in no more Redshanks. Or they will find themselves my guests here." In English he concluded, "Like Mary of the Scots."

He threatens us with Mary's execution! thought Ineen, biting her tongue so as not to scream at him.

"Oh, and what is this?" He asked. Fitzwilliam noticed the purse on the table. "An offering?"

Ineen stared at him.

Fitzwilliam grabbed the gold. "I kept your Mary Queen of Scots' rooms very warm." He stumped to the door, which he jerked open and slammed behind him.

"Sir William Fitzwilliam," Perrot said. "My successor, as custodian of your son."

Neither O'Donnell spoke.

"You may yet regret my withdrawal from Ireland, Ineen Dubh," Perrot chuckled.

Ineen took a step back, out of any firelight she hoped, for she did not want Perrot to see she had begun to tremble, as though icy water infused her every limb.

With only a nod to Ineen and O'Donnell and a glance to O'Neill, Perrot took his leave.

A blare of trumpets sounded to greet Perrot's appearance, along with escalating drumrolls, a prelude to the ceremony.

"Jesus, Mary, and Joseph!" Ineen moaned, the trembling becoming a quaking that nearly dropped her back against the stone wall. She was determined not to shed tears, not to give way before Red Hugh was safe home, and then to weep for joy.

O'Neill said, "You know I must attend the installation of the new Lord Deputy Fitzwilliam, and I advise O'Donnell and you to do the same. The Crown did permit Red Hugh to see you. Although it is not all I hoped would happen."

Ineen said with fury, "There was no mention of Red Hugh's release!"

But before she could say more, O'Neill cautioned, "If you want to see your son again, I urge you to attend the ceremony."

Ineen took but a minute to think. She recognized Hugh O'Neill's sound judgment but hated it. "Aye," she said.

But she told herself, *I'll see Red freed. Despite any old or new Lord Deputy.*

XIX

Armada Storms
Tyrconnell, Michaelmas 1588

*A*s the summer days passed slowly by, when cliffs shone amber and white high above the bluest of seas, no good news came of Red Hugh's release.

Then near Michaelmas, Ineen stood, wrapped in drenched black mantle with her boots soaked deep in wet sand at Killybegs, looking out at an enormous ship, a galleass. The Girona was one of only four of these large ships sent in the Spanish Armada to the Channel between England and the Low Countries. And the only one to survive. It landed at Donegal's prized harbor.

The Girona survived, racing up the North Sea around Scotland and down through the Isles to Ireland's west coast for the arduous route back to Spain. The battered but not broken Girona moored for repairs. Built to hold hundreds, it now took on thousands—sailors and soldiers from other ships wrecked along the west coast of Ireland in the wake of the defeat.

"A sorry lot they are," Ineen said to McDunlevy, O'Donnell's and one of Ineen's physicians. She stood near him by the rocky strand as they watched the Spaniards board the boat. "Will you tend to any of them before they leave on the repaired ship?"

"All depends on Captain Spinola," McDunlevy replied. Dressed as the high noble he was, the physician wore a saffron mantle with a fur collar that reached to his thick dark hair. "The Spaniards do have physicians of their own."

"Saxons must practice the blackest magic that the strongest ships of Spain should be destroyed so utterly. Such hopes I had, such prayers the Armada would be the end of the *English Monarch*. I prayed Spain's might would quicken Red's release."

"Aye," The physician commented. "You know what Bingham—" McDunlevy began.

"I care not that Bingham swore death to any who aided Spaniards foundering on the shores of Ireland. 'Tis our duty to God to rid us of the English evil. Mind you, too, that the King of Spain is Red Hugh's godfather."

Ineen and McDunlevy were not alone in watching. Along the strand, a throng milled of peasants and kerne as well as friars and O'Donnells. They cheered to the strangers climbing the gangway or staring from the taffrail. Those seeking treasure were not at all abashed to walk into the water and search or cry out in Irish for gold or precious jewels that floated from the ship.

The O'Donnell himself stood upon a high rock with Donal and Father Conan. Ineen's eye caught a look at the dark figure with trimmed glib beside her husband. She wasted no time in climbing up the rock to find out what Donal, her stepson, was about. She arrived just in time to hear him saying, "Only gold they will get out of these Spaniards they will get in Dublin."

Ineen nodded to each, noticing Donal, dressed notably noble as his position required.

Donal returned the nod.

"What gold?" O'Donnell said.

"Turning Spaniards in at Dublin," Donal answered.

"Sell Christians to *heretics*!" Ineen raised her voice.

"'Tis *I*, not you, that my son Donal has addressed, woman," retorted O'Donnell.

Ineen held her tongue, staring at Donal, holding in her agitation at seeing him. With all the times that Ineen had covered up her husband's increasing senility, he somehow came to his senses when dealing with Donal.

"There's some who might do such—trade Spaniards to the Crown. Many comb the beaches at Glencolumbcille and elsewhere for Spanish gold and even for Spaniards," Donal said.

O'Donnell thought a moment.

Ineen was suddenly silent and thoughtful. Then she asked, "Father Conan?"

"Yes, my daughter?" the friar replied.

"Not for gold for us," Ineen said, "but would there . . . would it be sin, do you think, in taking Spaniards to Dublin in trade for my son Red Hugh? Spain can ransom them with gold."

The friar was speechless, but not Donal. Donal looked directly at his stepmother. "They will not trade for Red Hugh. When they have him, they have you, Ineen Dubh."

Ineen turned to her husband. "Will God . . ." she could not finish the thought.

"Father Conan," asked O'Donnell, "would it be wrong?"

The friar fumbled, clutched the holy beads hanging from the cincture that circled his brown robe. "I can only give you my Franciscan answer. What a Jesuit might say, I do not know; but then Donegal Friary is Franciscan, is it not?"

"Of course, an O'Donnell would only take a Franciscan answer," the O'Donnell said.

"Dublin sinned," Father Conan managed to say, "by stealing young Red Hugh—not even a proper hostage arrangement—and holding the other pledges as well."

"Would it be a sin to trade Spaniards for Red Hugh?" Ineen pressed.

The friar thought aloud. "God's will be a mystery. Mystery or not, I think it not grievous sin to return Spaniards to the Crown—but only in trade for your son."

"Of course, and I will add gold to assure the Spaniards go back to Spain. Now we must return to Donegal," Ineen told her spouse in a low voice.

O'Donnell looked at her.

"We must be at Donegal Castle," she answered. "You and I—alone."

"Father," Donal spoke up, "as your Seneschal, I must warn that this is dangerous talk. If Bingham plans to kill Spaniards, do you think anything less will happen in Dublin!"

Ineen glared at her stepson.

O'Donnell ordered Donal to go mind the beach. "I shall stop at St. Catherine's Well," O'Donnell said. "We shall pray about this Spanish situation."

Three of them, O'Donnell, Ineen, and Father Conan, made the pilgrimage to the little circle of stones in the grass below the ruins of Castle Kit. One of the many ancient Holy Wells of Ireland—sacred, as it happened, long before St. Patrick reached the island—this one was now dedicated to St. Catherine of Alexandria, patroness of Killybegs. St. Catherine graced the little village with the most abundant fishing in all of Ireland. Such encouraged the naming of the O'Donnell as "The Fisher King" on the continent.

Ineen watched O'Donnell take the first cup lying about, murmur a prayer, and swallow greedily of the holy water. In the year since Red's kidnapping, the hair on his head and in his beard had turned so soiled white, into something like one of the tatters of fleece tied to nearby bushes. These bits of fleece mingled among other tokens of thanksgiving, brought there by persons grateful for healings and answered prayers. The old king handed the cup to Ineen.

Then Father Conan drank of the water from another cup and left them with an inspiration. "Red Hugh's 'like unto' a martyr—not a dead martyr," he hastened to add, "but a witness, which is the true meaning of the word *martyr*."

"Praise be to God," Ineen said.

"But," Father Conan began, "if the English ransom the Spaniards instead of executing them, then they are merely pledges exchanged for Red Hugh. If no blood is shed, it is an unbloody sacrifice—martyr for martyr. *But only if no blood is shed*."

"Sure enough," O'Donnell said. "In thanksgiving I offer a new chapel for the Friary."

Turning to O'Donnell the Friar proposed, "May I suggest, we have need of an oratory."

"Then an oratory it shall be!"

Later, as Ineen thought all of this over, a rider arrived at Donegal Castle from O'Doherty of Inishowen. Another ship of Spaniards had sunk in Glennagiveny Bay, off Lough Foyle, and boatloads of sailors had beached on Inishowen. They managed to march within a short distance of O'Doherty's castle at Ellagh.

"That is surely a sign," Ineen said. "We cannot leave these Spaniards in such a perilous situation. If I pledge gold enough to ensure Fitzwilliam receives my gold and in addition the Crown exchanges the Spaniards for gold from Spain . . ."

"Of course," O'Donnell responded.

"I'll meet you up at Castle Ellagh, after passing through Mongavlin," Ineen said.

O'Donnell kissed his wife on the cheek.

"We shall rescue our son. Pray God we will," Ineen whispered as she stayed in the warmth of her husband's embrace.

XX

March of the Spaniards
Ulster to Dublin, October 1588

When Ineen arrived at Castle Ellagh, northwest of Derry, with one hundred more of her own Redshanks to meet up with O'Donnell, she learned he had preceded her by only a short while. This did not surprise her. He was no longer the Hugh O'Donnell who could ride two or three horses the length of the day with hardly a pause from one end of the kingdom to the other. Besides, he spent time before leaving Donegal, making arrangements with Donal should he and Ineen proceed to Dublin.

The afternoon was one of high clouds and bright, windy, blue sky above O'Doherty's castle grounds that clamored with soldiers dressed in the remains of English armor. The armor, with deep dents and rusty edges, was no doubt retrieved from dead English soldiers, a custom in certain parts outside the Pale. Castle Ellagh was one of a string of strategic castles from Lough Foyle to Lough Swilly defending Inishowen, the wild and mountainous Isle of Owen, surrounded on three sides by water.

Spaniards in uniforms milled here sullenly. They were devouring chicken legs or sprawled like battle dead upon the damp hillside. Some five hundred exhausted Spaniards from the sunken *La Trinidad Valencera* were surviving on food from nobles and peasants as they marched to Castle Ellagh from the beach at Glenagivney.

Ineen did not intrude immediately upon her husband's business, that is, except for observing the contentious Hovenden brothers, Captain Richard and Lieutenant Henry. They were notorious for their mutual abuse in otherwise vehement agreement. Like the Hovendens, this Kelly was encased in English armor.

By the castle entrance stood or paced a number of Spaniards whose clothes, despite dirt and rips, marked them as officers or noblemen. At times the lone Spaniard conducting the negotiations turned to address his brother officers in Spanish. The first time he noticed Ineen he doffed his helmet and lowered his head. He was wearing a ruff no longer white, a short cape of shredded wool, and black hose with runs exposing bruises. Yet his dark eyes attempted a smile on thin lips within a short beard he stroked to keep sharp, and he braced his spine to maintain a courtly figure.

"Lo siento," Ineen returned his greeting with her own apology. Though her saffron léine was simple, she wore a rich velvet mantle suitable for meeting Spanish nobility.

The Spaniard responded brightly with his own thanks: *"Gracias, su merced!"*

O'Donnell also nodded, but with a look that made Ineen keep to the side. This was for him to arrange. He was the king. His Spanish was more fluent after decades of trading fish for wine with Spanish grandees and merchants.

The Spaniard, whom O'Donnell repeatedly addressed as Don Alonso de Luzo, was not the captain of the lost *La Trinidad Valencera,* but commander of the infantry *tercio* it had carried. As he spoke to O'Donnell and Captain Hovenden, he frequently glanced at Ineen.

The Spaniards wanted transport to Scotland. None of the Irish talked about Scotland, not even O'Donnell; they spoke only of Dublin and trading Spaniards for gold. What little gold Don Alonso and his fellow officers and nobles had rescued from the ship was already in Hovenden pockets. Given that, Don Alonso pled for courteous treatment and removal to Donegal to await the next wine ship from Spain. But for the natives there remained only the question of who took charge of the Spaniards. The Hovendens claimed the Spaniards by right of arrest at the Crown's command. O'Doherty claimed the Spaniards by right of territory, and O'Donnell let it be known that by his own right of O'Donnellship, he took charge of the Spaniards.

"These Spanish nobles stay with me," O'Donnell proclaimed at last to Captain Richard Hovenden.

The Hovenden brothers' faces had the same red eyes, the same shaggy red moustache, the same rudely shaven jaws. Brambles of hair stuck out the same way beneath their dented English helmets, and the younger one stood so close to his brother's back, the older one's shoulders seemed to support two redheads. Ineen knew they, too, had assisted in the hunt for Alex McSorley. They were as guilty of the claymore plunged into Alex's "grave" as Merriman and Hugh McDean.

Then Ineen whispered to O'Donnell that it was all about gold. O'Donnell gave a bag of gold to O'Doherty, indicating the Spaniards on the hill. "For their feed."

In the end, the Hovendens accepted O'Donnell's terms. They and their men were, after all, surrounded by Redshanks, and the most expeditious way to be rid of them was to let O'Donnell and his wife depart with the forty-five nobles and officers. Arms, plate, jewelry, and other goods enough would be left behind for expropriation.

Don Alonso asked that O'Donnell and Ineen send word to the Bishop of Derry to send priests to the Spaniards left behind, to say Mass and administer sacraments, and physicians to tend fevers and injuries. Four of the Spanish officers were too ill or injured to travel. O'Doherty supplied carts for the nobles and officers who would travel.

With a parting salute to his men, Don Alonso mounted the horse he was given, and with a flourish, bade O'Donnell and his wife to lead the way.

Ineen insisted that they halt for the night at Mongavlin. There Ineen refreshed herself, changed her léine, and saw to it the O'Donnell bathed, put on clean clothes and ate a meal of salmon and fine Spanish wine. She instructed her servants to do the same for the Spanish nobles and gather blankets for them as they were bundled together in the great hall.

At first light she put on a fresh dark mantle and ordered porridge, bread, and mead for all. Then they set out again with provisions for the Spaniards, including three dozen additional Redshanks and O'Cahan, one of Ineen's own physicians, to tend to any who became ill.

The weakest Spanish nobles were given horses to ride, but even this was too much for one or two of the officers who lay in horse-drawn carts, which could do no better than bump along. The column proceeded in intermittent autumn rain up the Foyle past Lifford.

It proved best if the column of Spaniards continued along the tributary Finn. After fording the Finn, they turned east into Tyrone. It would be at least a three-day march to the east coast. That evening, after winding along wheat fields and with some difficulty through forests, over the lower Sperrin hills and fording more streams, they stopped between Strabane and Enniskillen at Castlederg. Here, first thing in the morning, they buried one of the Spaniards after he rolled with fever, crossed himself, and died.

"*Requiescat in pace,*" Ineen prayed, then said to her husband, "'Tis an omen."

"Tend to the living, woman," replied her husband.

After breakfast and burial, ever southeastward, they skirted Omagh by filing up through the mountain gap between Dooish and Pollnalagh. Despite O'Cahan's ministrations, they had to bury another Spaniard in the yellow gorse of a hillside chapel yard.

Then O'Donnell, who could have claimed hospitality rights, paid gold to have the surviving Spaniards bedded under a ceiling, out of the never-ending spells of rain.

With these deaths, Ineen became increasingly disturbed. Could she herself trust the English in Dublin to prize ransom above bloodthirst? She heard that the Armada, despite defeat, had cost the English crown its treasure. That miserly queen needed the gold these Spanish nobles would bring her. Surely Fitzwilliam knew that. Surely Fitzwilliam would want both her gold and gold from Spain for the exchange. But fewer nobles delivered to Dublin would diminish the chance of ransoming Red Hugh. So, leaving Castlederg, she offered her horse to Don Alonso, who courteously declined, but she remained for a time on foot beside a cart holding two more Spaniards who could no longer ride. Ineen helped O'Cahan, which consisted mostly of replacing cloth after cloth soaked in cold river water on the feverish brows of the dying men.

Veering into Maguire's country, with a view to spending the night at Enniskillen, O'Donnell all the same sent a runner north to Dungannon in hopes Hugh O'Neill would supply fresh horses and spare some of his own troops.

Maguire welcomed all generously. Room was made for the Spaniards in the cottages but also in the castle; yet two more Spaniards had to be buried the following day. Ineen could not help keening—the only person to keen—though she kept it low and short.

Meanwhile, a runner arrived from Dungannon. "O'Neill was at the northern coast dealing with Spaniards himself."

Maguire generously offered fresh horses that he passed on to O'Donnell.

Intermittent exchanges with Don Alonso refreshed Ineen's Spanish. At one point, nodding an appreciative smile for her attention to the sick men, he thanked the queen for her kindness: *"Gracias, mi reina, de su bondad."*

This caused her a twinge of shame. *Bondad* meant not only "kindness" but "goodness." She answered coolly, "The more Spaniards delivered to Dublin, the better exchange for my son."

"The English will cut off our heads?" said Don Alonso, still with a smile for her.

"Oh, no, Señor! Gold has been pledged to the Lord Deputy—a great deal of gold. Some of the gold shall only be delivered to Fitzwilliam upon your return to Spain. You must know that the English queen needs your ransom money."

"God willing," he sighed. The Spaniard shrugged.

"He will." Ineen sighed as well. *"El tiempo viene,"* she said. In time. And she moved away to busy herself with her captain of Redshanks.

Ferrying across the Blackwater next day, one of the swiftest rivers of Ulster, three more Spaniards fell in and were swept away—one of them trying to save the others. When at last the column reached the Pale and inside the walls of Drogheda, fifteen of the forty-five Spanish officers and noblemen were buried or drowned.

Ineen Dubh dreaded entering the English town, especially as O'Donnell agreed to an escort of English troops since they were marching Spaniards to the Crown.

They proceeded along a road the English had banked and graded past miles of deforested fields. Every moment Ineen expected the escort to turn on them and confiscate the Spaniards. *Mother of God, protect us!* she prayed.

Nor was it reassuring that the English could sweep out from what woods remained between the Pale and the Irish Sea. Here she stayed on her horse, closely guarded by her captain and his men. O'Donnell refused to shelter himself the same way, riding ahead of the column. He seemed almost the O'Donnell of old, but she instructed her captain, "Form a detail to spring to O'Donnell's defense at the first sign of treachery by any English soldier."

As they continued along, Ineen's senses reached a pitch of alertness almost unbearable as they were assaulted by a hell-noise of outcries, curses, and howling jeers from people in the street, who pelted them with mud and stones. The Spaniards were the main targets, but the Irish were not spared. The English horsemen and foot troops ranged along the column's sides, pushing and kicking a path through the mob. It did make Ineen wonder if the entry into Dublin would be any less savage.

This fear increased as they were all marched into a guard's station just before Dublin. Three men stepped forward with an air of judges and proceeded to inspect the bedraggled Spaniards.

O'Donnell appeared as interested in these proceedings as he remained unafraid of them. After he and Ineen dismounted, they accompanied the magistrate into a little room.

The English considered the situation and then commanded, "Only the Earl of Tyrconnell will be permitted to continue with the Spaniards to Dublin, with a few of his bodyguards and a larger English escort."

Ineen objected, in English. "I am the mother of the hostage Red Hugh for whom we are exchanging these Spanish nobles!"

The magistrate dismissed her with a headshake and pointed her back outside. "That you are the mother of that half-breed pledge means nothing to me."

Two English soldiers stepped up beside Ineen. She glanced furiously at her husband, who made a face that said, *Wait outside a moment.*

When O'Donnell stepped back outside, he said, "You know what Hugh O'Neill says—they grabbed Red Hugh to stop you bringing in Redshanks."

Ineen gave her husband a pained look. "You say that to me when our son is in Dublin Castle and it is I who have also put up gold to free him."

"I do."

She could say nothing to that except, "And do you think the English of *this* town would not try to grab me when you're gone!"

"With all your Redshanks about you? I'd love to stay and see that battle!"

"Without *my* Redshanks, they could take *you*."

"My cattle they might want, not me," O'Donnell uttered.

"Hugh." Taking his arm, she pulled him close. "Red Hugh is your son of prophecy. I am his mother!"

O'Donnell looked troubled, for he depended much on Ineen, more than he cared to admit. "Begone to Dungannon, woman! I'll bring you *your* son of prophecy before the week is done!"

Deeply stung, she made no riposte. Soon enough, she turned round and called her captain, who held her in a perplexed and measuring gaze. Angrily, she gave orders to prepare to proceed to Dungannon.

The last she saw of the Spaniards was as they were herded into the middle of Saxon pikemen.

Don Alonso looked back at her. He ventured one last thank you, "*para vuestra ayuda, mi querida reina*." For your help, my dear queen. He gave Ineen half a grim bow, and then turned to look ahead.

Every effort, thought Ineen, *every gambit must be taken to get Red home safe*. Yet the bow and Don Alonso's last look sent a shiver down her spine.

XXI

North to Dungannon
Samhain, All Hallows Eve 1588

*I*neen hardly removed her rain-soaked mantle to give to a servant when Hugh O'Neill raised his voice.

"You devised a plan to sell noble Spaniards to Fitzwilliam!" Hugh O'Neill bellowed; eyes shot with furious tears.

Ineen gasped. "What—whatever do you mean, Hugh?" she asked as he met her in his great hall at Dungannon. "We are ransoming the Spanish nobles for Red Hugh's release and Spain will ransom them with gold."

"'Tis your prayer and mine that shall be true," said O'Neill more evenly, wiping his eyes, though his breathing was just as agitated. He offered her wine or mead.

"Not Spanish wine, Hugh. Mead, yes."

"Come, we shall sit by the fire in my chamber," he said.

"Surely, Hugh. As you wish."

"So, you have not heard!" O'Neill began, as they walked to a chamber off the great hall.

"Heard what?" It was all Ineen could do to say this much.

"As soon as your column of noble Spaniards left Castle Ellagh—before your messenger even reached Derry and called on the bishop to bring sacraments to the Spaniards you left behind—the Hovendens and their Sergeant Kelly and all their men began butchering the Spaniards."

Ineen Dubh was speechless. She shook. Rare tears filled her eyes.

O'Neill went on, anger between his teeth. "Butchered the sick and all the able-bodied they could catch."

Ineen felt behind her for a chair but found none.

"We never heard," she tried to explain with her right hand clutching her crucifix. "No one told us. No spy came to warn us."

"Why didn't you just kill the Spanish at Inishowen with the rest? Send a gillie to Dublin with a bag of heads? With your best regards!" He spat out the words.

"No! No! We made a plan to save the noble Spanish," Ineen pleaded.

"Where is the O'Donnell and why is he not with you?"

Then Ineen's cheeks ran with tears as she explained, "O'Donnell went on alone with the Spaniards and a contingent of Redshanks, surrounded by English troops."

"You let him do that!" O'Neill exclaimed. "We both know that he is becoming more and more frail."

"Hugh," she said, "the English did not want me to go. We thought it best—for the Spaniards, of course—that I not be in the way. That they would negotiate with O'Donnell."

"How foolish!" O'Neill responded.

"I hope not," Ineen sighed. She barely managed so say, "Thank you," as she sat down. "All four hundred Spaniards?"

"Thanks be to God, a hundred or more escaped in the dark. They fled across the Foyle, and I sent them on to Scotland. Ineen. I was myself up north dealing with Spaniards."

"Scotland," Ineen repeated. "So 'twas on the coast you were, sending them to Scotland, when we sent for you at Enniskillen."

"That I was."

"Jesus, Mary, and Joseph! I'm mourning a hostage son!" Ineen cried. "Now these Spaniards left behind and killed." The grim parting gaze of Don Alonso appeared to her eyes. "'Tis sure, sure," she licked her lips, "the avarice of that Fitzwilliam will . . . save the men marched to Dublin Castle. The Crown needs their ransom!"

"Where do you meet the O'Donnell?"

"Here."

"Whatever happens, and I do hope it is what you hope, you will be responsible as well as O'Donnell. I am grateful Rose is not home to hear of this, though someday she will. And my dear wife Siobhan is not here either."

231

"Hugh, this time gold will work. Red will be free. The Spaniards will go back to Spain."

Just then, one of O'Neill's servants brought wine and mead, and O'Neill asked, "Would you like venison or beef?"

"No, no. I cannot eat at the moment with this news," Ineen answered.

"'Tis rest you need." He called down the staircase for another servant to bring more mead up the staircase for Ineen.

So, next day Ineen walked about the treeless hilltop on which Dungannon stood, peering time after time at the distant line of Lough Neagh, seeking to hear any new clatter of hooves at the castle gate. One hour after another waiting for the O'Donnell felt interminable.

Then, days later, O'Donnell did turn up in the midst of a thunderstorm.

A sudden commotion in the sleet below the windows was followed by a servant shouting up the lower staircase. Ineen was halfway down the stairs when she met her husband trudging up, face streaked in the dimness, white hair stringy, eyes red and evasive, his tunic soggy, his legs and feet as wet as they were bare.

"Where is Red Hugh?" was the first thing Ineen could say. "Is he not with you?"

O'Donnell closed his eyes and turned his head, shivering.

"But he is alive?" she shouted. "Our son is still alive?"

He gave a weary nod. "Yes."

Then it further alarmed her that he let her take his arm and lead him to the great hall.

O'Neill sent a servant to bring a clean mantle and tunic from his Irish wardrobe for O'Donnell and ordered another servant to bring food and drink.

Once the O'Donnell—face now soft and bloodless as an old woman's—was dried and dressed, he sat in a chair at the long table. And waited.

To meet Ineen's stare, the effort it cost O'Donnell's eyes seemed that of a man wresting a tree trunk out of a field. When he looked into Hugh O'Neill's eyes, he was held as though by the gaze of a Brehon about to pass a dreadful sentence.

"The Spaniards?" O'Neill asked.

O'Donnell gave his head a slight shake.

"Hugh, what happened?" his wife screamed in a voice she rarely used.

"Fitzwilliam," he began, glancing at Ineen, "refused to release our son 'without an order from the queen,' says he."

Ineen and O'Neill exchanged alarming looks.

"'You have Her Majesty's gratitude,' says Fitzwilliam, 'and sufficient reward. Besides,' says he, 'you don't pay your cattle rent, and your wife,' he says, 'brings in Redshanks, and you expect a reward for the mere doing of your duty?'"

"Jesus, Mary and Joseph!" Ineen interrupted.

His lungs heaving and licking his lips, O'Donnell continued, "'You but demonstrate Her Majesty's wisdom in keeping your pledge where he is. Would you herd these Papist Spaniards here, if your son was not being held pledge? You'd have turned these devils into kerne!'"

"So Red remained in the tower?" Ineen questioned.

O'Donnell nodded. "Yes."

Nobody spoke.

Ineen pushed the cup of *usque baugh* to her husband's hand. He took it and quaffed. She nudged the dish of venison, but he held out the cup for another drink of whiskey. O'Neill filled it.

"And the Spanish nobles?" O'Neill asked again.

After another deep swallow, O'Donnell thumped fist and cup on the table.

"'Tis one reward we obtain, says the Lord Deputy, 'One grand reward Her Majesty owes you. You may be Her Majesty's honored guest at the hanging of these devils.'"

O'Donnell emitted a sigh like a croak. O'Neill drew in a large breath, turned away from the table to let it out, then himself pounded the table and stepped away.

"And he's hanged them *already?*" O'Neill asked. "All!"

O'Donnell wagged his head. He looked at his son-in-law and closed his eyes. Then he opened them and looked at his wife. "He took the gold, Ineen Dubh. Little good it did the Spaniards or . . . our son."

"Fitzwilliam always takes the gold!" said O'Neill, standing up and pacing before the log fire like a man in a cage.

O'Donnell went on. "He also says, 'As a token of personal gratitude,' he informs us that he, 'the Queen's Lord Deputy shall soon be touring the west coast to inspect the wreckage and the treasures of the Armada.'"

"Confiscate any Spanish gold that's washed ashore," O'Neill interrupted.

"And he shall be pleased to bestow the privilege of a visit to Castle Donegal!" O'Donnell whispered.

"Did you see our son, at least?" Ineen asked.

O'Donnell hesitated a beat. Then he stood up and pushed away the table. "No. No, no. After . . . after Fitz—"

"What? What!" Ineen struggled not to scream again.

"I could not face the lad. Too great my shame."

"They could hang Red Hugh, too!" Ineen gripped her face, shook and shook her head, walked off, threw up her arms.

But O'Neill intruded with a calming voice as he squeezed and patted Ineen's quaking shoulders. "No, 'tis sure I am, Red Hugh shall not be harmed. Do not forget the gold you delivered," he hissed, "went to Fitzwilliam."

"The gold bought nothing!" yelled Ineen.

"It bought some of Fitzwilliam's—can I call it good will? His good greed, then. Where this gold came from keeps Red Hugh alive. Fitzwilliam," he hissed again, "expects to win more and more gold to keep Red Hugh alive."

Too horrified for an answer, Ineen slumped into a chair.

Pacing, O'Neill tore a sword off the wall then slammed the hilt into the scabbard. "I'll hang Fitzwilliam myself." He went to the stairwell and called down for more whiskey.

"But, of course, 'tis no way to free your son."

The three of them remained in the hall drinking, cursing Fitzwilliam and the Queen of England who dug him up out of his government grave. But as they left to sleep, the last words the host managed to articulate: "Too soon, then. Not yet. Not yet."

Next morning, O'Neill's parting words were clearly spoken but all the sharper. "May you never have to seek refuge in a strange country, Hugh O'Donnell—neither you nor your sons nor your grandsons. I cannot speak for the kindness of fate."

Ineen Dubh accompanied her husband back to Donegal, not going on to Mongavlin. She realized even more that she must be her husband's strength until Red Hugh could take the white wand of kingship himself. Until then, she must hold the white wand.

XXII

Argyll to Carrigans
Winter 1588

*I*neen Dubh knew in a moment's prayer what she must do: bring the rest of her children to safety—to Campbell country, to Argyll. Bring them to her highlands in Scotland.

The autumnal day proved fair. Nuala held Caffar as Rory and Manus raced to the boat. Annag came along with them while Ineen saw to it that as well as her own bodyguard of Redshanks, there were ample ones to protect her children.

Once aboard, the galley went with the wind, with minimal use of sails or oars. From Lough Foyle north past the Mull of Kintyre they sailed and landed by the beaches of sand made golden by the footsteps of Columcille. This shore where he landed on his way to exile on the Isle of Iona invigorated Ineen.

She felt the Holy Man's presence with Scottish winds sweeping a strong reminder of his prophecy: *When Hugh is fathered by Hugh . . .* Belief in Red Hugh's destiny strengthened her.

Further, it was the union of Ineen's parents—MacDonnell and Campbell—that brought peace to Argyll, making her mother's clan, Campbell, the most powerful in the region. Their Campbell kinsman, the Fifth Earl of Argyll, relative of Mary Queen of Scots, settled Ineen at the Stuart court.

He had even arranged for Ineen's and her widowed mother's marriage to Irish kings and procured 1,200 Redshanks apiece as wedding gifts to mother and daughter. They both married on the same day on Rathlin Island. Ineen to Hugh O'Donnell and Agnes to Turlough O'Neill.

Under the present Seventh Earl of Argyll, the Campbells remained most powerful, and the Earl helped enable Ineen's procuring of Redshanks.

As Ineen's party trotted in a large black carriage along the bluest blue waters of Loch Flyne, *River of the Vine*, the bodyguard of Redshanks trotted on horse beside them. The twin conical towers and gray stone walls of Inveraray Castle rose before them as Ineen took in deep breaths of upland air, familiar to her since her own childhood. The green mountains, lush with beech and fir, reinforced her sense the children would now be safe—safe from Fitzwilliam, safe from Bingham, safe from any minions of the accursed Crown.

All of her children safe but Red Hugh in the hands of the English in Dublin Castle.

The little ones, no longer so little, Mairghead and Marie, lived in this safe world already from within days of Red's kidnapping. From the castle gate, the girls raced each other to the arriving carriage and hugged and danced in their blue, green, and black plaids. For the hundredth and almost final time Rory and Manus pestered their mother to let them run to the armory in the castle. But first Ineen told her sons to climb with her to the great hall she knew so well to greet and thank the Seventh Earl.

He was there to welcome them all formally, making a great effort to smile. Ineen heard Rory stifle a laugh and saw Manus grin without shame at the young Earl of Argyll's long nose and severe black doublet, accented by a large unruffled white collar. It confirmed the rumors of his nickname, *Gillesbuig Grumach*, or Archibald the Grim. Their mother nudged them to stop.

Archibald was much closer in age to Ineen's older children than to her. The children exchanged courteous greetings, and then tossed off mantles and cloaks before racing down the stone steps to the armory. Nuala took her young sisters by the hand and followed Annag, long acquainted with the castle. Still holding Caffar, Annag led them to the kitchen for refreshments.

On an intricately carved chair Ineen took her ease by the flames of the central firepit to relax with this Earl of Argyll, who had reason to look severe with the weight of the Campbell power on his shoulders.

She smiled after thanking him for his recurring hospitality. "I shall wait another day or two before contacting MacCleary to begin recruiting the thousand Redshanks upon which you and I agreed."

"'Tis no cause for hurry, Ineen Dubh," he replied, and with smiles they both let out a breath of relief. The Seventh Earl of Argyll carried on the custom of the Fifth and Sixth Earls in procuring Redshanks for his cousin.

Wintry weather seemed to come too fast in the highlands. Spies brought Ineen more and more disturbing news about Donegal. She shared much with her Argyll cousin. "Captain Willis, Bingham's minion, invaded and suppressed Donegal Friary, destroying holy objects, killing the guardian and garrisoning his English troops there."

"Aye. 'Tis as I feared. With Red Hugh held hostage and your husband in waning health, the English are becoming bolder," her cousin said.

"The friars fled to the woods and mountains," Ineen told him. "And now the O'Donnell has become a prisoner in his own castle."

The Earl responded, "'Tis the news I also received. 'Tis not like Scotland where those of the Roman faith and Protestant often regard one another as our dear relative Mary Stuart urged. Though, I must say there is effort going into undoing that."

The two sat quietly as the firepit flamed their thoughts.

"With such news, I dare say that I must depart for Ireland and leave my children behind under your protection."

"Surely, cousin. There are many here to see to your children's safety," he promised.

"I must see my permanent agent, MacCleary, before I go. Enjoin him to step up Redshank recruitment in my absence."

"I will see to that as well, and that you are sent only the tallest and strongest Redshanks," her cousin promised.

Ineen was able to bring six galleys with her, each with up to three hundred Redshanks, when she left Scotland and safely landed at her fort at Carrigans despite the cold and intermittent snow flurries. Carrigans was only a short distance to Mongavlin. The fort, hedged by a tall forest of oak and evergreen, not only added downstream defenses for Mongavlin, but its thatched buildings, grounds, and huts also provided shelter for throngs of Redshanks.

Something out of the ordinary, however, made her turn to her counselor, O'Toole, who greeted her.

"Owen! O'Neill's banner at the gate."

"'Tis indeed the red hand banner of Hugh O'Neill." O'Toole pointed, "Tyrone himself."

Striding rapidly from the gate, flipping the wet edge of his fur mantle over his shoulder, Hugh O'Neill gave Ineen a hurried but warm embrace.

"'Tis something urgent we must discuss, Ineen—alone. Pardon us, Owen."

O'Toole gave a gracious wave and turned heel toward the assembling Scots.

"Red?" she all but cried as thunder rumbled back in the mountains.

"No. He fares well enough at the Tower, as you have been kept notified," he said. He stared at the Scots plaid of her mantle and the scores of new Redshanks assembling behind her, shouldering their battle axes or positioning the sheaths of their claymores.

She saw the concern in O'Neill's usually unreadable gray eyes.

"The O'Donnell?"

O'Neill hesitated.

"Tell me! Is he not safe in Donegal castle?" she said.

"Safe enough."

"What then?"

Kicking his boots against the frozen ground, O'Neill said, "Let us go inside."

O'Neill's horse-boy leaned to hear the conversation, but his master yelled at him to watch the horse.

Ineen led O'Neill through the iron gate, past long-residing Redshanks warming themselves by small bonfires on the bawn as they stood watch. Others were in their tents. She took O'Neill up the spiral staircase to the great hall, small as it was. On the way she ordered a servant to bring up refreshment. Turf was already smoking lightly in the fireplace.

"Well, then?" she said.

"Fitzwilliam came to Donegal Castle."

"So? This I know from my spies."

"There's more." He whipped off his wet mantle, looking to toss it on a wooden chair.

She waved to a chair by the fireplace.

"Just tell me!" Ineen urged.

"Shortly before Fitzwilliam arrived, Donal came and stayed long at Donegal Castle."

Outside, another roll of wintry thunder came then ceased, leaving an uneasy quiet.

"Donal's after doing that, especially whenever I am gone," Ineen said.

O'Neill shrugged. "As I knew Fitzwilliam was coming, I wanted to reach Donegal. I did not want O'Donnell to face Fitzwilliam alone. As for Donal, his arrival just before Fitzwilliam seemed no coincidence. But then I saw Donal swagger himself about the castle bawn."

"As my husband's Seneschal, he does swagger. But you're implying something more?"

"Fitzwilliam has appointed Donal the Crown Sheriff of Donegal."

"Sheriff!" she shouted. "There is no sheriff in Donegal." She flung her fists in the air. "Why has no one informed me of that?"

"It happened so fast. Sure, and I knew Donal was there and Fitzwilliam coming. But it was all arranged before I arrived."

Just then the servant came up the staircase with brimming goblets. O'Neill took wine. Ineen ignored the mead, which O'Neill took for her, and placed it on a trestle table.

"This is all Donal's doing," she said. "The O'Donnell would never permit that. He vowed there would never be another Crown Sheriff in Donegal."

"On the contrary, O'Donnell approved," O'Neill asserted.

For an instant, Ineen Dubh was speechless.

"O'Donnell told me," O'Neill said, "an Irish sheriff will keep out an English one."

Ineen huffed. "No such thing as an Irish sheriff. The English have sheriffs."

"O'Donnell trusts Donal," O'Neill reminded her. "Donal has long been his Seneschal."

"How could my husband do that with English garrisoned in the Friary? And son Red a hostage in Dublin Castle." She reached for her mead. She took a sip so that she did not scream. "Has the Crown Sheriff removed the English back to Connaught?"

O'Neill replied, "'Tis a father's trust, Ineen."

"Trust! I ask you, has *Sheriff Donal* expelled the Saxons from the Friary? And freed his father's Donegal Castle? And is his half-brother safe home?"

O'Neill shook his head three times. "No!"

"An outrage! Is it not enough that they hold Red hostage in that tower? There must be no sheriff, English or Irish, in *this kingdom*!"

"'Tis done. Fitzwilliam is already back in Dublin."

"The fools!" Ineen said with a glare that O'Neill found most unbecoming, but surely warranted.

"The O'Donnell has long considered he owed Donal something—something more than Seneschal as his oldest son."

Ineen hung her head. "We both know that my husband's wit is not what it was even a few years ago. Doesn't he realize . . . ?" She could not finish the thought.

"O'Donnell believes this accommodation secures Red a while longer, and I must add that Donal being sheriff keeps his father safe from the English."

Icy rain pelted the nearby window slit as darkness began to fill it.

Ineen sniffed. "Indeed, it does. Now both my husband and my son are prisoners of the English. Donal is after replacing Red Hugh as successor to O'Donnell. What could be plainer?"

"'Tis a ceremonial office only, High Sheriff of Donegal. In England, and in the Pale, High Sheriff is a judicial officer."

Ineen looked over at O'Neill with a pleading look. "Donal hasn't been knighted by the Crown as well?" she asked as she clutched her golden cross.

"Aye. He has. But no English court exists in Donegal," O'Neill assured her.

Brooding, Ineen made no response. Then she stated, "if Donal is the Crown's Sheriff, he will have to abide by English laws. That means Donegal will have English laws. So, he leaves the English garrisoned in the Friary. Will he garrison them in Donegal Castle, too?"

"I know not what Donal will do. But the deed is done. And it must remain so until Red Hugh is safe home," O'Neill warned her, and he drank the rest of his wine until he put down an empty goblet.

"You're as Saxon as the rest of them, you who sit in Dublin's Parliament!" she hissed.

"Do not be bitter toward me, Ineen. No better place for me to be than Dublin Parliament—to keep Red Hugh in good fortune."

"And what good fortune is rotting in an English prison?"

"To see that no harm comes to Red and to get him freed. Home to wed to my daughter Rose, who pines for him. That is what you and I both want. We must further our efforts."

Sleet outside pounded the slit window as Ineen listened. "Harshly I spoke to you, Hugh O'Neill. 'Tis my horridness in this whole ... matter. And my shock at this news of Donal."

"I realize that, Ineen." He took her hand, which was unusually cold. "And you will see that Donal has begun to adopt some English laws over Brehon law, but nothing dire as of yet."

"Just what I fear. If Donal does not free the Friary and my husband, who knows what more he might do?" Ineen said before she reached over for the mead, for her entire body became colder and colder despite the now blazing turf fire.

"That I know. There is one last thing," he said, removing his hand and drawing a folded parchment from his tunic. "'Tis a copy of a letter that . . . the English queen sent to Fitzwilliam." He handed it to her.

She stood up, took a candle from the fireplace mantle, and lit it from the flaming turf to read the English words. Some were familiar enough, given her days at the Stuart court:

And hereto we add the remembrance of one thing that,
being well ordered, may breed quietness in those parts,
videlicet, the continuing in prison of O'Donnell's son,
'Red Hugh' and O'Gallagher's son, 'Owny,' lately
seized upon and remaining in our Castle in Dublin.
Elizabeth R.

"Evil she is!" Ineen crumbled the copy and threw it into the smoking turf. Even in the candle flicker her face turned a deep red of rage. She collapsed into O'Neill's arms as sobs wracked her, and in response tears stung his own eyes.

"Ineen, Ineen, we will get through this. We will bring Red Hugh home."

All she could do was lift her head to signal her agreement.

They held one another for some time, O'Neill's tears falling onto Ineen's shoulders, before she stepped back and turned to dry her face.

"This appears," O'Neill recovered himself, "to be an answer to my letter to Walsingham. That offer—he did not mention it was for Rory in exchange for Red Hugh—has not been taken."

Ineen's voice fell quiet. "Red would have none of it anyway."

O'Neill tried to strike a reassuring note. "Being in some favor with the English queen, she still regards me, *as a creature of our own*. I will send her my latest concerns and pleadings for your son's release. I will even go to London and plead for Red, my son-in-law's, release in Her Majesty's privy council. I will offer her a bribe."

"You will?"

"Aye, I promise."

"That may make all the difference," Ineen whispered, and sighed.

"'Tis time I am buying—time," O'Neill reminded her, as he so often did. "We must keep Red in Bermingham Tower till we free him."

"God's curse on Bermingham Tower!"

"Much better Bermingham, my dear Ineen, than that other tower he could be sent to—the one in London."

"Jesus, Mary, and Joseph! My constant prayer that never happens."

"'Tis a prayer of mine, too."

"But how will I see my husband? I must find a way into Donegal Castle," Ineen said.

Hugh O'Neill looked upon her—the wife of a senile and aging husband, a mother whose son was kidnapped and held hostage, and yet a woman resolute and fiercely determined.

"You shall come with me. Neither Willis or Donal will challenge you when you are with me. I have been going to and from Castle Donegal in your absence."

She felt herself breathe more easily. "Then I must count on you, Hugh."

"And I, dear Ineen, must count on you."

"Of course, Hugh."

"That my Lady means if I go to London, you need be strong but do not do anything that affects O'Donnell's kingdom or Tyrone or anything to upset things in Ulster."

The sleety rain was tapering off as she sat down. She picked up her cup of mead and sipped it as O'Neill finished his wine.

"Your children are well settled in Argyll?" O'Neill asked.

"Sure, and they are. I left Annag up with them and the servants there delight in my children. They have been given the run of the castle and the wee daughters so enjoy being together with their sister. They all ask about Red Hugh, of course."

For some moments, Ineen and Hugh were comfortably silent.

Then Ineen asked, "O, Hugh, what does Siobhan think of her brother Donal being the Crown's Sheriff?"

"Much like her father that 'tis better an Irish Sheriff."

"And must I just sit here and wait to hear from you?"

"Ineen Dubh," O'Neill said and stood up, as did Ineen. He placed his hands on her firm shoulders, kissed her on the cheek. "I have never known you to sit and wait for anything. God be with you!"

With that he flexed a knee in parting and headed for the staircase.

She took a deep breath.

All the same, she thought, *Donal must not remain the Crown's Sheriff.*

XXIII

Ambush Near Mongavlin
Lough Foyle, Tyrconnell 1589

O n a dew-drenched morning at Mongavlin, Ineen
Dubh walked her customary spring path by Lough
Foyle when she caught sight of purple loosestrife
and yellow primroses stretching through the grass. The
flowers, for the briefest moment, eased the anguish she
always felt for Red Hugh and the thoughts of her ailing
husband. From the Mongavlin area on the west side of the
river and her fort a few miles north, she could see some of
the numerous tents and small thatched structures that spread
for five miles across the fertile lands bestowed upon her by
the O'Donnell. Many tents housed her Redshanks, those
temporary and those who now lived permanently in Ireland.
Here on her lands, the English were kept out.

Her castle-constrained husband remained free of the
English who were still garrisoned in Donegal Friary. She
herself, with the help of her Redshanks, managed to burn a

goodly part of the floor of the great hall of Donegal Castle with the knowledge that the English could not now garrison themselves there. Her husband's chambers remained secure on an upper floor with a hallway that led to the curving stairway. The stone steps remained for the Earl of Tyrone, O'Donnell's scribe, O'Clery, and Brehons as well as guards and gillies to reach O'Donnell in his chamber. His physician, McDunlevy, occupied another chamber nearby him. The burning was done, of course, to keep the Saxons out, for Donal, now Sheriff of Donegal, continued to leave Captain Willis and his minions in the Friary.

Word reached her through Hugh O'Neill that Red fared well enough in Dublin Castle and that food from Tyrconnell and from his friends in Dublin reached Red and the other two pledges.

Donal was on her mind as she strolled back to Mongavlin when a wounded harness-man staggered out of twisted trees in the deep woods near her castle. He teetered, devoid of any armor belonging to his master, armor that he carried for his Redshank. Ineen, recognizing a Scot when she saw one, for the plaid slung over one of his shoulders, strode toward the struggling man as her guards surrounded her.

When Ineen reached the bent man, he managed to say, "'Twas a raid! I've escaped. A raid on new Redshanks to arrive from Scotland! Killed me master!"

"Who might that be that has done this?" Ineen probed, bending down to see the extent of the man's injuries, but she could not understand the name that he uttered. "Do you know who they were, the raiders? Did they fly a banner? Where are the others?"

"'Twas dark. I was hit on the head. I saw no banner. Those Redshanks that survived are making their way to Carrigans. But why? Why kill us?" He shuddered, trying to speak in a hoarse voice. "Only a small group of Redshanks I be with."

Ineen dug her leather boots into the wet ground while blood dripped from the Scot's shoulder onto the wide sleeve of her léine. She dared to think, *Would the knighted Donal be so emboldened as do such a thing?*

She continued to tend to the harness-man. Then she burst out instructions for her guards, "Stop any bleeding." To another Ineen ordered, "Run for the local healer." And still to another, she said, "Go ahead—order drink. And don't have this man moved until a physician approves it!" And then to all, "I will also send my own physician from Mongavlin."

The first thing she did at Mongavlin was send a runner to alert her physician and lead him to the injured Scot. Then she changed to a clean léine to meet with Owen O'Tool, one of her most competent advisors in the great hall. "Could this raid come from Castlefinn! Hugh McDean, I warrant?" Ineen asked.

"'Tis likely. Too small a raid for it to be the Crown's Sheriff," Owen said.

"Jesus, Mary, and Joseph!" Ineen reached into a pocket to find her holy beads and thumb them. "And here I am after worrying on the threat of Donal as Sheriff of Donegal. 'Tis our counterattack—the infernal Hugh McDean is also waiting for us with his desires to succeed the O'Donnell with Red Hugh still held hostage," she said.

Soon came rapid interrogation of neighboring peasants that confirmed one of Ineen's suspicions. The Castlefinn O'Donnells—at the least Hugh McDean—were seen not far from Mongavlin. But no one knew more than that.

"Hugh McDean indeed! 'Twas not enough that Hugh McDean should be one of Captain Merriman's party who slew Alex McSorley," Ineen raised her voice when she confirmed it was Hugh McDean who led the raid. "Ever since Alex's slaying, I have counted on the sworn allegiance of Redshanks to avenge the death of my foster brother. Time for justice!"

Hugh of Dean was not one of the sons of Conn but married a sister of the Conns and managed to become their leader. All Tyrconnell knew that the sons of Conn descended from O'Donnell's deceased brother. The Conn brothers, including Neal Garbh and his brother-in-law, made clear to one and all their claim to succeed to the kingship. But enmity grew between them and Donal, so their fiery in-law, Hugh McDean, led the Conns to recapture a great many of the Conn cattle that Donal raided. But they failed to kill Donal.

Emboldened by this swift victory, nonetheless, Hugh McDean started raiding cattle herds of less threatening *sub-kings* around Castlefinn. It was, of course, all about Red Hugh. 'Twas not enough that he was a hostage in Dublin

Castle. Hugh McDean as well as Donal, and who knew how many more, would challenge the absent one for the right to succeed the aging O'Donnell.

Ineen saw advantage in the situation. "We will avenge this without delay!" she proclaimed to the Redshanks in her hall as she stood up and felt the warmth of the nearby turf fire. "Hugh McDean and his brothers-in-law want cattle. We will entice them with cattle."

"'Tis true. We'll ambush and make an end of it," Captain Crawford assured her, raising his claymore.

"Aye!" another shouted. "A Redshank cannot be properly buried before his honor is made whole! We will ambush McDean."

Ineen looked at her captain, her eyes dark with intrigue. "We'll see if Hugh McDean will come to us for cattle."

"Aye," a chorus responded, sitting around the central table where ale and wine were copiously placed by Ineen's able servants.

Ineen called for a pause. "With Hugh McDean we must be deliberate—and successful."

By noon that same day, Ineen Dubh had the plan thought out.

Soon it was executed. Mongavlin and Carrigans kerne, guarded by Redshanks and their harness-men, spread out to all the farms under their protection. Cattle were herded to the grounds of Castle Mongavlin. Even some of Ineen's numerous stud mares and horses were rounded up to make them all the more alluring to Hugh McDean. Ineen made sure, by the usual means—well-paid—that reports went out of the enlarged herd at Mongavlin and spread to the environs of Castlefinn. Redshanks, harness-men, and kerne were deployed about all the approaches and watches. They took turns throughout the night despite heavy rains. But no raiders came the next dawn along the muddy roads and paths in the continuing cloudbursts. This was not entirely a surprise. Hugh McDean was likely assembling a large troop of Castlefinn kerne and drovers to handle the reported increase in the Mongavlin herd. Hugh McDean was no fool, but he was a hothead. Ineen Dubh counted on that.

She knew her man. By next morn in light fog, it all ended within moments. Hugh McDean, his hair flying about his long head like smoke, yelled the Dean Gallagher victory cry, *"The Faith is My Glory,"* then charged with his horsemen out of woods near the river Foyle. He proved to be as rash as he was brash. He led his troops down along the river road until they neared Mongavlin. When they filtered into the woods to spring upon the castle and its cattle in the customary way, Ineen's spies, hidden in those same woods along the Foyle, had already sent alerts, some by arrow. Likely Hugh McDean knew it and cared not, nor did he try to find and kill them; he felt that confident.

Leading his horsemen and kerne out of the woods, Hugh McDean—tall in the saddle, waving a broadsword—was struck instantly by two well-placed Redshanks. He was hit by a number of arrows as well, taking out his horse's left eye, which reared and dumped Hugh McDean on the ground.

Sword hand empty, sword arm useless, a rosette of blood growing on his chest under its futile coat of mail, Hugh nonetheless tried to lurch to his feet, but three Redshanks were already around him. Before he could look up, he was axed into three or four pieces.

A few of his fellow horsemen also fell, but none of his Conn brothers-in-law.

Most of McDean's troops turned tail in the woods and beat it back to Castlefinn. No matter. Hugh McDean would no longer press a claim to what Ineen knew belonged to Red Hugh by prophecy—and by her desire.

Ineen Dubh sat in the great hall of Mongavlin crocheting lace items for her daughters; her hands were as delicate as they were steady. She waited for word from the ambush with a cup of mead by her side.

Captain Crawford arrived first, bare legs muddied, his smile broad as he boasted of the skills of his Redshanks' arrows.

The next day, a message arrived from Donal noting the ambush near Mongavlin and aware that Hugh McDean killed the harness-man. He added that she must desist in bringing Scots into Ireland.

Ineen crumbled the parchment. She knew since the day she gave birth to Red Hugh that Donal was a threat. Surely, as the Crown Sheriff, he now considered himself the next O'Donnell by the English rite of Primogeniture.

XXIV

A Visit to London
1590

When Hugh O'Neill learned of the ambush near Mongavlin, he paced in his chamber at Dungannon and gazed out the glass window, looking at lands that cast a warning shadow these waning days of winter. Catching a view of his helmeted English soldiers, a renewed urgency to leave for London struck him.

He decided to make sure word reached Donegal, and specifically Mongavlin, that he planned to leave to see the English queen. He gambled that upon hearing this, Ineen would be held back from any further ventures since she knew that she told her he would make a personal plea to her Majesty to release her son, his son-in-law, Red Hugh O'Donnell. Although he cared not a whit for what happened to Hugh McDean or any of the Castlefinn O'Donnells, he did care how another of Ineen Dubh's actions would only complicate his endeavors to get her son freed from Dublin Castle.

With the ambush of Hugh McDean, he realized the beginning of a deeper change in Ineen; there was no more telling her to wait. And she kept bringing in Redshanks from Argyll when his plan was to keep the Crown at bay till Red Hugh O'Donnell came safe home.

As preparations ahead of the journey preoccupied him at Dungannon, he gathered every detail about the ambush he could without asking Ineen or anyone else directly involved. If and when asked for these details in London, the Earl of Tyrone could claim he knew no more than rumors. To keep the "rumors" only and avoid Ineen, he wished to leave Ulster as soon as possible, but it was not until late January 1590 that he sailed to England to see the queen. In velvet cloak, wool doublet, and beard newly trimmed, the Earl suffered the wet bitter winds of the Irish sea to seek official pardon for any past offenses the Crown considered him liable for and to plea for the release of Red Hugh.

Meanwhile, Hugh O'Neill hoped that Ineen Dubh honored his message, waited for his return to Ireland, and did nothing to further upset the situation in O'Donnell's kingdom.

After receiving O'Neill's messages, Ineen had sent various pleas back to Dungannon to remind O'Neill that he must convince the English queen that Red Hugh must be released for the good of all of Ulster. So, reassured by O'Neill, Ineen waited through the icy winds of St. Bridget's Day and beyond the fair spring at Mongavlin.

She received little information from Dublin, though now and then one of O'Neill's Irish men would ride to Mongavlin and report, "O'Neill's friends in the Pale and Dublin keep the provisions you send flowing to your son and fellow hostages."

Then came ominous reports from Ineen's spies that O'Neill still remained in London—having exchanged the wet cold of winter for a long hot drought in which horses cantered about the bed of a waterless Thames. And the Earl of Tyrone still had not won an audience with England's queen.

Mongavlin felt too quiet. So, Ineen kept riding by the river Foyle. Sometimes just pacing her mount among the parklike beeches and oaks by her fort at Carrigans. She rode in disguise a few times with her bodyguards to visit her ailing husband in his bedchamber in Donegal Castle.

One of those times she interrupted his consultation with Donal, the Crown Sheriff. "I see that you are with O'Donnell," she began.

Donal, who was cool but courteous to his stepmother, said, "I must be my father's Seneschal in these trying times as well as Sheriff."

"When do you propose to send the English back to Connaught so the friars can return to the Friary?"

"Well, Lady Ineen, 'tis something only I can work out with the English," Donal replied.

She hissed and glared at Donal. "Do it now!"

260

Donal turned back to his father and said nothing more to Ineen. "Father, I have been with MacSweeney Banagh such that all goes well there."

Donal intended to stay for a lengthy time, so Ineen asked him to step outside the chambers that she might have a brief visit with her husband.

"Husband," she greeted him as she moved over to the chair in which he sat.

"Ineen, 'tis grand that you have come." He painstakingly stood up and kissed her on the cheek. "Donal is here helping me in many ways," he said as he sat back down.

"I have seen him, husband," she commented, and then shared news of their children and how Red Hugh was still in Dublin Castle, though in the same Bermingham Tower in which they had visited.

They spoke of such things, for Ineen was sure that Donal must be listening to them.

Looking out the slit window, Ineen saw something that caused her to hold back a gasp. She noted the surprising number of unfamiliar warriors and kerne inside the bawn and tents around the walls of Donegal Castle. There were also English morions and pikes parading down the Eske by O'Boyle's castle.

What is Donal doing to stop the cattle-thieving and rapine and plunder of Captain Willis and Bingham's minions? she thought. *Why does Donal of Glencolmcille supply Captain Willis all the beef he desires?* The time of reckoning for Willis and the English and those in league with them was coming, if only Red Hugh would be in Donegal and out of Dublin.

After Ineen sat by the O'Donnell and a servant served them both wine and a plate of beef and fresh bread, Ineen took her leave without any other sight of Donal.

Once back at Mongavlin, she was prisoner to O'Neill's promises and warnings, except for the Redshanks she continued to receive from Scotland.

She rode her Spanish stallions, ones Fitzwilliam heard of but never found, the strongest and most highly prized horses in Ulster and the rest of Ireland. Riding her white stallion, Niall, she was free in all the lands she commanded.

Once, in mantle of green that was striped with crimson, she led a party of horsemen as far west as Farsetmor by Lough Swilly, where O'Donnell, in his much younger strength, had won the battle.

Finally, from her spies who came up to Mongavlin, she learned that Hugh O'Neill was on his return from England, rewarded with a parchment pardon for any offences of his against the Crown. But he received no assurances about the release of the Crown's prized hostage, Red Hugh O'Donnell.

Ineen counted so on Hugh O'Neill's powers of persuasion that she turned from her spies, rushed into her private chamber, and sobbed. She stayed there the rest of the day, and as a thunderous nightfall came, she realized that with no good news of Red's release, she might have to act alone.

For all of O'Neill's efforts—and they were many and steady—it was now three years that Red Hugh was held in Dublin Castle. And with the English in Donegal Friary, Donal the Sheriff, and her husband ailing more and more each time she saw him, she knew that she could not wait any longer for Red Hugh to come home.

XXV

The Crown's Sheriff
1590

*I*neen did wait through the celebrations of Lughnasa, the harvest time a few weeks before Michaelmas. The sun began its descent toward the inevitable wintry darkness. Along with hurly games and spear throwing came the cutting of the first grain. A bull was roasted and eaten. Cereal was plucked and apples were ripe for the eating as the bards shared their stories around the bonfires.

Ineen was in no mood for feasting.

A brief time after Lughnasa, Ineen was surprised by the sudden appearance of MacSweeney Doe. "Owen Oge MacSweeney, you have come with no messenger to alert your arrival?" Ineen asked, after he was escorted into her chamber in Mongavlin.

Owen Oge's beard looked a weary white, his manner grim and abrupt and his mantle a dreary brown.

She ordered wine and salmon brought up. She was not prepared for Red's foster father and was dressed in a simple léine of little color, her dark hair hanging loose.

"From Rathmullen I come," he said.

"From MacSweeney Fanad?"

"Aye. And from your stepson, Donal."

"From Donal!" she startled. "About Red Hugh?"

"Red's alive," he said.

"Then O'Donnell. He still lives?" she asked.

Owen Oge replied, "Aye, O'Donnell is much the same."

"Then what?"

"I came," he said with a stern voice, "because Donal's after canvassing sub-chieftains for leave to become loyal to him and *not* loyal to his father. He says his father is too old and senile. And that the English queen prefers him and may *never* release Red Hugh, for even the Earl of Tyrone could not persuade her to do so."

"Jesus, Mary, and Joseph!" Ineen gasped. "Please, take a seat. Tell me more."

"MacSweeney Banagh has beheaded one of our MacSweeney kinsmen and pledged loyalty to Donal. And another MacSweeney south of here as well. 'Tis how I learned this. And your old neighbor on the Eske, O'Boyle, he's with Donal."

"Ach, Donal took him in when Willis chased him out of his castle. Has no one told him 'tis Donal who does not expel Willis from Castle Boyle and the Friary!" Ineen raised her voice.

Owen Oge took a deep breath, as though the next he was about to deliver was an axe he held over her head. "My Lady, 'tis said that from Bearnasmor above Donegal to Drowse, on the border of Connaught, Donal has brought over the nobles and their people with the help of the English."

Ineen jumped up. She pointed her finger at MacSweeney Doe. "And why have I not heard all of this before? Not all loyal to Donal have I known about. So many unloyal?"

"'Twas quick once O'Donnell found the presence of mind to tell Donal that he would not step down," MacSweeney said. Donal even has English troops to support him in his quest to succeed O'Donnell," Owen Oge sighed.

"English troops," Ineen said. "A good many loyal to Donal? But Ballyshannon even?"

"Ballyshannon I have not heard about, but . . . all the way to Connaught. We are loyal to O'Donnell—and to you. Me. And Fanad," MacSweeney Doe reminded her.

Ineen paced in rising anger, then spun on Owen Oge. "Have you spoken with Donal?"

"Aye, 'tis why I know so much about this. I told Donal a very heavy thing he ponders, one that a loyal *ur-ri* like myself cannot take lightly. For his father's peace and the kingdom's peace, says he. 'And because Red Hugh is still held hostage.' 'Tis one thing for a king to step down, says I, 'tis another to wrest him down."

"Indeed!" Ineen affirmed. "And with this grand plan, what plan has this Crown Sheriff and his father's own

Seneschal have to get rid of Captain Willis and his English troops?" she snarled.

"That I asked him as well. 'In good time,' says he, 'as the Crown High Sheriff . . .'"

"Crown Sheriff!" Ineen scoffed. "The king himself Donal means to be!"

Owen Oge MacSweeney gave an unhappy shrug.

"Red Hugh O'Donnell is the prophesied king," Ineen declared, "and the only king there shall be!"

"And so, I ride here, my Lady, to inform you of Donal's threatening doings."

The conversation went into the wee hours. Owen Oge spent the night at Mongavlin, and in the morning Ineen rode with him to Rathmullen to see MacSweeney Fanad.

On the strand below Fanad's castle she gazed across Lough Swilly at the heights of Inch, the isle where Alex was beheaded. And on the dark and choppy waters between her and Inch, the treacherous English merchantman had kidnapped her son, whom Holy Columcille prophesied would drive out the foreigners that bedeviled Ireland.

Time was short. In the few hours remaining until the sun fell below the rugged nob behind Castle Fanad, Ineen and the two loyal MacSweeneys discussed plans and contingencies, not to rescue O'Donnell but to keep him at Donegal.

The one true lord of Tyrconnell until Red Hugh was safe home from the English. If harm befell her husband—if he died, so died all hope for Red Hugh as king.

Both MacSweeneys Doe and Fanad vowed to stand by the O'Donnell.

With the vows of the two substantial MacSweeneys, Ineen returned to Mongavlin, only to be greeted by a face she had not seen for many a month.

He was waiting in the great hall with six Redshanks, who, like him, stood bare legged under mantles of green and blue plaid.

She recognized the intense stare as soon as she matched it with his ragged moustache: McAteer Crawford, known simply as McAteer. She thought of his guttering face in the torchlight, which seemed a century ago when her impetuous son led his friends on a raid to bring back stolen O'Donnell cattle.

"I come to tell you, milady O'Donnell, 'tis all amiss at Ballyshannon."

"Sit," she ordered. "Will you have whiskey and beef?"

"Aye," McAteer said.

"This has already concerned me," Ineen told him. Ever since the arrest and imprisonment of her counselor Owen O'Toole O'Gallagher, by order of Lord Deputy Fitzwilliam during his west coast quest for Armada gold, Ballyshannon had been in turmoil. "What more must I know?"

"Donal has recruited many of O'Gallagher's mercenaries and kerne to be loyal to him and not the O'Donnell, but not all."

"Oh, how I hoped it would not come to that," Ineen said softly.

268

"But your Redshanks I have kept out of all of that," McAteer proudly announced.

"You are stout and loyal, McAteer."

"'Tis to tell you that rumors abound that Donal may do something within the fortnight that I have ridden here, given his help from the English in pursuing those loyal to him."

"Sure, and I have long thought he might do something— as if he has not done enough becoming the Crown's Sheriff."

McAteer said, "Donal tells that as long as O'Donnell remains king while he ails and weakens, and, milady, you bring in more Scots from Argyll and the Isles, Red Hugh O'Donnell shall not be freed, nor Owny Oge O'Gallagher with him, nor Owny's father Owen O'Gallagher."

"Donal would say that," she said with bitterness.

"But 'tis more he says."

"What more?" Ineen raised her voice.

"As Crown High Sheriff taking over 'administration,' he calls it, of the 'shire of County Donegal'—as he has conducted 'administration' as O'Donnell's Seneschal—he will show the Crown a new day in this part of Ulster, and then the Crown may release Red Hugh and the hostages. He, of course, would become the O'Donnell king by right of the firstborn."

Ineen felt too much anger to respond immediately.

"A promise from Fitzwilliam, he says." McAteer hesitated, then added, "Ye know the Lord Deputy and the English queen prefer Donal to your Red Hugh."

When Ineen was able to speak, she said, "That I know. So, Donal confessed he deals with the devil himself."

"He thinks putting forward some English law to replace Brehon law is to Donegal's benefit."

Ineen responded, "Sure, and Donal would."

She knew the time had come. No more waiting for O'Neill's promises. There was no time to waste. She began making arrangements, grateful that all her children were in Inveraray with the exception of her son of prophecy.

She took McAteer and the other four Ballyshannon Redshanks, along with her own large contingent of Redshanks, to Rathmullen. She sent a summons ahead of her.

So, Owen Oge MacSweeney brought down a substantial contingent from Castle Doe and joined McSweeney Fanad, who had already shaped up his own contingent. They all felt it. They all knew it. There was no choice but to stop Donal O'Donnell.

XXVI

A March South
September 1590

*I*neen strolled among her Redshanks wearing a shirt of mail over her shortened léine and sturdy trews, over which a long scabbard was tethered to her belt. She encouraged her men, letting them know that they would be the most valuable in stopping Donal O'Donnell from setting himself up as the O'Donnell's successor. Whatever it cost.

She ordered McAteer, "Go back south. Bring loyal Redshanks from Ballyshannon. Go to McGroarty and tell him you have orders that he come with his men and that he bring the *Cathach, The Battle Book of The O'Donnells.*"

"Aye, my lady, 'twill be done," he answered.

"We shall meet on the cliffs above Lough Glen where the river flows into Teelin Bay. Do not go on to Glencolmcille until we meet," she said.

As McAteer left with his group of Redshanks, Ineen walked back into Fanad's great hall where MacSweeney Doe and MacSweeney Fanad were. They too had once been Scots mercenaries, and it comforted her that she was surrounded by Scots. There Owen Oge asked Ineen to speak with him apart.

They moved to an empty corner away from the turf fire. A large wooden table nearby held beef and salmon placed on platters near small bowls of salt. Goblets of wine and mead were filled to the brim.

Owen Oge went to the point. "Tell me, milady, what do we tell O'Donnell if Donal, his eldest son and Seneschal, dies?"

"The truth," Ineen said. "Donal conspired to dishonor and depose his father."

"'Tis true, 'tis true. But also hard," Doe sighed. "He has never done me ill, Donal. He served his father well, till now," he said.

"'Twill be much harder if we fail," Ineen reminded him. "Do I hear you wavering, MacSweeney?"

"What you hear, milady, is the sadness of my heart about all this."

"I would prefer to hear your anger at this turn of Donal's. Are you with O'Donnell and with our Red Hugh, your own foster son?"

"Of course. I am angry, angry and sad at the same time. And you," Owen Oge went on with some difficulty, "I'm after dreading to utter the words, and praying God it can never happen, but if 'tis yourself that should lose your life . . ."

Ineen rubbed her forehead with vigorous fingers. "If that happens . . ."

Owen Oge looked down then into Ineen's eyes. "And if . . ."

"Tell the O'Donnell his wife went to battle to keep himself king and so his true son Red Hugh fulfill the prophecy of Columcille. That Red free the kingdom of its enemies and become king."

"Aye." MacSweeney could say no more.

MacSweeney Fanad came over to them. "Is there something I should be knowing?"

"No," Ineen said. "'Tis talk of Donal."

"You must eat, Ineen," Fanad said, leading them to the table.

But Ineen could not eat. "Best I rest now. In the early morn we begin the march south. We must all get our rest," she commanded.

Once she undressed upstairs, she slipped on a simple smock and knelt by the bed in prayer. She prayed that the Lord would fulfill His prophecy for Red Hugh; she prayed Donal would never plant English in O'Donnell's lands; she prayed the Lord's will would triumph on the morrow; she prayed her husband would not die. In the unfamiliar bed she tried to see her son's face, gray eyes mischievous. But the only face in her mind's eye was Donal's, breaking through her thoughts like a ghost, appearing in the guise of his grandfather, Shane, the *ri* responsible for her father's death. Donal's dark beard was trimmed like a Saxon's, and his hair neat as a Crown Sheriff. But this night she needed sleep to prepare to face him. *Out of my mind, Donal,* she pleaded.

From the time she married the O'Donnell, and heard jubilant cries of how Donal, her stepson, resembled her spouse, so valiant and strong, she could barely stand the sight of the boy.

Startled by the viciousness of the howling wind, she sat up in the bed shaking her head. She fought the thoughts on a feathered mattress. She turned this way and that. She must have managed to doze off before MacSweeney Fanad's wife nudged her awake.

Darkness surrounded the lit candle. Ineen wasted no time dressing in the shortened léine and trews. A maid brought her roast beef, eggs, and mead to break her fast, but she could stomach little if any of it. Just enough mead and eggs for strength.

Once outside and seated on the embroidered padding of her warhorse, the pre-dawn dark softening to dawn, a shirt of mail over her léine, iron skull tight on her head, and with the long, plain scabbard now wrapped with hilt tethered to the padding beneath her right leg, Ineen Dubh was surprised how fresh she felt. Sleepless, yet all the same her eyes were awake, her head was clear.

She felt a peace in her breast she would never have expected during the night. She felt quite right as she, MacSweeney Fanad, MacSweeney Doe, and Sean Oge

O'Doherty of Inishowen, who had joined them, spurred their horses and commenced their joint column south and west.

Her spies already sent surprising confirmation that Donal was located near Glencolmcille this 14th day of September. And she wondered, were they already betrayed?

XXVII

Arrows at Derrylahan
14 September 1590

C ommencing in the torch-lit dark, with air that was cool and sweetly scented with the harvest, Ineen's lungs filled. Filled with hope. The drizzle was light and intermittent. She touched beneath her mail coat where Alex's medallion was secured in her pocket. *For the O'Donnell and Red Hugh I do this, and for the prophecy*, she reminded the Lord.

The retinue marched to the cadence of a low chant that passed in uneven waves from the Redshanks and other warriors back to the pikemen. In the softening dark, the marching of hundreds formed a worm of fire winding south down Lough Swilly and then to the west.

Escorted by torch-bearing kerne, a detail of Ineen's Redshank archers, in saffron léine kilted up to their belts, headed the column. They were followed by the vanguard battle of seventy axe-shouldering warriors, in seven ranks, wearing coats of mail reaching to their calves, accompanied by their harness-men.

Together with the MacSweeneys and Owen Oge O'Doherty of Inishowen, bodyguards came next. MacSweeneys Doe and Fanad called on troops of their own. Another contingent from Castle Doe would join them near Glengesh Pass. These numbers might be fewer than what Donal O'Donnell had at his disposal, but he did not have hundreds of Ineen's Redshanks.

Most Redshanks marched barefoot and bare-legged, no matter whether islanders or highlanders. And others, especially Ineen's bodyguards, rode horses. Bagpipers marched as well, ready to fill their bags and skirl as soon as the field of battle neared.

Any one up and about would know that O'Donnell's wife was on the march, heading somewhere.

A little past the River Swilly, McAteer joined the column just as troops began to snuff their torches in the daylight. He rode with McGroarty on from Ballybofey, as it was McGroarty's office to carry into battle the sacred battle-book of the O'Donnells, the *Cathach*, at the head of any O'Donnell hosting. *The Psalter*, a book of psalms, was inside the gilded box inscribed by the very hand of Holy Columcille himself.

"Would I be heading off without you and the holy book?" Ineen greeted McGroarty.

"Surely not," the noble said, pleased. He held it up like a shield for her to see. Then McGroarty fell into line beside her and her Franciscan confessor, the rugged Father Donohoe, trotting along on his chestnut mare.

From Rathmullan with only brief rests, it usually took at least three hours of steady quick time to reach the junction called Ardara. Although it had its ups and downs, this trek passed mostly along the glens of low rolling hills and skirted craggy mountains to the east, and there were plenty of little lakes and rivers for any halt for water.

It was still morning when the march reached Ardara. Sunless but warming under high, gray clouds, the wet earth gave off the smell of ripened oats. The party of troops sent by pre-arrangement from Castle Doe awaited them.

Here Ineen decided the march should separate into two contingents, as there were two clear approaches to the area around Glencolmcille. One was at the far west of the peninsula above Donegal Bay, and the other the road up Glengesh Pass in the peninsula's interior.

Owen Oge MacSweeney Doe left the main column to consolidate his troops, knowing the mission was not to attack unless summoned by Ineen, but to block any retreat by Donal and provoke surrender.

Ineen Dubh preferred to keep MacSweeney Fanad beside her; his preference, too. So, they went toward Killybegs in MacSweeney Banagh's territory. That meant going near Donohoe MacSweeney's Castle at Rahan, about two leagues east of Killybegs.

To this MacSweeney Fanad looked forward keenly. He hated Donohoe MacSweeney for beheading the previous

MacSweeney Banagh and because Banagh became loyal to Donal.

As it turned out, not far east from Ardara, Ineen and Fanad were met by one of the spies with news that Donohoe MacSweeney was not at Castle Rahan. He had left behind guards at the road into Killybegs.

"Where would this MacSweeney loyal to Donal be heading? Do they know?" Ineen asked her men.

No one had information about that.

"'Tis no desire of mine to waste arrows or men on MacSweeney Banagh's men," Ineen said to Fanad.

Outside Killybegs, at the crossroads called Straleeney, the column halted when they reached the guards near Castle Rahan, the waters of the inlet glittering just beyond. Ineen let Fanad do the talking.

"Good day, Clan Sweeney!" Fanad greeted.

"You shall not pass, MacSweeney Fanad, honored sir," replied a Banagh guard who stepped forward.

"'Tis no desire of ours to enter Killybegs, let alone impose on Castle Rahan. God be with ye good men of Banagh. We are on our way to the meadows of Teelin Bay. West we go, not east. And we intend to recompense you," MacSweeney Fanad went on, handing gold to the guard, "and welcome your escort to the coast road."

In a voice as stony as his eyes, but his free hand clutching the gold, Constable McDiarmuid said, "West you may go, MacSweeney Fanad. No escort being called for."

So Ineen sent spies ahead in widely spaced tandem to relay back any indications of Banagh kerne lying in wait.

The wind off the Lough cleared her eyes, filled her nose with a clean smell, fragrances from the earth as well as the sea. She ran her gaze over the growth along the banksides, grass green and thick, yellow furze, purple heather.

The only intelligence run back by the spies was of a company of troops, almost certainly MacSweeneys, moving down the slopes of Derrylahan in the direction of Glencolmcille.

But as Ineen's and her troops' final stretch neared, she found it easier not to think about what was about to happen, because happen it would.

It seemed quite sudden: in less than an hour from Killybegs, shortly past the little crossroads called Kilcar, the muddy road turned right and the land fell toward a long gray stretch of water off the sea. As the green and rocky cliffs and peaks of Slieve League rose beyond, shouts distant and near went up.

"O'Donnell!"

"O'Donnell!"

Ineen commanded Captain Crawford to call a halt to the vanguard. Ineen and MacSweeney Fanad spurred their mounts to trot ahead, bodyguards with them.

Far down the lush slopes a blue banner on a staff firmly planted flapped in the wind with the unmistakable O'Donnell banner of silver unicorns, framed by three silver stars and silver hand palm up. Behind it, axe-bearing men in

280

saffron tunics hanging to the knees and other troops—Donal O'Donnell's men. And the disloyal MacSweeney's troops were there as the spies had reported. Startled, Ineen and Fanad looked at each other. The assembly point was by the O'Donnell banner below on the fields near Derrylahan.

Ineen called back, "Captain Crawford! Double-time to that cliff ahead!"

The entire column, unit after unit, followed her command. Ineen and Fanad and their mercenaries galloped, Ineen signaling McGroarty, Father Donohoe, and the other horsemen. Then Ineen slowed, knowing better than to make herself a clear target.

The place they were near, Derrylahan, or Broad Derry, had the bay below, called Teelin, and a mountain stream feeding it known simply as the River Glen.

The slopes of Derrylahan down to the edge of the narrow bay were not smooth but fell in waves of heather and furze and irregular gullies and ridges, thick with bush, scrub conifers, and isolated stands of oak and beech. Scattered dots of sheep cropped a swell of grass to the left below. Ineen rode this road many times and often paused to take in the beauty of the bay, the magnificent rolls and peaks of the hills across the way—which also loomed above Glencolmcille on the far side.

Not this day.

Atop the granite outcropping, Ineen Dubh looked down at Donal's assembling entourage. Her standard bearer planted the same O'Donnell Banner, blue with silver

O'Donnell unicorns rampant and the same three silver stars and same silver hand palm up as Donal's banner below. It snapped grandly in the breeze.

Not all Donal's men, in a long string from the right, could be seen through the thickets here and there. Ineen looked for horsemen. She made out the largest white horse prancing back and forth, the tall figure on it gesturing impatiently in the direction of the assembly above. Donal.

Then Ineen peered toward her far right, where Glengesh Pass would open above the broad valley. MacSweeney Doe did indeed hold his men just below the top of the Pass until her arrival. So, now all troops were together again.

Gray clouds roiled in from behind Slieve League, but for the moment they did not look like rain. The wind kept a steady breeze. Ineen said to Fanad, "The traitor Sheriff of Donegal has spared us an hour's further march to Glencolmcille."

"I wager 'tis definitely himself, Donal O'Donnell, on that white horse," Fanad said.

Meanwhile, a considerable number of Ineen's forces had massed and formed on the upslope behind her. As instructed, ranks of Redshank archers, short recurve bows in hand, arrow quivers at the belt, some with iron skulls, most bare-legged though a few in hosen, fanned to the right and the left of the outcropping. It was a respectful pace behind the front battle of axe-shouldering MacSweeney gallowglass and harness-men, seven ranks deep. Constables and captains barked orders. The extended vanguard commenced a low concerted hum. Bagpipers behind them bleated tuning-up notes.

Ineen, still on horseback, peered at Donal's troops. The noises coming up from it were random. She thought she recognized, by beard and bearing, some of whom were long loyal to her husband, and she keenly resented Donal's expropriating them.

"McGroarty!" she cried. "Unpack the holy *Battle Book*!"

Father Donohoe joined McGroarty and the two men nudged their horses gingerly forward, McGroarty breathing hard in this solemn moment.

Ineen turned her horse around and stepped it in from the outcropping before the assembled mass of her column. She dismounted and stood on a high, smooth rock before she unfastened the long scabbard from its tethers. From the scabbard, slowly she drew its sword, which shone dully with the scratches, nicks, and dark stains of a thousand years. That she had removed it from Donegal Friary to Mongavlin even before the invasion of the Friary was not generally known. To the gasps of some who recognized the sword, Ineen raised it high.

"Behold the ancient sword of Conall Gulban! Behold the sword blessed by the holy Columcille before the Battle of Cúl Dreimhne. By this sword, the true son of O'Donnell, Red Hugh, shall drive the enemies of Tyrconnell and the enemies of all Ireland into the sea. Until Red Hugh comes safe home, I hold it for him."

"O'Donnell Abu!" rose out from the mass of men before her, swelling to roar upon roar: *"O'Donnell Abu! O'Donnell Abu!"*

Ineen promised, "No English or their minions shall take it or turn and slay our people in the name of the foreign queen. Remember this other prophecy of St. Columcille:

> *"There will come a man, glorious, pure, exalted,*
> *Who will cause mournful weeping in every*
> *territory;*
> *He will be a holy prince,*
> *And he will be king."*

"'Tis a sword I have in my heart," she announced, her raven hair falling beneath her skull cap, her blue eyes fierce with hope. "My great and valiant O'Donnell, a man with all the qualities and virtue that make a champion king has been betrayed by his own flesh and blood. This unnatural treason," she raised her voice higher for Father Donohoe and the throng of warriors to hear clearly, "cries out to God for vengeance. A treason that has already bloodied the fields of Tyrconnell by the swords of the English. You know the names I curse: Bingham and Connell and Bowen and Willis. And God's curse on any Crown Sheriff who would sell the kingdom to the English! They burned the feet of our people with brimstone. Today we shall avenge such things."

Lowering the sword, she returned it to its scabbard, moved off the rock and nodded to McGroarty.

He had robed himself in ceremonial mantle with ancient Celtic figures in silver and gold, and he now held the box

284

containing the *Cathach*. He raised it as a priest raises a Host at mass and offered it to the Franciscan, who slid from his own horse, received it, and also raised it high. In color a dull gold on an overcast day, the lid was studded with polished crystals round as pearls.

Amid its painted, teeming figures sat a long-haired, young and beardless Columcille holding in one hand a book and raising the other hand in blessing; to one side stood a smaller St. Patrick, hand also raised in blessing; and to the other a smaller Christ on the Cross, flanked by His Mother and Beloved Disciple. Although old Hugh O'Donnell had required McGroarty to bring it on many a raid over the years, by tradition the *Cathach* stayed with its official custodian in a small chapel at Castle McGroarty.

Father Donohoe kissed the box three times: once each upon St. Patrick, the Crucified Christ, and St. Columcille. In a strong voice, he read the words embossed on the bottom of the box: "Pray for the soul of Caffar O'Donnell, for whom this *Cathach* was made!"

Remounting his horse, Father Donohoe raised it high. A gillie, taking the reins of the horse, walked horse and priest three times round Ineen Dubh, MacSweeney Fanad, and over by MacSweeney Doc. With the book the Franciscan made a solemn Sign of the Cross and blessed the warriors who, after a moment of silence, again roared, *"O'Donnell Abu! O'Donnell Abu!"*

Ceremony concluded, the constable of the vanguard ordered them to turn and march. Each flank of Ineen's

Redshank archers contracted into tight formation to make a flat, obtuse V at the front.

If Donal's troops took the initiative, they would have to march uphill through those ankle-wrenching gullies. Ineen ordered, "Captains, ready bows and arrows."

Atop the cliff, a detail of kerne stacked up a palisade of leather and deerskin shields from behind which Ineen, MacSweeney, and others, dismounted, could view what was happening and give new orders.

Ineen Dubh assessed the assembly below and recalculated the strength and disposition of her warriors. Both sides could see each other straight ahead.

"We shall let Donal make the first move!" Ineen pronounced.

"Let them wear themselves out, we shall!" agreed MacSweeney Fanad with an excited grin.

Ineen and her archers held their lines until ordered otherwise.

From behind the shield palisade, Ineen watched Donal on his white horse move to the side of his formation. She saw MacSweeney Banagh taking counsel with O'Boyle far from the river's edge. Then the first line of Donal's troops spread sudden gaps between them, and spear-brandishing men ran out, descending immediately, and awkwardly, into the first gulley.

Up on the ridge, MacSweeney Fanad's men remained shoulder to shoulder, solid as a rear guard. Ineen's front lines of Redshank archers held bows and arrows down.

From both forces, Ineen's above and Donal's below, the skirls of bagpipes rose high.

But nothing happened. Donal and his troops just waited.

Finally, Ineen bellowed, "Archers!" to her right. "Archers!" she called out to the left.

The Redshank captains cried orders. In unison both lines drew arrows, raised their bows to shoulder level, fired. The air hummed like thousands of maddened bees. The captains cried new orders; the air again filled with a terrific hum. A third set of orders were cried and the air buzzed with murderous speed.

It was this third volley that felled all but a few, who were struggling within a spear's thrust from Ineen's line. But the battle went on all day. The cries reaching up from below now were howls and screams instead of bellowing war cries. But to his credit, Donal O'Donnell on his white horse rode out before his vanguard. The horse reared and pranced sidewise, no doubt to avoid dead bodies. Arrows from above whizzed down around the rider.

Donal's surviving vanguard, behind him now, marched down into the first gully to make their way toward Ineen Dubh.

But Ineen saw his kerne break into a run across the lower fields toward the river, beginning to flee.

"'Tis one thing will end this, milady," McAteer said.

Recognizing the voice, Ineen looked behind her. Redshank that McAteer was, his belt sported only dirk and short sword. He went back into the deeper ranks of Redshank archers and presently returned with a Scottish short bow and a gillie clutching arrows. McAteer stepped round in front of the shield.

But Ineen herself reached for one arrow after another from her arsenal, keeping her eyes on Donal's every movement. She aimed until one of her arrows pierced Donal. She watched the Crown's Sheriff fall from his horse, his blood spilling onto the field upon which he lay. She saw the arrow come out the hollow of his armpit.

The sound of his remaining men lamenting their leader rose in the twilight sky.

The succeeding front ranks of Donal's force stopped coming. They halted, and one of Donal's men grabbed the banner. Hundreds of bodies lay strewn about them as they started walking backward. It seemed some two hundred of Donal's men were dead. The extreme rear of his assembly dissolved toward the river.

The battle was over, but not before Banagh's son was slain by one of Ineen's archers.

Ineen herself felt numb with relief as her troops rang out, *"O'Donnell Abu, O'Donnell Abu."*

Ineen sent a runner to those still below to call a halt.

"'Tis mine to do," yelled McAteer before she said more. Down he leapt and sprinted across the field, dancing away from bodies. When he reached Donal, he probed with his sword, took off the Crown Sheriff's helmet, and waved—a signal that Donal was dead.

Ineen gazed at the waving helmet. Donal was really dead! Of a sudden she felt empty. She stood, staring. Breathless. Her troops moved toward her on the outcrop with a rolling chorus of more *O'Donnell Abus.*

She turned her back on the scene below where bodies lay dead or dying. She addressed her troops in a raised voice, "There is no longer a Crown Sheriff of Donegal."

The *O'Donnell Abus* rose up again.

Knowing what she must then do, Ineen, fingering her sword, said to Father Donohoe, "I want to inform the O'Donnell that his son received the Last Rites of the Church. Dispense them to Donal."

"Our Lord is merciful," said the Franciscan, caressing the rosary beads hanging from his cincture.

"I *must* know that Donal received the Last Rites," Ineen ordered.

"Aye," he said as he prepared to walk down the slope to Donal.

"But first," she took a deep breath, "I ask you to bless me, Father. Bless me for this battle I have fought for my husband and for my hostage son."

Father Donohoe blessed her: "*In nomine Patri et Filii et Spiritus Sancti.*"

She bowed her head and whispered, "I shall go to O'Donnell now. And to tell him of Donal's death will surely be another battle I must fight."

XXVIII

Donegal Castle
September 1590

*T*he air turned cooler as the sun, fully down, gave way to a starlit night as Ineen and her bodyguard of Redshanks rode north toward Lough Eske, *Lake of the Fish.* They were following thickly wooded paths to reach O'Donnell Island where O'Donnell's loyal Redshanks as well friars who had fled the English were. From the island it was but three and a half miles to Donegal Castle by boat.

With the fields of Derrylahan behind her and the victory hers, Ineen breathed deeply the night air before Donal appeared in her mind's eye, pointing to the bloodied arrow coming out the hollow of his arm. She shivered at the intrusion that brought an unexpected feeling that Donal might chastise her all the days of her life.

Before Ineen left Derrylahan she had commanded that any dead on the ridge be buried before troops returned home.

She looked down to be sure that Father Donohoe anointed Donal.

They reached the shores of Lough Eske in cover of darkness and dismounted at the southwest corner of the Island, where Redshanks greeted her with flaming torches and *O'Donnell Abu's*. They were eager to hear every detail of Donal's demise as they walked onto the bawn, its bonfires ablaze. Ineen entered into the castle where once O'Donnells celebrated summer festivities before Red Hugh was kidnapped. She asked the few servants left that her Redshanks be given ale and beef in the great hall.

She refreshed herself in a familiar chamber that held an old but large armoire. She took off her mail coat and skull, placing them inside. Then she exchanged her short léine and trews for a long saffron léine and took out a gray mantle from the trunk nearby. When she returned to the hall, one of the numerous Crawfords offered her mead and fresh salmon sent up from a friar who once cooked at Donegal Friary. She accepted with thanks, knowing she must strengthen herself for the ordeal ahead.

She took two boats, one for her and her bodyguards and another for some of her Redshanks. The boats slithered the few miles to Donegal and reached the O'Donnell's castle at first light. The boats arrived at the back of the castle by the river gate without difficulty. A dense fog obscured the gray stone of the castle as Ineen and several bodyguards moved onto the ground as quietly as possible. The howl of a lone wolf as the moon slipped away helped. The forest of trees and red berried bushes offered a welcome. The first castle guards she saw were ones she recognized.

Ineen did feel a surge of gratitude that O'Donnell insisted on remaining in his seat of power. She hoped that he was still where Captain Willis left him.

She found her way to a murder hole she knew she could climb into to reach the inside of the castle just as the ancient bell rang out from the Friary, calling friars to Morning Prayer; yet no friars were there. Ineen entered the bottom floor where her Redshanks were to meet her.

A startled castle guard saw her, bowed his head, and said, "Queen, you were not expected."

"Aye, I have come to see my husband," she said, noting that her bodyguards were now there.

"May I be bringing you a goblet of mead?" said one of the few gillies left as he came forward.

"No," she answered, for she intended to remove the scabbard she still wore beneath her mantle. "Perhaps after I refresh myself, but my bodyguards of Redshanks will stay here below and surely agree to what mead or wine you can spare."

Then she walked up the stone steps, still there despite her burning part of the great hall. The chambers on the next two floors were intact. She hurried into a room where she untethered the scabbard and rolled it and the sword into a wool mantle at the very bottom of a trunk. She reached for the comb on a nearby table and arranged her black hair until it fell to her shoulders; just the way her husband liked it.

As she exited the chamber, Friar Conan stood there startled, almost stuttering the words, "Dear Ineen, I was not knowing you were after coming here."

"'Tis a need to see O'Donnell. I have not wakened him," she answered. "How are things with my husband?" Ineen asked.

The friar's white hair, spectacles, and bent stature told of what he endured with each tolling. "As well as can be expected. No English but those in the Friary."

"Bring the physician, immediately," Ineen ordered.

"Sure, and I'll do that now," The friar answered.

Ineen caught a whiff of incense—preparations for the grand feast of Michaelmas, no doubt requested by the O'Donnell. Faithful Father Conan risked his life by staying in Donegal to care for his king, to the point of living in a chamber above O'Donnell.

Footsteps jolted her. *For the love of God, help me tell the Crown Sheriff's father,* she pleaded with the Lord.

Father Conan returned with the physician.

Urgently, Ineen asked McDunlevy. "The O'Donnell?"

"Ineen, an unexpected visit," he remarked.

"Aye, but it is necessary."

McDunlevy, in a cream-colored tunic, his white hair flowing to his shoulders, let his worried eyes meet Ineen's questioning ones. "I've just come from your husband," he said. "He's awake. How I'm wishing to be telling ye better news. He's been most disturbed this last day and night."

"What is your meaning?" Ineen asked as she shuddered.

"Tossing and turning throughout these last hours. Terrible nightmares. He screamed 'Donal!' He's often confused."

"I bring hard news. He needs to hear it from me," Ineen said.

"I will take you to him. I'll give him a goblet of strong ale with potions. I think it might comfort him to see you," the physician said.

Ineen cringed. She knew well that O'Donnell would not be comforted. Somberly, she walked to O'Donnell's chamber. The door was open. Her husband lay in the large bed with burgundy curtains hung around it to keep out the cold. In his night clothes, he looked so white with thinning hair on his pale scalp that he seemed ghost-like. Scotty, Red's wolfhound, lay beside him in the bed, the only dog left in the castle. He barked happily to see Ineen, and she reached down to pat him. She walked past the room's stone fireplace, turf blazing red.

The O'Donnell must not have heard her enter. He started when she said, "Husband, I am here."

"'Tis yourself," the O'Donnell said. "I have worried." Seeing her seemed to clear his mind. "Is Red all right?"

"The same. In the Tower, Hugh O'Neill reports," she said.

"Aye, good," he mumbled.

"And you, Husband?" She offered him a drink from the goblet on the trestle table by his bedside. After, she touched her hand to his cheek, a cheek burning with fever.

"Could be better. I'm after missing you."

Ineen waited as he sipped until the pause became noticeably uncomfortable. She decided to tell O'Donnell now, when he seemed lucid. "I've difficult news to bring."

With that O'Donnell sat straight up. "Tell me."

"A grave battle."

"Where?"

"At Derrylahan."

The O'Donnell appeared confused. "Sure, and Donal took care of that. 'Tis his responsibility, his being my Seneschal and now a Sheriff."

Just the word Sheriff caused Ineen to shudder. "There were traitorous Irish and numerous English there," she said.

"Where was Donal?"

"With disloyal Irish and the English."

"Not possible. Who told such a lie?"

"I was there, Husband. I saw Donal assembled with his men as well as with MacSweeney Banagh's and O'Boyle's. I saw them from a cliff above the fields near Derrylahan. Donal enticed O'Boyle and MacSweeney Banagh and much of the south from Barneasmor to the border of Connaught to be loyal to him and *not* to you."

O'Donnell began coughing. Quickly, Ineen gave him a sip.

The physician hurried in. "What's happened?"

"'Tis the news I bring. But he must hear it."

"Then I insist on staying with him, as his physician."

Ineen nodded. "You will hear it sooner rather than later."

A long silence ensued. For a moment, she cupped her hand over her own mouth, dreading to say more. At last, she spoke, softly, "Donal was slain in the battle."

"Donal, what?" O'Donnell raised his voice and stared at her.

"Donal died in the battle."

"No. Not possible!" he shouted in a raw voice. "How?"

Ineen lowered her head. "Arrows pierced him."

O'Donnell began sobbing. "Donal! My son! My eldest living son!"

This time the physician gave him the medicinal ale.

"Whose arrow?" O'Donnell yelled.

Ineen could not look her husband in the eye when she said, "'Twas my arrow, Husband."

"Then you who killed him. You killed Donal—my son!"

She looked away. Then turned and reminded him, "Fitzwilliam preferred Donal to our son Red Hugh. And Donal betrayed you."

O'Donnell spoke with surprising care. "If 'tis true, Donal took to the English—others followed—" then with fury he said, "'tis for me to deal with my son. The gravest killing in all Brehon law—slaying one's own."

"You did not kill Donal and he was not my own son." Ineen looked straight at O'Donnell when she uttered the words.

The physician gasped, stunned by Ineen's statement and the clearing of O'Donnell's mind in this moment of shock.

"And did ye not think killing an English Sheriff that Red's head could end up spiked atop Dublin Castle Gate alongside your beloved Alex McSorley's? Did you not think *that,* you fool of a bloody woman!"

Ineen stared at him, speechless. Tears came to her eyes.

The physician plied the O'Donnell with more medicinal ale. "Ineen," he whispered.

But Ineen would not stop. "The traitors and the English are after destroying us. I did what I did for you—for Red— for the prophecy!"

O'Donnell coughed and coughed. Stopped. Swilled the ale and with every fiber of his ailing voice. "I have no sons of my own now! All are gone," O'Donnell shouted, then lowered his voice.

Ineen knew O'Donnell would be upset. Knew he would grieve even in his senility. What she did not expect was for her husband not to consider Donal's disloyalty. She reached over to take O'Donnell's hand, reminding him, "You do have a son, one I bore for you—Red Hugh, and he is our son of the prophecy, and you have other sons."

He pushed her hand away. "You kill my son; no son of yours will the nobles let succeed me as king."

"Do you not understand your son Donal was deposing you, overthrowing you—with MacSweeney Banagh and your O'Boyle—and English troops loyal to him!"

"No, no. Donal would never do that! He was only doing what he deemed best." O'Donnell began another fit of coughing.

Again, the physician attempted to intervene. To no avail.

"Woman, I can call my Brehons that they judge you for this grave offense."

The physician broke out of his unsuccessful attempts to monitor the exchange between his king and Ineen. He was determined to see to O'Donnell's physical health. "Ineen, stop!"

"As king I can kill you. Go, woman!" O'Donnell shouted.

"What's to become of us?" Ineen sobbed.

"Woman, I know you not."

Ineen looked at McDunlevy, who grimaced, then she pleaded to her husband. "I saw to Donal having Last Rites."

The O'Donnell ignored her. He said to McDunlevy, "Tell that woman she must get word to Donal's son, that I grieve for his father. I will tell that fatherless Donal Oge that I shall care for him as soon as possible. Now tell that woman to go back to Scotland! 'Tis the O'Donnell king I am!"

The physician nodded to Ineen that she should go.

"I shall be at Mongavlin—" she began, then jumped aside as O'Donnell took the goblet and threw it against the stone wall, splashing its contents all over.

"Out of my sight, out of my castle, you Scotswoman!"

When the goblet hit the wall, the chamber door banged.

"Who harms O'Donnell?" said the guard running in.

"No one harms O'Donnell," O'Donnell said, falling back on his pillows. "Get this bloody Scotswoman out of here."

Ineen hurried to the upper chamber, took the sword wrapped in the mantle, and went to the stairs.

She was the de facto power in the kingdom.

But the sounds of O'Donnell's coughing sobs followed her all the way down the cold stone steps.

XXIX

Bermingham Tower
Dublin 1590

T he key clicked in the door in the state prison room as Red quickly put on his Saxon shoes. In walked Captain Wood, decked out in puffy pantaloons, ruffled white shirt, doublet, and high leather boots. Relief surged through the hostage, for by then he trusted Captain Wood.

"Captain, 'twas not thinking you'd be coming," Red said.

"Come quickly, Red Hugh," the Captain ordered in a brusque tone. "A visitor for you in the courtyard."

"What about me and Owny?" Donny whined from the cot, his young age taking a toll.

"No," Captain Wood shouted. To Red he said, "A cool day for the approach of St. Crispin's. Take your cloak!"

Red grabbed it from a hook near the chess set. "Who?" Red asked as he moved into the hall.

"Richard Weston, come to see officials on behalf of the Earl of Tyrone," Captain Wood answered, speaking curtly so that no one hearing would connect him in a favorable way to the prized hostage. "Weston's already been searched and cleared."

Richard Weston, an English friend of the Earl of Tyrone, hailed from Dundalk, just below Ulster, and came frequently on behalf of Tyrone.

Red said nothing more. He stepped down to the Tower's ground level where Wood took him through a lavish hall before reaching a door to the interior courtyard. Pompous castle officials moved about in earnest. They glittered like the candelabras.

"All the way from Venice," Wood boasted in a loud voice, noticing Red's glare at the intricately crafted glass. "Her Majesty must be represented most regally in her Kingdom of Ireland."

If Red did not know the heart of Captain Wood, he would have moved to punch him.

When they exited the door to the courtyard, they found Richard Weston pacing back and forth on the cobblestones, dressed in a crimson cloak that blew in the breeze. His black hat featured a plume on one side.

"Richard, I'll accompany you and Red; we've permission to take a stroll."

"Greetings, Red Hugh," Richard politely acknowledged.

"Sure, and 'tis grand to be seeing you." Red, enthusiasm bursting, started to hug Weston when he noticed the Captain's hand signaling *no*.

Weston stood tall and lean, wearing a half smile on his fair face, stepped back. "I've brought a letter," he said.

Red reached for it as Weston pulled it from a concealed pocket in his doublet. "Slow down, I'm handing it to you."

Red opened the parchment. Longing filled within him as he looked on Rose's delicate handwriting:

My Darling Red,

I'm after aching for you. 'Tis hoping I am that you'll be released for Christmas. You know how special the feast is to me and to your mother. She also desires you home for Christmastide.

We all pray about it. Come safe home for Christmas.

Your loving Rose

Red looked perplexed. He went over the note. Rose repeated "Christmas" many times. "May I keep this letter?" he asked.

Captain Wood nodded *yes*. "For a brief time. Then I must dispose of it. Red Hugh, it can take a long while for news of home to reach you. But Weston found passable roads despite foul weather to give you news from Ulster."

"And how is my father-in-law, O'Neill?" Red asked.

"As eager to see you safe home as his daughter is," Weston said.

Red's smile lit up his gray eyes for a brief moment.

"But there is news that has not reached you," Captain Wood said.

"What more can there be?" Red inquired as the smile left his face.

"Keep walking," Captain Wood ordered, ever aware of observant castle officials.

The footsteps of the three pounded on the cobblestones. Buildings enclosed the courtyard, beneath a sky that loomed a dark gray.

"Pause by that stone wall, Master O'Donnell," Wood pointed.

For a moment Red considered the possibility of betrayal. Would he be executed? Hanged like the Spaniards brought to Dublin Castle by his senile father and urged by his desperate mother? He leaned up against the stone.

Weston's gray eyes appeared grim. "There was a battle." Here and there he mixed Irish with his English. "At Derrylahan."

"Mother?" Red stifled a scream.

Weston spoke very carefully. "Donal was slain by one of your mother's arrows."

"Can't be. A mistake?"

"No mistake," Captain Wood assured him.

"Donal—my father's son and Seneschal. My half-brother!"

"Yes, and Donegal's Crown Sheriff," Weston said.

For a moment the three stood silent.

Then Weston commanded, "Walk slowly now, Red Hugh! We must not be seen as if we are huddled together."

Red walked step by step between Captain Wood and Weston.

"Red Hugh, you've been here three long years," Weston confided. "Donal tried to usurp your father, even asked the O'Donnell to step down. Once Donal became the Crown's Sheriff, he brought in English ways and left the English garrisoned in Donegal Friary."

Red became physically agitated. "Whatever else about Donal, I can't imagine him not following Brehon law," Red said, shaking his head.

"With your father more senile, Donal began gathering supporters and the English helped him. Your mother recognized that was a danger to you succeeding your father, from what we have learned," Weston added.

"My mother would be thinking like that . . . She has never liked Donal, of course. She let me know that there were those who considered Donal a bastard," Red said.

"There are always rumors, whether true or not," Weston responded. "MacSweeney Banagh and O'Boyle and their men became loyal to Donal. It's said that before the battle most all from Barnesmore down to the border with Connaught supported Donal. Ready to depose your father."

Red Hugh said nothing. He could only sigh at that point.

"Mother . . . there—at Derrylahan?"

"She brought her Redshanks and led MacSweeney Doe, MacSweeney Fanad, and O'Doherty to where Donal was reported to be that day," Weston said.

"She must have desperately needed to do it," Red whispered.

"'Tis true," Weston replied quietly.

Red kept walking, but his mind raced. *I have to get out of here soon. I must get home.*

As if he caught Red Hugh's thought, Weston went on, "The situation is perilous. You must get out of this Royal prison!"

Captain Wood emphasized, "And that letter tells you that Christmastide is the timing for you to escape. I'll bring festive English cloaks during one of those days. That night, have a rope. A carol will ring out: 'The Twelve Days of Christmas.' Go to the window above the drawbridge, where—"

Red Hugh stared at Wood and asked, "And just where am I to find a rope?"

"Weston brought a basket of food for you and the lads. 'Tis been checked and will be brought once you are back in your state room. There is a goodly strand of rope to put together. More to come. Tell no one! Not even your fellow hostages," Captain Wood said.

"I take your meaning," Red answered. He thought of Rose's brief litany of *Christmas*. And now, *A piece of rope. More to come*. With urgency, he walked alongside Captain

Wood. When Captain Wood ended the visit, Red wished Weston, "Safe home!"

When the hostage reached his room, he said nothing more to Owny and Donny than, "A letter from Rose. And I'm not after reading it to you lads. You can enjoy food from home when some oat cakes and apples are delivered."

Then Red sprawled out on his cot and prayed: *Thanks be to God mother's still alive. But I must get meself and the lads out of here very soon.*

XXX

An Escape
Dublin 1591

ecember came colder and darker than usual, but the promised strands of rope kept coming. They continued to arrive, hidden in food baskets from his mother or brought up by Captain Wood himself, though it was a risk. Red stuffed some pieces of rope in cracks in the wall and others inside his cot that was rarely checked, if at all. A few days before Christmas, in the deep of night, Red sat in the farthest corner of the room, after the lads fell asleep, braiding rope parts together. From time to time he touched the string that would hold Alex's medallion when he was safe home. Hope warmed him even more than the logs that blazed in the fireplace. Once he finished the braiding, he placed the combined rope in his cot and tried to sleep, grateful he was forced to make his own cot each day.

Then one icy eve, with sleet hitting the barred grate, Red heard carolers singing "The Twelve Days of Christmas" from somewhere outside the drawbridge. *This must be the designated signal for escaping.*

Red jumped on his cot and spread out his arms. "Lads, this night follow everything I do. Ask no questions."

"What's with you, Red Hugh? Ye've been lacking sleep and now ye're lacking sense," Owny commented.

"A celebration of a kind," Red laughed, pulling out the rope from underneath his mattress.

"What are you after doing with that?" Donny stared, his eyes wide.

"It's what we are all after doing," Red raced his words and motioned to the lads to move toward him when a key turned in the door. He hid the rope as fast as possible.

Captain Wood came with festive cloaks to escort Red and the hostages to a secure room where they would partake of mead and bread.

"Are we going to celebrate the Christmas? Will we be given mulled wine and sweetbreads?" Donny asked.

"In a way," Captain Wood said with a wink toward Red Hugh.

"Lads, we've been here more than three years. Take your chances with Captain Wood and me or take them with Lord Deputy Fitzwilliam."

"If you are after doing something foolish, Red Hugh . . . we'll be sent to the Royal Dungeon, if not beheaded," Owny groaned.

"We'll be captured," the two lads joined in anguish.

But they followed the Captain to the secure room where they were informed that a trusted man, Art Cavanaugh, would be outside the main gate wearing a red cloak, carrying two swords.

Red Hugh pulled out the rope now twisted around his waist, "We'll be sliding down from this window and getting out of this hell hole," he informed them.

The two other hostages sat in silence then nodded their heads, *yes!*

They drank the mead and ate the wheat bread. Red put on a green and red cloak with golden sleeves that the captain gave him. One fellow hostage received a red one with silver beads and the other a green one.

Captain Wood took Red aside. "There is news from Hugh O'Neill that his wife, Siobhan, your stepsister, passed away with December's foul weather. I am sorry to have to tell you this," he said.

Red fought back tears, given that Siobhan was dear to him and was also the deceased Donal's sister. He thanked Wood for sharing the news, sad though it may be.

After looking out into the hallway, the Captain nodded, *Now!*

Red Hugh hurried the lads to the open window. He found the large nail that allowed for him to hang the rope upon it. First, he helped Owny slide down, and then Donny. Then he held onto the rope as he slipped down, landing on Dublin's frigid, wet ground as sleet fell upon them.

The near starless night provided coverage as the lads raced across the long, wooden drawbridge over the dirty moat. Red took a quick look back to the place he remembered Alex's tarred and spiked head—*I'm off, Alex*. At the main gate, guards were mysteriously absent, so Red pushed at it. It was already unlocked.

A man in a red cloak stood on the other side and greeted them. "I'm Art Cavanaugh. Ready to lead you out of Dublin town." He gave Red a piece of wood to jam the gate shut from the outside to delay Crown troops coming after them.

Without a word, Art tossed open his cloak, brought out two swords with a flourish, and presented them to Red Hugh. Red gave one to Owny. Art sped the lads through the festive streets of Dublin. They reached the gates of the walled city undetected, the gates remaining open for Christmastide.

Moonbeams silhouetted the Wicklow Mountains against the night sky. Bonfires rose above low cottages scattered on hillsides, and the glow of Christmas candles could be seen inside. Art accompanied them south toward Slieve Roe, or Three Rock Mountain, not taking the usual roads before leaving them.

In the escaping, taking paths filled with briars and icy ground, Red Hugh's shoes fell from his feet—the very Saxon shoes he detested but nonetheless needed.

Still, the lads made their way up to Three Rock Mountain and rested until first light. The sun did not rise golden that day of Christmas. It hid behind a cold cloud, and as they looked down, the escapees saw English troops at the bottom of the slope with weapons and torches held high. They were about to drop back into the brush when they realized the troops below were turning around, heading toward Dublin town for Christmas goose.

"Nollaig Shona," Happy Christmas, Red pronounced to the lads. "Our first happy Christmastide in more than three years."

"To you, Red," the lads echoed.

"We must be moving ahead," Red said. "We must reach Feach O'Byrne, as there is danger of other English out on patrol." But when Red stood up and went to walk, he could not move fast enough for the bleeding cuts and surging pain in his feet. He needed shoes, even English ones. He knew the other lads must go on ahead.

"What's wrong?" Owny asked.

"These wet, cold hose are not strong for keeping me from slowing you down. 'Twill be best for you to keep going. Castlekevin is not far. I'll reach it by getting sturdy Irish boots. From Phelm O'Toole at Castle Kevin. And I'll be catching up with you before you know it."

"Not without you, Red," both lads said at the same time.

"Ye must! Now leave. Go as fast as you can across the river to O'Byrne's castle. Feach, the fiery Gael of the Southern Mountains, will get you Irish lads to the north and safe home."

Owny held up the sword he'd been given and proclaimed, "If this is what you command, Red Hugh, we shall do it."

Tears froze as they fell from Red's eyes. All he could say was, "I do."

After the lads were out of sight, with winds blowing bitter, Red dropped beneath the heavy branches of a dripping evergreen. The pain from his feet shot through his legs. The freezing rains of the night before returned. He thought about Feach's sister, who was married to Phelm O'Toole, and hoped they would both help him if he was able to reach the O'Toole castle.

But after a few hours of thinking and resting, Red stood, determined to make his way to O'Toole's castle no matter how much pain it cost him. But he heard the sound of horses' hoofs. *Must be O'Toole.*

He raised his head and saw the O'Toole standard bearer, then glared at a contingent of helmeted English. An eerie chant began. "Behead him!"

Red's head fell to his chest. His shoulders sagged. What was going on with Phelm O'Toole?

"I shall bring this rebel back to Dublin. Then we shall see if Red Hugh O'Donnell shall be beheaded," Sir George Carew shouted to his soldiers.

He could see that Carew's silver helmet fit his harsh and angular face with its pointed nose. Carew spoke as one who knew that he was a favorite of the English queen.

"The Avonbeg River flooded," Sir George said as his greeting to Red. "No way for Feach to get to you and no way for you to reach that Firebrand."

Red said nothing. But he hoped that Owny and Donny crossed the river before it flooded.

Carew's men shouted, "Behead him!" again.

"What I am entitled to do," Carew said, for the Crown ordered that an escapee of a royal prison be beheaded. "But I shall take him back to Dublin Castle and see about what is to be done there. And Phelm here will escort you as well."

Red Hugh called on heaven to let him live.

As darkness surrounded them, Red and the Crown's troops rode out of the Wicklows and back to Dublin Castle.

As the entourage entered through the main gate of Dublin Castle, Red was still alive. And Phelm and his troops departed. Red rode across the long drawbridge, hanging his head for disappointing Alex. Then he looked up and promised, *I'll not let this be the end of leaving this bloody place.*

Castle guards jeered as the entourage entered castle grounds. "Ah, the rebel Prince Red Hugh. Behead him. Behead him!"

Red dismounted his horse as ordered; his feet still filled with pain. He was led to the entrance of the dungeon.

"Couldn't be satisfied with a comfortable Tower room," Sir George sneered before leaving Red to the guards and to Lord Deputy Fitzwilliam.

Before they opened the dungeon doors, a guard pushed the escapee to the ground. Fitzwilliam, standing proud in gilded cloak, his golden chain of office rattling, put a gouty foot upon Red Hugh.

Fitzwilliam smirked, "You half-breed son of that Scotswoman—you filthy rebel. It is my privilege to behead you as Captain Carew did not. Perhaps I should invite your Scots mother to join you. After all, she did kill the Crown's Sheriff. But I shall think upon the timing of such an event—whether to be sooner or later."

Red glared. He stood up and fortified himself with a vow that he would never forget what the English were doing to him. He would live to tell of this evil place. He would find a way to escape and let all in his homeland know, and then all Ireland.

The guards opened the dungeon doors.

And the smell of Fitzwilliam's foot and sounds of threatening words, Red would remember the rest of his life—if there were a rest of his life in this world for him.

XXXI

Donegal Castle
Tyrconnell, January 1591

*I*n the snowy days since word came from Hugh O'Neill's messenger that Red Hugh escaped the confines of Dublin Castle, Ineen held her breath, looking out the window over and over and at the still-burning Christmas candle. Mongavlin Castle was still empty of her children; yet at Inveraray under the Earl of Argyll's protection. Her Redshanks and servants were who waited with her. One particular night when she could hardly sleep for the worrying, she sat bolt upright in bed, shivering from a dream. In it, a very young Red Hugh looked up at Alex McSorley launching a falcon, but all too soon Red became older and stared at Alex's tarred head. She started dozing off; but something was in the wind. The sound of horses clattering.

Ineen reached over to the bed table to light the fat beeswax candle. Once up, she clutched a fur-lined mantle against her nightclothes, darting to the slit window. Ghost shadows guttered on the snow below. *So many ghosts.* Then she saw a banner flicking in the torchlight with the red hand of O'Neill. Soon she heard his familiar male voice downstairs. She tore off the mantle and nightclothes, pulled a fine mantle on over a linen gown, slipped on boots, and smoothed her sleep-disordered hair. She straightened her shoulders, closed her eyes, and tried to calm her wild heart and breathing, for the voice she wished to hear was not yet heard. She hurried down the spiral stairs to the great hall just as Hugh O'Neill, beating snow off his own mantle, handed it to one of her servants.

"Hugh, thank God! My Red Hugh is with you?"

But all he said was, "Greetings, Ineen. Let us sit by the fire."

She grasped her crucifix.

He moved two chairs nearer to one another, close to the burning turf. After she sat down, he did the same.

"Jesus, Mary, and Joseph, tell me where my son is!"

"Red is alive, Ineen," O'Neill said.

"*Deo Gratias.* At Dungannon? At Enniskillen? Not at Donegal Castle, of course?" But at the sight of O'Neill's crimson doublet, she guessed that he came directly from Dublin.

"Ineen, dear Ineen," O'Neill said softly. "He is alive, though taken back to Dublin Castle."

She stood up and let her lungs wail. "But he escaped!" she said when she could form words.

A servant ran near to the fireplace, but it was O'Neill who said, "Bring whiskey!

"Indeed, he did escape," he said, and stood. "But he injured his feet fleeing in the Wicklows, wearing shoddy shoes in cold, stormy weather. And champion that he is, he bid his companions go on without him. Red was taken by Sir George Carew." Briefly, O'Neill recited the rest of the story, adding, "It cannot be known whether an O'Toole betrayed Red Hugh or whether Sir George, who was combing the Wicklows in search of your son, found him."

Tears ran down her cheeks. Smoke from the turf stung her eyes. At last, she asked, "And where is my son now in Dublin Castle?"

"In the dungeon," O'Neill sighed, shaking his head, unable to look at her.

Ineen put trembling hands to her eyes and broke down in sobs.

O'Neill leaned over and gripped her shoulders softly. "It could have been much worse, Ineen. Red's now deemed a rebel. Under English law, Sir George could have beheaded him then and there. But some order from the Crown—I don't know who gave it—stayed his hand."

Ineen raised her head. How she desired to be angry with Hugh O'Neill, for all his promises, his many assurances, but she saw the tears in his own eyes.

O'Neill moved closer to her, and without a thought, Ineen placed her head on his shoulder.

They said nothing until O'Neill, in a whisper, said, "We will rethink our plans. And we will get Red Hugh safe home."

Ineen lifted her head, looked into his teary eyes, and all she could say was, "We must!"

A servant came with whiskey and bread for both and a dish of cold beef.

"Do you go to Donegal at first light, the snow permitting," Ineen asked after a swallow of whiskey, "to inform O'Donnell?"

O'Neill looked at her. "We both go to Donegal to inform O'Donnell."

She was shocked. "But you must know that he may not speak to me."

"I have seen your husband and spoken with him twice since Derrylahan. He is more and more unwell, but I think he will speak to you. He may not even remember he wasn't going to speak to you."

"'Tis a risk. With Red in the dungeon and the English still in Donegal Friary."

But O'Neill said, "You will be with me and the English will do no harm if I am with you." Then he sat there, thinking back, deciding what to say to her as turf flared and the wind resounded outside the window slit. "I heard that MacSweeney Doe himself also visited the O'Donnell. The first moments of that confrontation were stormy, but the storm spent itself quickly."

"What makes it so that my husband will speak to me?" Ineen asked and swallowed more whiskey.

"You are now the strong one in the kingdom. If O'Donnell means to remain the O'Donnell, he must speak to you."

"Aye, but he may still not want me there."

"All these years he has loved you. I think he must to talk to you. You must be the one to tell him your son was recaptured and cast back into Dublin Castle. We must lose no more time in telling him."

"But what if he blames me for that? Because Donal was slain?"

"Ineen," O'Neill warned her, "there must be no what-ifs. The failure of Red's escape was shoddy shoes. And the damn wicked weather! This has nothing to do with Donal being killed."

It surprised Ineen that she shared with O'Neill so painful a thought: "Sometimes, I feel as if anything that goes wrong is because my arrow slew Donal."

"Be done with that, Ineen," he said. "When Red is safe home, you'd not be wanting him to find more English than those Donal left garrisoned in Donegal Friary, would you!"

By first light they found the snow much lighter, the air keen, but when they left Mongavlin the snow-slick roads made trotting slow for Ineen and O'Neill, who both rode with a strong contingent of bodyguards. Without sleep, with misery that her son now languished in a dungeon, with immense dread of confronting his father, Ineen Dubh managed to endure the ride, tears frozen to her cheeks.

Before noon they arrived. Days earlier, Ineen had sent excited word to Donegal of Red's escape. Now she entered the castle, walking into parts of the castle where much of the kitchen remained. She greeted McDunlevy, the physician, who happened to be down there, with a cheerless, "How is the O'Donnell?"

At first smiling with surprise and delight to welcome her, the physician answered, "Oh, much better than he has been in a long time, thanks to news of Red's escape." Then his smile fell as he took in the faces before him.

Ineen looked at O'Neill, who cleared his throat: "Red Hugh was recaptured. Taken back to Dublin."

"Oh, dear God," said McDunlevy. "'Tis dreadful. This will greatly affect the O'Donnell—set him back."

O'Neill summarized the end of the story to the point that Red Hugh was known to be alive in the dungeon of Dublin Castle.

Ineen shut her eyes to stop her tears, and not for the first time felt God had abandoned her.

"We must inform the O'Donnell," O'Neill stressed in a firm voice.

McDunlevy glanced with appeal from one to the other. "Must himself be told every detail?"

"He must know Red was recaptured." She grit her teeth. She whispered, "He must know his son's alive. Nothing more."

O'Neill broke the awkward moment. "I will speak to O'Donnell now," he turned to Ineen, "then send for you to join us. You may be outside, physician, should something go amiss."

Ineen nodded at O'Neill and hid her face. She paced below, near the kitchen cauldron, exchanging glances with servants but attempting no words.

McDunlevy led O'Neill up the stairs and into O'Donnell's chamber.

The O'Donnell was out of bed, wrapped in a fur mantle and seated in a large, carved chair by a table. He looked round eagerly at the visitor, still murmuring prayers from a prayer book. Pushing to his feet, his rosary beads knocking against the chair, he spread his bushy face in a trembling grin.

"My dear friend, Hugh!" he managed. "Is Hugh Roe with you?"

His words hung in the air. The old man looked anxiously from one to the other.

"Not home yet, is it?"

"Why don't you both sit down?" said the physician, pulling another chair over to the table, and at the same time picking up small plates of differently colored powders, tapping them one by one into a mortar, and lighting a candle under a beaker containing a dark liquid.

O'Neill did not take the chair but looked soberly into his old friend's eyes, grateful his own frozen face kept his tears solid in his eyes.

"Red Hugh is alive," he said, "but weather has forced his return to Dublin."

"Weather?" O'Donnell stared at his friend. "No O'Donnell has been born that minds weather."

"Heavy rains, sleet, and floods. He was unable to reach Glenmalure. The English captured him and returned him to Dublin Castle."

O'Donnell stared at O'Neill. "They will have his head!" Once again, in some circumstances, O'Donnell showed himself clear of mind. "My son, who I pray that nobles elect to succeed me," he wept. "My son is in grave danger."

"His life is spared," O'Neill said quickly. "The English find him of greater value alive. He shall yet reach home safely; this is my vow to you. That he was able to escape the castle and the city tells us it can be done. It will be done."

O'Donnell looked about him. His hand picked up the rosary and pressed a bead.

"Does the lad's mother know?"

"Aye, she knows."

O'Donnell grimaced, nodding, and pressed the bead so hard it broke. He tossed the rosary on the table. "'Tis long since I have seen her."

O'Neill said nothing.

"Good reason because . . ." O'Donnell faltered.

O'Neill let him go on.

"Oh, my Donal, my Donal!" the old man sobbed. He sank into the chair. "I don't know where Donal be." He looked O'Neill in the eye. "I know Donal meant no harm to me, but he comes no more." He looked O'Neill in the eye again. "You may tell my wife, who I have loved, no one can gainsay it. You may tell Ineen, MacSweeney Doe has told me something happened to Donal. I know he tells me true."

The physician stepped over by O'Donnell. "Take your potions, 'tis time," he said.

After he took the physician's potions, O'Donnell wept.

O'Neill said gently, "What you have told me now, you may say to Ineen herself. She waits to see you at the bottom of the stairs."

O'Donnell looked up wildly through tears. "Here? Ineen?"

With that, McDunlevy dropped down the stairs for Ineen.

"Himself is asking for you," he told her, as she was indeed there at the bottom of the stairs.

She had not strained to hear what was being said above, but as she paced, she hoped a clear word, a phrase would reach down. Nodding to McDunlevy, she stepped immediately onto the staircase and straightened the heavy gold cross that hung from her neck.

Then came a ridiculous thought: *When Red Hugh is safe home, I shall wear the emerald necklace O'Donnell gave me.*

She reached her husband's chamber, stepped into it for the first time since she brought the news about Donal only months ago. O'Donnell stood up abruptly and fell to coughing. The physician urged his patient to take more of the medicinal drink.

At the sight of her husband, Ineen fell to her knees. Everything that had happened, everything she had done, righteous and terrible, crashed in upon her. She was bloodied, her husband was bloodied, for she had bloodied him. Parting O'Donnell's mantle, she buried her face in his dressing gown against his wobbling leg.

"There, there," O'Donnell patted her hair uncertainly.

O'Neill caught McDunlevy's eye, and they both stood back.

"For—" O'Donnell kept patting her hair, then smoothed it and patted again. "'Tis pleased I am to have you here, Ineen."

Ineen wiped her eyes and looked up. "In truth, Hugh? Do you speak truth?"

"Wife," he patted her head again.

She got to her feet, pressing her fist against the floor and sliding her face up along her husband's gown and mantle, holding his legs steady. They looked in each other's eyes. She saw a touch of the old affection and, yes, a little evasion and confusion in his eyes. She kissed him on the thick whiskers of his cheek. "You know what's happened to our son, Red?"

"Aye, aye, sad news Tyrone has given me," he responded.

"'Tis atrocious—" she started to say.

O'Donnell squeezed her hand, brushed his whiskers against her cheek, worked his lips to brush her cheek. "But alive he remains, alive! And we shall yet free him and bring him safe home. Is it not so, Tyrone?"

"I shall not rest," said O'Neill, "till Hugh Roe O'Donnell is home at Donegal, in good health and good condition."

"There you hear it, Ineen!" O'Donnell coughed, again. He coughed through the words as he said, "My successor . . . Red Hugh." Then when his coughing stopped, "And it shall not be long, shall it, Tyrone?"

"As soon as possible, O'Donnell."

No mention was made of Red Hugh's being in the dungeon of Dublin Castle where few if any ever escaped.

Ineen kept a strong grip on her husband's arm, her heart beating hard. Her prayers answered. The prophecy lived. She gazed at her husband with more gratitude than she expected since this day began.

XXXII

Twelfth Night
Hampton Court, London 1591

Her Majesty said, "Do tell, Wild Horse," to the famed explorer, whose hand she took as they processioned to the Twelfth Night banquet. "Are your Virginians in the New World as savage as those Irish?"

"Perhaps, Good Bess," replied Sir Walter Raleigh, Lord of Lismore and Youghal in Munster. "They are all of the same tribe."

Elizabeth, eyes merry, glowed in a white velvet gown and wearing a rich jade necklace while Sir Walter, correspondently festive in a large, lacey collar above a rich velvet doublet, ambled with her through the six hundred guests assembled in the great hall of Hampton Court. The noble guests followed their queen into the large room with row after row of benches as well as musicians and jugglers. A fool already strolled about as Sir Walter accompanied his patroness, trumpets blaring, to the head table on its dais.

"The Queen of England and Ireland," announced the herald preceding her.

Gold threads in the tapestry behind the table glittered in light from the large candelabras, which assured all of seeing their queen. The winter's cold was warmed away by the massive hearth. And no guest dipped a hand in perfumed bowls of water before their queen refreshed hers.

"My lord Bishop," Elizabeth ordered, "the Blessing."

The reformed cleric, in black velvet robe, stood up. "With meek heart and thanks, we partake of this Twelfth Night banquet that celebrates the kings who came to honor Our Savior. Grant that all here confess salvation."

When the bishop sat down, a flourish of trumpets announced the commencement of the feast. Hundreds of servants bustled in with silver trays piled with grapes; then came platters of hens seasoned with cloves, ginger, saffron, and salt, followed by beef with mustard, pork chops, swan neck pudding; and after twelve more varied courses, hot apples and pears, sugar candy and other sweets.

Sir Walter raised a cup of claret. "A toast to Gloriana. I could not have ventured to a New World without her indulgence."

The guests cheered, toasted the queen and one another. Mead, ale, and wine filled and refilled their tankards. After the Twelfth Night cake was eaten and the prize bean found inside by Elizabeth, the musicians began to play dancing tunes.

Sir Walter rose. "Your Majesty, may I have the honor of this first dance?"

"Wild Horse, you shall." Elizabeth took his hand, and as guests crowded them to watch, the queen danced Italian steps and French pirouettes.

But a series of drum roles interrupted the music for announcement of a new guest.

"Your Majesty, your envoy from Ireland, Sir Henry Sayer."

Reaching his queen through an aisle of parting guests, Sir Henry bowed. "Your Majesty, I am late, very late. The sea's rough, the Irish weather fouler than ever, but I arrive with the best of news from your western kingdom."

"Come, Badger," his Queen greeted him. "Come sit and eat while you relay this wonderful news, whatever it is."

Raleigh's face did not hide his displeasure at the interruption, nor did he fail to smirk when Elizabeth addressed the envoy by her pet name for him.

Those at the head table scrambled to give the envoy a place at the English queen's right hand where Sir Walter had been sitting. Sir Walter held his tongue and, with a bow, motioned the aging courtier sitting on the queen's left hand to vacate. Huffily, and clumsily, the old man obeyed. Simpering to Sir Walter, Her Majesty now enjoyed the unvoiced rivalry of two of her favorites.

She turned a wide smile to Sir Henry, whose festive doublet sparkled with gold buttons. "Tell, tell, Badger."

With a sip of claret, Sir Henry licked his lips and smiled. "That Scotswoman's son, Red Hugh O'Donnell, escaped Dublin Castle—"

"You call this the best of news, Badger!"

"And was almost immediately recaptured by Sir George Carew, Master of the Ordnance," he managed to speak.

"That is good. Sir George must receive a suitable reward," the Queen said.

"O'Donnell is now confined in iron manacles in the deepest dungeon of Dublin Castle," Henry reported.

"Ha! That Scotswoman will never see her son again. Wait! *Only* confined to the dungeon? He's an escapee of one of my royal prisons; he must be beheaded!"

"Your Majesty, Sir George has your discretion in mind. Surely in the dungeon the lad will succumb. An act of beheading, at this time, would set Ulster aflame."

"Ireland! More savage than your Virginians, Sir Walter," she turned to her other courtier, who, smiling, started to reply, but she turned again to Sir Henry. "Sir George Carew does enjoy some leeway. We shall see if that half-breed succumbs to allow us to avoid an *unseasonable* beheading. But the law on escapees is the law!"

"News that might entertain you," Sir Henry continued. "The Earl of Tyrone is smitten with Mabel, the Protestant daughter of Sir Nicholas Bagenal." He chuckled.

"Excellent! It will serve the Earl well to marry a Protestant now that his Papist wife is dead. You exceed yourself in good news, Badger." She leaned over and whispered: "With news so good, I can even enjoy this feast so much more."

She clapped her hands. The banquet noise rippled into near silence. "Let the revels go on!" she commanded.

Sir Walter stood up and addressed Her Majesty with a half-bow. "I have composed a poem in honor of Your Majesty, which I beg your indulgence to share with you."

Elizabeth, bemused, nodded assent.

In a sweet voice Raleigh gave voice to his words:

"What is our life? A play of passion,
Our mirth the music of division,
Our mother's wombs the trying housed be,
where we are dressed for this short comedy . . ."

The queen clapped to interrupt the recitation, standing up. "My dear Raleigh, we desire gaiety this night, not melancholy. Steward!" she addressed the liveried servant waiting nearby. "Bring us someone with a merry verse."

Sir Walter, infuriated but not stupid, bowed, took his seat once again, and covered his angry mouth with his tankard. The great hall buzzed, excited to see a favorite shamed. The queen cast a grim eye on every face that whispered to another face till the guests crowding the front of the head table fell quiet, but presently the steward returned and bowed with a message for Her Majesty. "Young Shakespeare is here."

Behind him a young man, handsome in an embroidered vest over a festive doublet, rounded the head table to present himself before her. "I beg the honor to offer you words which I have written." Extending his arms in a dramatic arc, he began in a loud voice that carried throughout the hall:

"How sweet a thing it is to wear a crown.
Within whose circuit is Elysium.
And all that poets feign of bliss and joy . . .
Which God shall guard
And put the world's strength
Into one giant arm. It shall not force
This lineal line from me."

Even before he finished Her Majesty was smiling. When he bowed the guests burst into energetic applause, which caused the queen to cast them a quieting glance, since they clapped before she spoke her own praise.

As the bowing, new playwright stepped backward to exit, the queen said, "I wish to inform you that we are not averse to hearing more from you, William Shakespeare."

Not long after that the revels settled into card games and other amusements in one or another of the four hundred and twenty-one rooms Hampton Court made available.

Elizabeth took leave of Sir Walter with a promise to see him in the morning. "You have been provided one of the finest state rooms."

But Sir Henry she bid stay with her awhile. "Come, Badger," she motioned with her finger. "You shall tell me more of Ireland. And we shall dance. And I shall remind you to tell Lord Deputy Fitzwilliam that the capital crime of escaping his custody may bring him ill if beheading is not applied to that Scotswoman's son."

XXXIII

Royal Dungeon
Fall 1591

Bermingham Tower had not prepared Red Hugh O'Donnell for the dungeon, or for the humiliation of Fitzwilliam's gouty foot on his neck upon his return. For that boot, Red would have the Saxon's head one day, that was that.

Nothing told about the Lord Deputy in the months that followed would ever change Red's mind a hair—Fitzwilliam's head, screaming through its tar—must replace Alex McSorley's over Dublin Castle's gate, and if he couldn't stick it there, then Donegal Castle gate would do. Would do just as well. Just as bonny. And the gouty foot, too. The last foot that would ever step on an O'Donnell neck till a sword beheaded every last Saxon on the Day of Judgment.

Fitzwilliam's boot changed everything.

And the dungeon added to it once Red Hugh was flung onto a rat-ridden pile of straw and clamped into wall chains. At the beginning, with an aching head, he nevertheless howled out of the darkness. A darkness damp as a cave. Howling, he tried to throw himself against the guard. A nearer howl startled him, ripping from his throat, and his face caught more flogging.

In the beginning, a human voice suddenly spoke up out of another quarter of the darkness, rose up in a pained and weary Irish curse and the long howling ceased. "Woe betide you—you'll soon like me with an old face about you."

"Who are you?" Red coughed.

"I be Art O'Neill," the voice said. "Guest of the dungeon now some five years and me brother Henry here, too, here for many long years."

"In the dungeon?"

"Aye, Dublin Castle Dungeon. And you must be Red Hugh O'Donnell—the guards are buzzing about ye."

With that knowledge, Red wept. He was with the sons of Shane O'Neill, and their father being the very one responsible for his grandfather's death.

How this all happened he pondered day after day, week after week, though he did not even know the days of the week.

Will my mother ever find a way to bring me safe home? And what about Hugh O'Neill's promises? What will happen now to the prophecy?

But without anyone's trying to wrestle him, Red tried to move, though hands and ankles were held by cold gyves. In a little while he noticed movements in the darkness.

There was, as his head rolled, a wash of blue light high in the darkness; his face no longer was flogged; he managed to rub one hand against it and try to shake the slime from his fingers; and so, he awoke, head ringing still to his new life in the dungeon in the Southeast Tower of Dublin Castle.

The dungeon cell, being at the bottom of a tower like Bermingham, was round but not as large as the room at the top of Bermingham Tower where he and Owny and Donny Gorm had been held hostage. But that old room they had kept clean, and daylight crisscrossed the floor there through two barred windows.

The only window in this dark hole was the little grate far above Red's head, all but out of his line of sight, that leaked its light into the dungeon down a long, sloping casement too small for a dog to climb up if his paws did not slip and slide on the wet stonework. It was a renowned Royal Dungeon. The Grate, as it was called.

Through its wee window, Dubliners passing across the moat would hear demon howls or piteous cries and would, as they were moved, cast stones or drop bits of bread or farthings. The prisoners ate only what they could buy or their families managed to send that got through to them.

In the Castle's dungeon, many had starved in its four hundred years. So, the farthings most always ended up in a guard's purse, and if he wished to collect more farthings, a crust of bread found its way to a wretched mouth.

The moat was not a dry ditch, as on the west side, but a widened puddle, which acted also as castle sewer, pouring its filth into the Liffey. The floor in the dungeon was such filth, dried somewhat and hard-packed but still damp and muddy, eternally cold, heaped and strewn with rushes long ago turned to straw. The straw was full of what made the dungeon, slop pails or no slop pails, stink like a cesspit. It also stank of rats, dead and alive.

An unending week of days filled with long hours came. Would he even know when it was St. Brigid's Day, the first day of spring? Or St. Patrick's feast, or Easter, let alone St. John's Day?

No matter the pain, to reassure himself Red moved a manacled hand as far as possible, arched his back and stretched his fingers to touch a part of the cord which had held the MacDonnell medallion his mother tried to give him. Oh, so long ago. The medallion device, *In Deo Nostra Spes—In God Our Hope*—became his prayer when he could say no other prayer. And when he could say no prayer at all he said, *Hope*.

For a long time, the only thing to look forward to was the pail of gruel, twice a day. Red learned of the legend of the castle apothecary, Bottle Smythe, for poisoning prisoners and politicians at the Lord Deputy's direction. No doubt by his own nasty "authority" as well. He feared poison; yet, had to eat to stay alive.

"Aye, this is a rotten hell hole," Art whined.

"And somehow you still live!" Red responded.

"If you be calling it that," Art spit out the words. "Or your tarred head would already be grinning on the gate."

And so Red was able to keep down a little of the gruel and drink a potion. So, Red Hugh did not die those first months. He even developed a hunger for the gruel.

Both O'Neills needed little provocation to torment the son of their father's conqueror, especially the elder brother, Henry. It was Red's own father and his mother's relatives who put an end to their father, Shane O'Neill.

So, it was indeed Henry, whose howlings and handfuls of slops and straw had flogged Red awake those first days.

"Henry's soft in the head," said his half-brother, Art. "Too long in this dungeon."

Henry had been in the dungeon since before Red was born. In what pale light leaked into their darkness, when Red could catch a glimpse behind the old Henry's glib, he thought he saw egg whites laced with blood, and black holes of burning turf. Hair and beard, paler than the weak light, hid Henry's head like a bush of brambles, a dry and dying bush that had not seen the sun in years.

Between pails of gruel the old man, chained only by the legs, would catch a rat and dash its head against the wall and pick at its raw meat for a day or two. His legs and arms were boney in their rags, but sinewy too. Henry raged and yelled and cursed. But his stillness could last days, and though his rages never lasted as long, they could go on. He had not attacked a guard in a long time, but that was why the guards slid his pail to him down their swords and forced him aside at sword point to retrieve his slops. They never knew when he might attack.

"Henry's head should have been on a spike many a time," Art told Red when no guards were present. "And the O'Neill, Turlough O'Neill, that is, would not have shed a tear."

"I'm after not remaining here long," Red said in a hoarse voice, almost a whisper.

"'Twas what I thought, too," Art sighed. "I eat the gruel and wheat bread, slide the pail toward the door, rearrange a bed of rushes, and ride off soundlessly to Tir-na-N'Oge, the land of the dead."

"'Tis not for me," Red said.

In the dusky daylight in their cell, the voice of Art came always from the floor, or at highest from a hand or two up the wall.

Even after the first weeks passed and the freshness of the Wicklows with them, at times it seemed it had all been a dream. Red told himself, out loud so he could hear, that he was fresh from outside compared to Art and Henry.

And Henry had not been out of that dark, dark cell in years. *Red's* kinsmen had just helped him escape. His mother was fighting for him every day for sure. Making all the arrangements she could make, intriguing and sending gold. Sprung once, he would be sprung again.

XXXIV

Mongavlin Castle

By harvest time, Red's mother prearranged with the Earl of Tyrone to come to Mongavlin from Dublin and the Parliament. She needed to know everything she could about Red Hugh and what she could do to prevent Fitzwilliam from beheading her son. From a slit window of her great hall, Ineen saw O'Neill's horse and his high English hat one night. Throwing a dark mantle round her léine, she ran out the front door and hastened across the bawn to order the gate opened. When Tyrone dismounted, dressed as English as a Lord Deputy, she assumed he came from Dublin. "My son?"

He nodded, "Alive." He would say no more till they were inside.

"What have you learned?" she plied him in the wan daylight of the great hall.

"Too much." He tossed hat and cape onto a chair by the fire and dropped into another to pull off his boots.

"Tell me! Tell me!" She paced, shaking her fists.

But they were interrupted by a servant running up the spiral stairs with a trencher of venison and two bottles of Spanish *rojo,* the best of the red wine, that she had ordered.

"We must get Red out of that dungeon *as soon as possible,*" whispered Hugh O'Neill, throwing both stockings on his cape. "Before Fitzwilliam decides the English queen will put more gold in his pocket for your lad's head."

"Go to my chamber near this hall. The turf is lit," she said, more cautious now that even someone in her castle might betray O'Neill for helping her. She went up to her bedchamber.

When she came downstairs, dressed in a simple gown and gray mantle, O'Neill was already in the chamber.

"How much, Hugh? How much gold?"

"Whatever the English queen thinks Fitzwilliam needs."

Ineen heaved three bags of gold onto her writing table.

"I shall add my gold to yours, Ineen Dubh," said he.

"When!" she panted. "How!"

"Weston and Eustace will get me word. They can be around and in Dublin Castle. And I will get word to you. 'Tis harvesttime now. We have but very few months at most to get Red out of that dungeon. Quick we must be—and perfect."

"Perfect," she said, feeling for the moment that with this much gold, her son would fulfill his destiny. And she chanted a phrase from a Mac Ward poem, *"When Red Hugh O'Donnell, hope of his country . . ."*

This line encouraged her.

"You really believe we can get Red Hugh freed from that devil's hole of a dungeon."

O'Neill looked with deep care at the woman before him, a woman that he had come to love but could never be his. "I do. Things are being arranged this very day. But you, dear Ineen, must continue to provide gold. And you must, for everyone involved including me, know nothing more until Red Hugh is inside Ulster. There he will stay with me, and I will get word to you that he will be coming home to you."

Ineen took O'Neill's hand. "'Tis a promise, for if it does not work, surely my son will be killed."

He held onto her hand, and he would have liked to hold that hand for hours as the turf fire warmed them both and deepened their collaboration. "The very best I can do. That is my promise. That is my hope."

XXXV

Christmas of the Stars
12 January 1592

*T*he cool, damp air somehow alerted Red that fall had arrived and foreshadowed the winter to come.

At times, meat came in the food pails instead of gruel—dry and maggoty, thanks to Fitzwilliam and the guards taking the best of it. But it became the one piece of news from home that could be trusted. Fitzwilliam had to account for the food that would keep Red alive in the cold months ahead. His mother's gold must be having an effect, he decided, and that gave him hope.

Hugh O'Neill must still be paying, too, for he was the one to come to Dublin. Even when the weeks, the months in that cold, damp rat's hole made him weep dry tears of despair, the meat in the pail told him he was not forgotten.

The first escape took over three years to arrange. The thought gave no cheer, but it told him he must stay alive. He must eat, stay warm in his rags. And keep his arms strong, his legs nimble, do everything the gyves would let him do.

He did not want to meet the dead heroes of Ireland yet. And so, sometimes after he ate, he sang, under his breath and out loud, of the green hills of Donegal and the kingdom he was meant to save. He sang to his mother, sang to Rose.

Then one night more bitter cold than usual, with rain seeping through the walls, a little torch flame flared against Red's eyelids. He squinted across the dark at the cell door, opening a large crack.

A figure slipped into the cell. Fearing an assassin, Red pulled knees as much as he could against his chest, ready to punch if he could, shouting to his sleeping cellmates. But the shadowy figure bent and shushed.

"Red Hugh O'Donnell, no harm do I mean you. 'Tis from Feach O'Byrne, that Firebrand who's free of the English, do I come."

Red still held himself ready to punch out.

"Here," said the stranger. Something hit Red's foot; he kicked it away. "No, no," said the stranger, groping in the straw. He picked the something up and placed it gently in Red's shackled right hand. "I cannot tarry," the figure went on. "Use this to file your gyves, and the gyves of your friends, but leave a bit of each chain unfiled."

Red groped. He took the object as best as he could and rubbed his thumb along its fine, serrated edge.

"Not yet the time for you to leave, but the time is coming soon. At Christmastide."

"Who are you?" Red whispered hoarsely.

"Eustace, a horse-boy of Feach O'Byrne."

"How I missed Feach O'Byrne when I last escaped."

"You shall see him soon. File your gyves."

"When! When is Christmas!" Red whispered. "My God, no knowing what day or week or month you have in this pit!"

"Ach, 'tis the best time for the guards being full of ale and celebrating the season. 'Tis some weeks yet, to file your gyves."

"Is it Feach O'Byrne who takes us out of here?"

"Visit over!" barked a sudden voice from the cell door, yanked wide, torchlight flooding the nearby straw, a growling Henry rising to his knees in response.

The shadowy figure rummaged in his mantle and pressed small broken loaves of bread in Red's mouth and handed bread to the other two.

Eustace whipped round to hasten out the door, which slammed shut, making the night blacker. Then followed the sound of Henry's body collapsing with a wild snort.

Red closed his eyes, the better to feel around for the bread pieces that dropped to his lap. Was this but a dream? No—his hand found the file, gripped it. No dream. He heaved his lungs, expelled a long breath. "Not today, Holy Columcille. But the day comes soon. In *Deo Nostra Spes*." In God our hope.

Again, Red Hugh slid his thumb along the file, down and up, till he slid it into his shirt.

"By Saints Patrick and Columcille, we're going to file these gyves away and get out of here!"

Art surprised Red with, "Let me begin filing the shackle on one of your hands, for I have only me legs to free."

"Aye, must when fewer guards are about," Red cautioned, letting Art slip the file from his fingers.

Henry thought it all a ruse. But in a few days, he began to believe the possibility.

Soon the excitement waned as the days passed slowly, and it seemed as if months went by since Eustace had brought the file. Red's hands were freed with enough chain left for rearranging the irons to fool the guards who came each day and checked, but with time their checking became less rigorous. And with years of such checking on the O'Neills, they hardly looked at Henry's gyves.

"Wisha, Red," said Henry when Twelfth Night came. "Who knows when these rat whiskers"—what the elder brother called the guards—"might keep that horse-boy away, or maybe they killed him? Don't ye hear the screams of the tortured at night? I'm not so trusting of any cozy of Feach O'Byrne as you be."

"He'll come back, Henry O'Neill," said Red. "I'm getting free of these chains—and this dungeon, and so are the two of you."

"I hope," said Art. "This is still Twelfth Night, as I still hear the buzz of their English ale this last day of Christmastide," And between coughs, he added, "I'll catch

me death in this wretched place before we see the likes of
your horse-boy again."

Red encouraged them, himself as well. "He'll come."

And the horse-boy did come late in the evening of
Twelfth Night.

As snow drifted in through the grate, Eustace slipped in,
saying, "Mr. Maplesden, the chief gaoler's health is
failing—near to death by St. Bridget's Day—or sooner. The
guards are lax this night because of that and busy celebrating
the feast."

"*Deo Gracias*!" said Red.

Of late, the guards did not delay quitting their duty; did
not linger to taunt, or bother to say a word, civil or uncivil.
It had become very evident that in recent weeks several
guards were intruding on them less and less. The chief gaoler
indeed must be dying.

"Stamp your feet, chains and all!" By then all three lads
were mostly free of their manacles except to drape them on
to deceive the guards. "You have to go down through their
garderobe—the privy."

"Right into all their filth!" Henry snapped.

"I dunno," said Art.

"Do you want to get out of here?" asked Eustace. "On
the far side you'll meet up with someone with fresh clothes
and boots for you.

"Already, you have fewer guards. Need I remind you
that all has been arranged? Do what I tell you, and you will
never see this place again."

Soon the guard, given gold for his help, motioned urgently for Eustace to leave. Eustace said, "God be with you."

"Wait," said Red. "Will we be tugging a rope to the garderobe?"

"It's already placed there. Even so, the drop is short."

"I dunno, I dunno," said Art.

"You whiner," said Henry, now ready to leave.

"Ready yourselves!" said Red as he touched the cord that he hoped would once more hold his mother's medallion. He prayed that his mother be strong and his father be well enough to see their son safe home.

Red urged Art, "Try to hold back your cough, lest the guards hear you."

But if the guards heard anything, they paid no attention, for they long thought Henry done in by the dungeon. For all Henry's soft mind, his physical sturdiness proved surprising.

A guard then stepped in, but said only, "Come with me!"

"Jesus, Mary, and Joseph, what is this all about?" Red said, concerned that the escape was already foiled.

"Someone awaits you outside," was all the guard informed.

Dim light lay on the spiral steps beyond their cell door.

Far up the staircase could be heard raucous voices, the clinking of tankards, and singing of Christmas carols. Red had to grip Henry's arm to hold him from running up.

"Do you know the garderobe—the privy?" The guard asked.

"Up there?" asked Red Hugh.

Red knew where the shaft dropped down four levels. He remembered vaguely the location by the guardroom from so many months ago. "I'll go up to scout the guardroom," he said to Henry. "When I kick the wall, you come up, quiet as a mouse. I'll point you to the garderobe."

Red was sure the dark area of the garderobe would protect them.

Never far from the front of his mind was the possibility it was all a set-up to trap him and the other two. Thus, three new heads would be on the castle gate.

He climbed slowly up the turning steps, knees just a bit wobbly from disuse, thinking of his mother's prayers, his mother's gold—of all O'Neill's help, until he reached, still in shadow, only a few steps below the entranceway to the guardroom.

The guards were in an uproar, competing song for song, which should cover little scraping or running sounds. He could not see, nor would he risk peeking around the corner of the doorway, whether a guard was on duty.

He listened, hearing loudly only the beating of his heart. But round the corner inside the guardroom no movements or breathing could be heard. Praying again, he kicked the wall. A body rubbed past him fast; Henry, not missing a step, vanished into the garderobe dark. Red held his breath.

Art, who could get them all caught, was another worry. All these weeks, ever since he had worried about Art, he nonetheless rejected the thought of leaving him. Red had given his word they would *all* escape.

Heavier footsteps scraped up behind him. He waved Art urgently ahead. The big, floppy body squeezed past him, with lungs breathing hard. On all fours, Art scraped up the remaining steps and into the dark.

Red blessed himself and darted forward.

"Where's the rope!" Henry cried in a whisper.

Red felt around hastily. It's in there."

"Jesus, Mary and Joseph," he breathed. He wound it round his waist and chest, nudged Art to grab hold of it in front of him, gave Henry the end length. "Get in the hole! It's not a straight drop; mind, it slants. You'll have to slide till you reach the shaft."

These stone slopes in the garderobes were infrequently doused with water to reduce the smell. "Mind the pail at the bottom! But if you dirty your rags on the way down there are fresh clothes waiting for us."

Henry squatted atop the small seat, facing the wall, then gripping the rope over his shoulder with both hands, slipped feet and legs into the hole and swung down out of sight. Presently curses flew up at them. "You drop same as me," Henry said as he ran off.

"I dunno," whined Art. "I'll get stuck."

"No, you won't. Just do what Henry did."

But Red had to push Art up and help him clasp the rope. For Red it was like trying to squeeze birds that couldn't fly.

"It's a short drop. Art! Bite your tongue till we're in the Wicklows!"

Art groaned and held onto the rope as Red shoved him deeper into the hole. Red listened, hearing footsteps on the stairs.

"Quick! They're coming!" he surmised, and with a sorry whoop Art slipped down the hole, scraping his head along the inside of the hole.

Red told himself, *"Short drop!"* as he slid into the hole, hanging by both hands but already wet from slime on the stone. The drop was short indeed, but his bare feet sank into the box before he steadied himself and tripped his way into sharp, chill air and prickles of sleet in his face.

"God be with us!" Red breathed, scraping and stomping his feet on the snowy grass. The castle wall, the ditch, and the houses across the way were still visible in the lowering nightfall. *"Deo gratias!"*

But Henry was not there. He must have gone on ahead of them. Red and Art made the short swim to the other side to meet up with fresh clothes and boots.

Now Red really prayed that they would not be caught. Not twenty steps away stood a bridge across the ditch to a back entrance of the tower wall. Not much further away another bridge crossing the moat ditch teemed with heads and torches moving from the outlying streets through a big castle gate toward the celebrations in the city. It was impossible to detect if any of those people noticed the lads' activity.

Something rough but soft hit Red's face from above.

"Catch this rope, catch this rope!" came a frantic whisper from above. He did not recognize it.

"Eustace?"

"No, Colum! From Eustace."

Red remembered Eustace said himself or another would meet them.

"Aye! Let me pull you and Art up. Eustace has horses waiting outside the gate."

It certainly surprised Red Hugh that both he and Art reached the top of the bank for sure, and much sooner than he had feared only moments earlier.

"Where's Henry?"

"Who?"

"The other fellow?"

"Aye! Dunno! Grabbed clothes and ran off."

"He didn't wait for us?"

"Didn't even wait for food."

"Food!" The word itself made Red's stomach growl.

A torch flared; Red hit the ground, but the torch was Colum's.

"Hurry this way!"

They followed Colum further along a stretch of houses away from the city bridge. But this holy night when torches and merry-making bearers moved everywhere, this stretch was for the moment clear.

Colum handed them doublets, hose, caps, and fur-lined capes and leather boots.

"These are more Saxon than our dungeon clothes," Red protested.

"Aye, what else but festive capes for celebrating Twelfth Night in Dublin town?"

Red and Art were still slimy wet. Red wiped his feet and legs with the fur of his cape. The hose was hard to pull on because of the stinking slime. But best of all for Red were the hardy boots that Colum gave to each of them.

Art's doublet barely closed around him.

"'Tis all there is," Colum said. "And these. Daggers and scabbards containing short swords."

"Give most to me," said Red, feeling by now a mighty temptation to leave Art to find his brother Henry.

"Last but not least," said Colum, who pressed a bottle to Red's lips. "*Usque baugh*, the best Irish whiskey to warm ye—but eat this to hold it down." He pressed rough oat cakes into both lads' hands.

Red took a sharp swallow of the whiskey that burned his chest.

"Don't swill it so fast, man! Ye've been away from the Irish drink."

Colum passed the jar to Art, who eagerly swallowed whiskey. Then again to Red who, this time, sipped the whiskey and let the warmth spread thinly in his chest.

Colum snuffed a torch on the ground and pointed, "We'll head toward the torches ahead. You," he nudged Art, "follow behind. And walk!"

"Just fast enough to get the devil out of this city!" said Red.

They did not go toward the city bridge but wound round the line of houses facing Dublin Castle and down the next street, passing parties of people heading Castleward. Colum greeted the merrymakers with Twelfth Night cheers, then found some folk moving away from the city, fell in behind them, and, as they were mumbling songs, joined their singing.

The roads out of Dublin passed through several gates, but the guards were as festive as the civilians and nobody stopped the trio, although it was necessary to reach the final gate before it closed.

Colum kept them at a quick march, and they arrived just as the gatekeepers were rushing the last country people out. There, Colum, whose orders were to remain in town, took his leave.

By this time the sleet had turned entirely snow; the wind streaming through the streets dropped now they were in the countryside, but the snow kept falling. Red gripped Art by the arm and began to trot toward the grand, soft dark to the south: the Wicklow Mountains.

"We're out, Art! We're out!"

When Art breathed heavy, Red realized his own feet in the leather boots had begun to hurt. "We'll soon be on horseback!" he promised.

"Lads!" a voice they knew cried out softly from within a coppice of bushes. "God be praised and bless you all this night of the stars!"

"Eustace!" said Red.

"The same!"

"I pay you thanks first, Eustace," said Red, "so that it cannot be said I have not. But where are the horses?"

"Ach, the horses," said Eustace. "No horses. They're gone."

"No horses!" Red grabbed Eustace by the shoulders. "You're supposed to be behaving like a horse-boy. What do you mean no horses?"

"Taken, Red. But does not mean we're betrayed. Likely, some English borrowed them for this night of merrymaking."

Eustace pressed a velvet purse in Red's hand. "Gold enough from your mother by way of Hugh O'Neill to buy a team of horses and help you get safe home."

"We have to climb the Wicklows on foot!" Red reminded Eustace of his last venture.

"We'll die out here," said Art. "At least in the dungeon . . ."

Red himself was not, after months in a dungeon, in the best shape to climb a mountain in the dark and the snow, Art was in very serious danger; and a collapsed Art would imperil them.

"Art O'Neill, my brother in strife," said Red, embracing Art's fat shoulder. "Aren't we the ones St. Patrick himself freed tonight? And wasn't St. Patrick himself a hostage who escaped as we have? He had to cross the sea! We have only to climb a hill. These heavy boots hurt me feet, too. But I know what happened when my shoes were not strong last attempt and Carew found me. 'Tis Patrick himself who will boost us up this hill."

"Aye," Art sighed. "I can walk till I can walk no more."

Red knew what a trudge and climb awaited them, having trudged and climbed this same way a year ago. He could not shy from marching himself up Table Mountain.

For surely, surely this time, for all the gold his mother spread and all Hugh O'Neill surely spread around Fitzwilliam and the Dublin Council, Fitzwilliam himself would pocket it and still mount Red's head beside Alex McSorley's.

No! There was no going back this time.

Art was indeed a challenge. Red swore to himself, but even this thought faded as all he could hear was Art's breathing and sighing.

Red could think no further thought. There were no thoughts to think but to keep the knees moving, the feet trudging.

They made surprisingly better time than Red expected within an hour after leaving the last city gate; other revelers

354

had passed through the turnpike ahead of them. And it was easy enough to wobble and stumble like the rest and let coins from the velvet purse make the difference if need be.

At last, the ground began to rise, but gently. The height was no trouble.

Eustace accompanied them, insisting on keeping off the roads up to Wicklow, not because their mud and ice slowed them, but because, for all they knew, English troops were already on the way. He also turned them west along the sides of the hills. He did not want to climb further till they passed where the Liffey rose to form a lake.

So, they went sidewise along the hillsides through what oak the English had not chopped and thickets of white blanketed bush. Over stone walls, too, and skirting huts and hovels.

Red kept peering and listening for horse sounds. He kept wrestling Art forward up the hill. His own eyelids were frosted with snow.

"Stop at the next hut, Red."

"No huts here. Maybe a cave," Eustace told them.

"First cave." But Red began to lose trust that a cave would be anything but a place to find their bodies. He shook that thought away.

They halted every so often, but never as long as they wanted. There were a few stars to guide them. They were heading where the English's Twelfth Night became Ireland's "Christmas of the Stars." They were heading out of the Pale.

Near the top of the mountain, they reached some glen. Red kept moving, as did Eustace.

Art was between them, helpless to do anything but groan and be carried by Red and Eustace.

After a while, Art also began wheezing and coughing. Soon Art and he were on Table Mountain with Red Hugh's aid. No sound could be heard but the howls of the wind and dumps of snow on their heads.

Suddenly the hillside leveled out.

"At the very top we are?" Red asked.

"Aye," said Eustace, "and I can't walk another league with Art. We'll find a cave. Here!"

Eustace turned them out of the blowing snow into an icy cave.

Red tried to force a sound out of his throat to hear if it echoed, but already his legs gave way, something heavy leaned against him till he realized it was Art. Red placed Art, whose teeth were chattering as he shivered and coughed and cried out, onto the floor of the cave.

But when Red shook him, Art only wheezed and snored. Snored and wheezed.

Already, snow slid down around the thickly iced entrance. The cold tightened Red to his hard chest. He moved towards Art's labored wheezing. He spread his cape out wide to best cover Art and himself. No longer did the snow blow in Red's face.

No longer did he hear the wail of the wind. He barely heard Art's wheezing.

The last words Red heard from Eustace was something about "being back with horses." Then echoed the sound of footsteps crunching away as Red Hugh wondered if he and Art escaped the dungeon to die in an icy cave.

XXXVI

Glenmalure
Wicklow Mountains 1592

Red Hugh did not know he was alive—he did not know what alive was. Not till Ineen's son remembered, face stinging from sharp slaps and light rubbing, his lips burning from ale, did he realize his eyes had been awake and staring at whiteness in the flickering light of a torch.

He began to remember when his arms and legs were tugged, tugged hard, and snow whisked off him—off his tunic and trousers, out of his hair, trickling down his neck—and gave him a start. Whatever was poured over his face mellowed into beer. He opened his lips to swallow. None of the men sitting him up had a familiar face, except one—Eustace.

"Aye, he's coming back!" was repeated by different voices before the words made sense.

After a time, Red was taken outside the cave. Wool was wrapped around him till he felt the cold begin to fade a little, even from his face as hands picked him up and kept turning him side to side by a lit torch.

"Leave the boots on," a strong voice said.

A long, white time passed before he recognized what was happening. "Arrr! Arrr!" were the first almost intelligible sounds to squeeze out of his throat.

Said someone, "He's calling for Art O'Neill."

Another body, snow-covered mostly but with a blanket on its face, lay placed beside the cave.

"Not Art O'Neill y'are. Sure, and you know your name, a great hero's name indeed."

Red Hugh looked from face to face of the men standing and clapping or rubbing hands till he found the one he had seen somewhere before.

"Eustace?" Red sputtered the words.

"Your name, lad," said the face with the glib held up.

After more moments back and forth his throat suddenly said: "Hugh," though it sounded like *You!*

And all the men cheered and clapped.

"*O'Donnell Abu!* 'Tis himself y'are, Hugh Roe O'Donnell."

A man with a very black glib took up Red's hands and shook them, "O'Byrne am I."

"*Feach* O'Byrne!" Red raised his voice as much as possible.

"Wonderful to hear me name on your lips, Hugh Roe. Sure, ye're back from the land of the dead, at last!"

After chewings of bread and no longer choking swallows of beer, the escapee realized who he was, where he was and why, and that Art O'Neill—poor, portly Art—had not survived. Then Red was picked up, settled on a litter, bound to it lightly but firmly with leather straps.

One of the two men who carried the litter was Eustace; the other an older man O'Byrne introduced as his physician, McHaggerty. He was the man who had busied himself with Red's face and limbs, and even ordered the boots be left on.

Only when Eustace, in front, holding the litter handles behind him, started straight out from under the cliff did Red notice there was no sheer drop. It was not a gentle slope, but neither was it steep.

Eustace and the man holding the rear handles at Red's head, with two or three others gripping the litter sides, stepped gingerly down to horses snorting breath in the snow and a wide drag of thick wood behind one of them. In the grey sky above, the sun burned a bright smear, and no more snow fell. The air was bright and clear.

"Art!" Red cried. "Take Art."

"Art we must leave for a bit yet."

"No! The English will get him," Red screamed such that the cave walls behind heard and shuttered.

"Not in Glenmalure, I assure you," said O'Byrne.

"Art must be buried then," Red insisted.

"Surely, Red," O'Byrne agreed. "He shall be buried under snow and rock now, and a priest will come to pray over him, another time. But the Lord Himself has taken him and he's quite safe from wolves and the English now."

A large bundle, wrapped in a blanket, was laid in the drag beside Red.

"Art," Red breathed.

Only as the drag slid along the snowy mountainside, slowly so as not to rock and bump too much, did Red discover his toes felt nothing.

By a stand of snow-shrouded firs they halted. O'Byrne ordered three men to dig a grave.

"We shan't delay," he said to Red. "We must be getting you under a safe roof. But now we pray a *requiescat.*"

As he added his own tongue to the responses, Red's teeth began to chatter, *"Rest in Peace, Art."*

The physician wrapped another blanket tightly round the woolens already wrapped round Red, now muffling his head but for a little opening to breathe. Red knew it was the blanket that covered Art. His eyes ached; a fever coming on. He just wanted to get under a roof and beside a fire before it took hold of him entirely.

After a short time, noticing Red's chattering and shivering, O'Byrne had him lifted from the drag and bound him in the saddle of his own horse, beside him to hold him up. This way they were able to hasten their pace.

Below them, O'Byrne's castle stood on a rise above a long, ice-frosted lake. But they rode on past it and up along

361

a far slope into woods before halting to dismount at a peasant hut. Red was lowered from the horse but insisted on walking through the snow to the door, although not without O'Byrne and Eustace gripping his waist and shoulders. Inside the sweet, warm, dark, he collapsed.

"Cead mile failte," A hundred thousand welcomes, shrilled an old woman's voice. But seeing the lad's condition, the woman, stooped in a black mantle, wasted no more welcomes but loosened his wraps, pulling him over to the turf fire.

O'Byrne, with a few words of explanation, and the physician, turned him around to set his feet by the fire.

Chanting under her breath, the old woman produced a knife with which McHaggerty cut the breeches. He then cut the woolens and leather boots.

"How do ye feel, Red Hugh?" he asked.

"Hot beyond all the heat of bonfires on St. John's Eve with this turf blazing."

The physician instructed Eustace to fetch a pail of snow and the old woman to bring rags and warm the snow on her settle. When Eustace returned, he scooped a palmful of snow from the pail and dabbed it gently on Red's brow.

"And your feet, lad?"

"There's pain in me ankles but in me toes—nothing at all."

"How do they look?" O'Byrne asked McHaggerty.

"Not the worst my eyes have seen. Time will tell. At least now we can dry them. Then warm them by the fire and wrap them in wool."

"I cannot see them clearly," said Red, squinting in the dimness.

"Blisters on the great toes, and a bit of black here and here; but a bit of red, too. Likely less than a day or two since they froze, though, which is good. I shall wrap them in a herb poultice, which may not be touched or changed for a day or two."

"And will me feet be well? I must get home to Ulster. My feet will heal, yes? As son of the O'Donnell, I must have no physical imperfection if I am to succeed him."

The physician peered at him in the dim light. "'Tis my opinion they will heal well enough."

"How long?" Red asked.

"As long as it takes. But you must keep in this hut a few days. The English will be coming to try to yank you back to Dublin, be assured of that. Mother Nora here will feed and see to your bathing. Eustace will keep you company and be of use. But I best be at my castle to greet the English when they call."

"Get word to me mother and father and Hugh O'Neill," Red urged.

"That I will. Your mother sent a spoken missive by messenger in these words: 'If my son Red Hugh arrives safely to Glenmalure with the grace of God, tell him to follow all directions that Hugh O'Neill has arranged. I approve of them.'"

"Aye. I will keep my mother's message in my heart. And when you send word to O'Neill, include Rose O'Neill, who is also my Rose," Red smiled.

"By all means to Rose," laughed O'Byrne.

"The Lord bless you, Feach McHugh O'Byrne," Red said and dropped his head and his voice, but he could not keep the tears from his eyes. "You are my friend forever more."

"'Tis the least these Wicklows owe you, Hugh Roe. The very least."

Red asked if it was too much to be after asking for a harper to come and play.

"Tomorrow, maybe. Today I see to our defenses. The Saxons would love to snare a harper along with an O'Donnell. If 'tis safe, my harper will come."

"Ach!" said the old woman. "Ye won't be leaving before ye've tasted my lamb stew, O'Byrne."

"Another reason to return, good mother, but I am off. Your stew is a godsend, though, to our heroic guest."

"O, himself surely gets a bowl!"

"Broth alone," said McHaggerty, "to sip only. The lad needs strength, but he must begin eating slowly for all he has been through."

The woman gave Red a wooden bowl steaming with broth.

As Red sipped broth, the physician laid his own bowl aside and opened his bag of ointments and herbs. He took out leaves of yarrow, bits of grass, and an herb known as finabown. He ordered the woman to bring him the white of an egg. He then took equal parts of each ingredient and ground them up thoroughly before mixing them. He applied the poultice to both of Red's feet, all the toes and both ankles. He wrapped three clean linen cloths around the poultice on each foot. "Now you must take your rest on the bedding prepared for you. And you must remain here for tomorrow and the next day."

"I have to get north. My father is a prisoner in his own castle, and my mother . . ."

"Nay, nay," said the physician, "not if you wish to heal—and avoid imperfection. After two days, I will put a new poultice for each foot, with fresh cloths. If they look to be healing, I'll put very large boots to cover your feet."

"I'm thanking the Blessed Mother to be free and to have such a fine physician as yourself. If I have to wait but a wee longer . . . May the Lord be good to you and to Feach O'Byrne—now and evermore."

"'Tis an honor to be serving you, Red Hugh."

But while the blankets were warm and the straw comfortable, Red could not fall asleep right away. He could not help revisiting the impossible climb uphill through sleet and snow that would not stop blowing in his eyes, and his feet freezing numb. He fell asleep fitfully, whispering, "Art, Art."

Eustace heard him and brought a mug of ale. Red asked for snow, which he rubbed against his hot forehead again, and held against his tongue between swallows of ale. Eustace hardly slept. Red's last thought, clear as the air at the cliff that morning, was, *I could not keep Art alive.*

Next day the physician returned. Red's fever passed without reaching crisis. The old woman added lamb and turnips to the broth. The rest of the day went long, though Red slept often between sips of broth and chews of meat or vegetable and sips of ale. Eustace made time pass asking him what Donegal and the kingdom was like and whether his mother the strong queen the Crown abhors . . .

As dusk fell, a visitor suddenly announced himself: O'Byrne's harper. O'Byrne came as promised but only briefly, so concerned was he to be in his castle to give no hint to any strangers that Red Hugh was nearby. The next hour or two delighted all with lively plucking and glissandos sweet.

Before sunrise next day McHaggerty came to change the poultices, bringing with him O'Hagan, sent from Hugh O'Neill, to travel with Red on the return north. The physician was pleased enough at what he saw that he fitted Red's feet into leather boots. O'Hagan tried to answer the lad's word-starved questions about everything in Ulster, especially "Me mother and father?"

"Last I heard, they were both as well as could be expected. Anything more is for Tyrone to tell you."

Red discovered that O'Hagan, who spent much time with Hugh O'Neill in the Pale, always referred to O'Neill as 'Tyrone' or the Earl of Tyrone.

"Tyrone has made all the arrangements for your journey north—our journey."

"When?"

"As soon as you put these on." O'Hagan handed Red a folded bundle which, when Red shook it open, revealed itself to be doublet and hose, a very large black cape with hood, and a large but modest feathered hat of English fashion.

"These are English!" Red said.

"A change of clothing awaits you when you are out of Dublin town. Best if we travel as Saxon, especially crossing through Dublin."

Red nodded, convincing himself. "How I hate Saxon clothing." Then he asked, "How many ride with us?"

"Only as many as do not attract an English eye, five or so."

"So which way do we go?" Red pushed, eager to get going.

"Tyrone has given me instructions. We must get past Dublin."

As Red made profuse thanks to the old woman who had housed and fed him, she doused his hood and cape, and as much of him as possible, with a bottle of water from a holy well.

"Sure, an' the Lord be praised for blessing me hearth with the visitation of the hero, Red Hugh O'Donnell, who escaped Dublin Castle!" Old Nora said.

"Safe home," Eustace called out to Red.

"I'll be thanking you and O'Byrne until the Last Judgment for all you have done for me," Red Hugh said.

Red rode between O'Hagan and a bodyguard and troops of O'Byrne's. Once over the mountain, they made their way down through Glendaloch, then up over the next mountain and down till Dublin lay below. There, O'Toole joined them with a contingent of bodyguards. With chimneys smoking, the bay dark and cold to the east, in the center stood the dismal towers of the dreaded Dublin Castle and the English within it that Red Hugh had learned to hate.

Red stifled a scream and asked O'Hagan, "What is O'Toole doing here? 'Twas not far from O'Toole's castle that Carew and his soldiers nearly beheaded me."

"'Tis different now, Red. O'Toole is here until we are out of Dublin. Tyrone thought it best. Red, his being here might fool the guards," O'Hagan explained.

Red just stared at him, remembering his mother's words to follow O'Neill's instructions.

"And thanks to the rumors and reports, the English do seem to be hiding troops by several fords along the Liffey to attempt to capture you. So, we go this way where bare bones are said to be at these gates of the city."

Down the last slope, passing peasant huts and fields, O'Hagan and his troops on horseback rode straight to the designated gate. There were but two guards, one on each side, who picked up their pikes just as Phelm O'Toole and party approached.

O'Toole galloped up ahead of them. Red was tempted to take off on his own, any way he could to get out of Dublin.

"Are ye coming from the mountains?" An English guard bellowed.

"Aye, that we are," O'Toole said, as if both parties were travelling together.

"Did ye see any sign of the Papist rebel, Red Hugh O'Donnell, who escaped Dublin Castle?"

"Hugh O'Donnell?" O'Toole answered, "He's not been seen in my lands. I am heading into Dublin but I cannot imagine he would be going there."

The guards looked at each other. "Pass on," both guards said at the same time.

"May your vigilance be amply rewarded," O'Hagan remarked to the guards as he took advantage of O'Toole and entourage going through.

O'Hagan's party trooped through and up the lanes over the little bridge to the gate in the extended castle wall. Then they no longer could see O'Toole.

Red's heart beat fast, his eyes dropping tears to be so near the castle once again. The feathered hat he pulled down. It felt as unreal as a dream, and he could not help it. And though he could not see Alex's tarred head, he tossed a thought his way: *I'm out, Alex—but I'll never be forgetting ye!*

Soon, they clopped over the cobblestones of the city streets, crossed the Liffey bridge amid a crowd of people streaming both ways, and climbed with those on the north side up to the near north gate where the two guards stationed there saluted without a word.

They ambled then on along a darkening road outside the city.

It was through a few remaining trees before O'Hagan called a halt at a hut and dismounted for refreshments and necessities.

Within very few minutes they resumed travel. A horseman bearing a torch led them to the next stop. The low rush of a river could be heard—one of many bends of the Boyne.

A slovenly, old ferryman sat by the fire outside a small cottage. For it was now dark. In the guttering flamelight, a torch boy showed the man a small gold medallion, which the man took, turned in the firelight, and with a nod returned. The torch boy motioned O'Hagan and Red Hugh forward.

Taking no chances, with one hand on his dagger, O'Hagan lifted and shook a small bag.

"I'm generous, as you will see, friend, and I'm wondering if my young man and I might hire you to cross the river. Six gold pieces, three now and three on the other side of the river. And my men will remain here and pay you upon your return."

The ferryman looked keenly at the purse, nodded, and without a word or a question, motioned the two down to his currach.

O'Hagan helped Red enter first. He could feel the way the lad rocked gingerly, but in the torchlit dark the limping was not so noticeable.

Red stared at the ferryman. He knew that in every town and village in the Pale there were people to whom gold spoke sharply—O'Neill's or the Crown's, it mattered not. A man could sell to either or both—and steal whatever dropped in his hand.

Red was confident he and O'Hagan could handle the old man if he tried anything untoward. But, of course, they could fall out of the currach in the attempt, and once in the river, in the swift icy cold, in the black night . . .

They reached the other side without incident.

But when O'Hagan said that they were headed to Mellifont, the manor home of Sir Edward, an English friend of O'Neill's, Red said, "I'm wanting nothing more of the English, O'Hagan. That manor was built from the very stones of a demolished abbey."

"Well, you'll be wanting a horse for your injured feet to get you across the border to Ulster. And Sir Edward will have fresh horses for us," O'Hagan reminded him.

"Jesus, Mary, and Joseph, is this what me mother would be wanting after me fleeing the English?"

"Aye, she would, for she's trusting O'Neill and she wants you home safe."

Red sighed as he limped up to Sir Edward's manor house. They came out at a snow-covered path as moon beams struck Mellifont, which meant *big abbey.*

Red knew that for four centuries the Cistercian abbey had flourished until the queen's father, Henry VIII, shut it down, scattered the monks, and confiscated the gold-wrought sacred vessels.

From the window of the bed chamber provided him— heated by wood, Red agonized that even the fireplace was built from stones from the old abbey.

But in the morning, he was even more horrified to see what the night had masked: almost nothing was left of the abbey. The bases of columns, like tree stumps axed to clear land for farming, were abandoned to ice-covered weeds thick all over the ground in the curve of wall where once stood the arches of a now broken colonnade. No coating of snow fully covered it all.

"The horses and me feet." Red looked down at his feet, realizing he needed horses!

Red prayed that this did not turn out to be a rouse and he be sold back into the hands of other English from whom a third escape would likely be impossible. There was only this escape, even if it meant risking a night at a ruined abbey.

He never wanted to see this abomination happen to Donegal Friary, already taken over by Captain Willis and his minions. He must rid the English from Donegal Friary, free his father in Donegal and the people of the kingdom and become his father's successor.

That is what his mother was counting on him to do to begin to fulfill the prophecy.

XXXVII

Hampton Court
England, Winter 1592

*I*n the winter of 1592, the Queen of England, though an aging monarch, prided herself on how she ruled her realm in an age of unsurpassed magnificence. Four years earlier, the mighty winds that had delivered the Crown a victory against the Spanish Armada brought enhanced command of the seas. The Crown's reach extended beyond England to most of Ireland and to places in the New World. Shakespeare, now an acclaimed actor and playwright, entertained Londoners at the Globe Theatre. And this day Elizabeth awaited a private performance by William himself.

All this Henry Sayer knew well when his barge sailed down the Thames and he exited at Hampton Court. He gazed at the majestic red brick palace, smoothed his doublet over the paunch the years had given him, and painstakingly took the privy stairs. He walked the dark lower rooms without his usual charming smile.

The queen kept him waiting an unreasonable amount of time in a room cluttered with oddities and courtiers. Cecil, Lord Burghley, old and an invalid, sat off to a corner.

Finally, Henry was led along another dark hallway to the privy chamber where Elizabeth sat with Essex at her side. Essex, the stepson of Leicester, and now himself a favorite of the queen, wore a silk doublet with gold threads that sparkled in the candlelight. His leather shoes were raised from the ground on cork and ornamented with buckles. Essex looked, for the entire world, like he ran England.

Henry bowed to the queen with profuse flourish. "Your Majesty."

His grimace indicated that it rankled him that Essex should be there. When Henry stood, it rankled even more that Essex stood taller than he did.

"God's rage, you've come to explain the deplorable situation in Ireland—after Providence granted me such a land," Queen Bess roared. "My men in Ireland can't keep one half-breed rebel in the dungeon and that Scotswoman's son of all rebels!"

"I have come to give you all that is known, your Highness." Henry bowed again for effect, calling on all his experience as a diplomat. "Should that escapee even reach Ulster alive, your English will apprehend him."

The pock marks that filled Elizabeth's face were more evident with her rage. She made a quick remark to Essex,

"Imagine that small man standing before us has the audacity in thinking that he can belittle the mess he and others have made of the Irish problem."

Henry fought back, "The English won *sub-kings* to your cause, Your Majesty, but this Red Hugh's escape brought renewed talk of the prophecy related to him. But Captain Willis is yet garrisoned at the Friary and the O'Donnell himself all but imprisoned in his castle."

She spat out the words and stomped her feet. "And is Ulster so secure for us?"

"Secure, Your Majesty." Henry took a deep breath. He did not reveal as much as he knew. "Hugh O'Neill is your friend." Henry shuffled his feet.

Elizabeth turned from Henry, "My cousin, Essex, what do you think I should do about this incompetent man before me?"

Henry listened while she did not once refer to him in any pet name of endearment.

Essex, Elizabeth's cousin by virtue of the blood ties between her and Essex's mother, stood so near Queen Bess that Sayer nearly choked.

Essex knew how to cajole her. "Most excellent sovereign," he began, "if Fitzwilliam be at fault, you cannot hold Henry entirely responsible. I do not like to see you so distressed, especially as we await Shakespeare, dearest cousin."

Elizabeth returned, "I have no proof of anything that he has done other than be incompetent. But I send men to the

Tower for less. Why, Raleigh is there now for marrying one of my ladies-in-waiting."

The room held its dank breath. The English queen, who looked so small in her throne chair, held the power of Henry's destiny and life in her aging hands. She sighed and heaved her chest. "I'm inclined to send Henry to the Tower."

"Yes, my sweet queen. You already told me that you appointed Sir Edgar Lesman as envoy to Ireland. That is where your energies go now."

"I banish you, Henry Sayer, from this court. As you heard, I already have a new and more faithful envoy to Ireland. You will be taken to the Tower this day. I shall hear nothing more of you. You shall hear nothing more from me unless I have further cause to command more than your stay in the Tower of London."

Henry gasped.

"Go now," Elizabeth ordered. "Guards are already at the exit. I prefer to hear Shakespeare with my dear Essex."

As guards dragged Henry from the chamber, Shakespeare began to walk up to the throne.

Elizabeth whispered to Essex, "I want to hear that splendid man speak himself these wondrous words that he wrote: '*Against the envy of less happy lands; this blessed plot, this earth, this realm, this England.*'"

XXXVIII

North to Ulster
Dungannon 1592

O'Hagan and Red Hugh rode refreshed horses lent by Moore until they were almost outside the Pale.

Then they passed sentries through a gap in the rank of stakes and entered into Ulster.

There, Red knew he was almost home, as the pines, birches, elders, and hazels welcomed him. There were oat fields covered with snow hedged by forest tree lines. Cold winds ushered him across the fields and made leaping little ice-choked streams feel like taking flight. Red began to feel how freedom really felt.

The sight of Castle Fews on its knob made his heart sing out, *"In Hoc Signo Vinces!"* In this sign conquer.

This provoked his companion to a loud and merry chuckle. "Best save those words for when you are home, Hugh Roe O'Donnell. You're in O'Neill country!"

Red laughed. He kicked his horse to gallop the rest of the way to the castle of O'Neill's mother.

Old Judith's greeting was as warm as the sweet smell of turf burning in her fireplace, "*Failte*, Red Hugh. Your grand escape is the talk of all Ulster."

"My mother knows, and my father knows?"

"How could they not, me hero! Are not the bards singing of it already? Not that they know where you be!"

"'Tis wise," Red said.

"Aye, to be sure by now even her wicked self in London must know you escaped if a missive made it across the Irish Sea."

With that, Lady Judith sent a messenger on to Dungannon and for the rest ordered beef, oatcakes, and wine, which were brought to the table in her great hall.

"To the mother of Hugh O'Neill," Red raised his cup, "and to those here—*Sláinte*—to your health. You brought me back into Ulster!" He felt an easing of his soul and a balm brought on by the embrace of the likes of O'Neill's mother, of beauty and the smell and warmth of the turf fire.

Next morn he and O'Hagan left and spent the following night at Armagh, concealed with another friend of Tyrone's. At the first hint of daylight, they rode off through woods to a ford on a bend of the Blackwater directly under Tyrone's protection.

Then iron helmets aplenty lined the road up the steep hill to Castle Dungannon.

"I cannot trust those English," said Red.

"Feed them and house them as well as Tyrone and they shall fight the Queen of England for you. None of their fellows in the Pale live so well."

O'Hagan, after presenting their pass to the first of these, nodded to the rest as they ascended. Red studiously ignored this, although he could not help, from the summit, a wary backward gaze. A few helmeted Saxons milled about the castle gate, but O'Hagan knew to lead Red Hugh to an entrance that would hide as best as possible Red's stay at Dungannon.

When Red and O'Hagan entered the great hall, Hugh O'Neill himself stood there, a delighted grin parting his long beard, his favorite gray wolfhound stretched out by the turf-burning fireplace.

O'Neill cried out, "So you've managed to escape, Red Hugh," gingerly embracing Red. "Safe home to Ulster you are, Hugh Roe O'Donnell, out of the Pale!" Tears ran unabashed from O'Neill's eyes as he embraced the younger man.

"God be—God be praised for you!" Red responded, tears stopping as suddenly as they broke in his own voice.

A pace behind her father, hands clasped, bowing with a light curtsey, smiled Rose.

He could not take his eyes off his Rose.

"And a man you are now, and more than a man," O'Neill said and went on holding him, then stepped back to look up at him. "'Tis a sorrow that I couldn't be seeing you in the dungeon. But I needed, for your sake, to keep my distance."

"I shall never be able to repay you, Hugh O'Neill, for freeing me from that place of hell—from Dublin Castle. And for seeing I had food all these long years."

And O'Neill answered, "'Twas with the help of your mother, Red Hugh—and you shall repay me, have no fear," he laughed. The Earl then noted the direction of the young man's attention. "Is she not a beauty herself, your Rose, who has abided faithfully for your return!"

Rose was staring to his left and his right, meeting his eyes, her head stiff from white ruff to small, sharp-feathered hat atop her red hair—hair tied up in braids. A heavy mantle of green silk draped her body, her breast plunging and plumped in a gown of gold velvet. His gaze dropped to the hem of the gown. Two black satin shoes could not keep from peeking out.

Red found the only thing he could say was: "You're wearing fancy shoes!"

"I told you, Father!" Rose reached up and gripped one foot, hopping—"He hates these togs of Mabel's!" She ripped the one shoe off, then the other, and, swinging the cloak over one shoulder, pulled the hem of the gown up her bare legs to her knees.

"I'm still your Irish Rose, Red Hugh O'Donnell, still your Irish Rose!"

"They're not Mabel's togs," her father cried back. "I bought them; Mabel left them; they're yours!"

"Red, if you don't know, you will hear that Mabel Bagenal eloped with me last autumn," he shrugged, "appeared to enjoy some months of contentment here, then ran back to her devil of a brother, *Marshall Henry!* So much for Pale wives, eh?"

"Surely, I am grateful that I never knew that," Red replied.

Then Rose continued, "My betrothed has been in an English prison these four years; he doesn't want to see me in English togs!"

"English, are they? Your cloak is Spanish, your gown is French."

"These pleats are English."

"They're Irish. Pleats are pleats. Do ye see, Red Hugh, what you have been looking forward to all these years!"

Hat flung away, Rose was already undoing her braids and now shook her hair to her shoulders. "There. Now you see me as I am truly, Red Hugh, my husband-in-waiting!"

"Husband already, is it?" said her father. "And I thought you were wanting a royal wedding first!"

Red, now recovered, laughed, "My dark Rosaleen."

"You have not gone and lost all love for me these years, Red Hugh?"

"Not at all. At this moment, I am after having more." Slipping both arms under her mantle, he hugged her hard, kissing both her cheeks till she stopped him and devoured his lips.

They parted, out of breath.

"'Tis your eyes, Dark Rosaleen, and your lovely mouth that I dreamed of in Dublin Castle. Never did I give a thought to . . . your clothes."

She laughed; they held hands. "So have I, Red Hugh! So have I dreamed of yours—your light eyes."

"Rose, I wish I could be marrying you this night and we could be off to see my mother in the morn and bring her the good news."

With a sharp glance at her father, who was greeting and embracing O'Hagan, Rose whispered, "I wish that too, Red. I have gotten to know your mother over these years and especially on her visits to Dungannon. She would do anything for you, and I will, too."

Her father raised his voice and clapped: "Our greetings are made, and now my physician, McManus, will see to Red's injuries. Rose, you may join us for supper."

"But, Father . . ."

"'Tis all right, Rose," said Red. "It seems word of my frostbitten feet reached Dungannon."

"Let me see your feet," she said. "I will nurse your toes."

"Go!" said her father.

"We shall see a lot of each other," said Red. "I'll be here a few days. And let me say, this Spanish mantle of yours,"—tugging it round her shoulders so it fell both sides of her gown— "it flows upon you like hills of springtime."

"Indeed, you will see each other," broke in O'Neill. "Be off now, Rose, and see that the servant sends in the physician."

Vexed, Rose turned to find the servant. O'Hagan said farewell, but O'Neill insisted on a toast. A servant followed with Spanish wine for three with Venetian glasses, and the three exchanged toasts before O'Hagan took his leave.

The physician, McManus, arrived. O'Neill pulled a cushioned chair from the wall rather than make Red climb a round of stairs. McManus conducted his ministrations where Red sat.

"Have you sent me mother word?" Red asked O'Neill as McManus unwrapped his feet.

"Day after tomorrow will be soon enough," O'Neill replied. "'Tis best to keep your arrival quiet until time for you to return home. Surely she knows that you escaped."

"I'd like to kneel at Siobhan's grave while I'm here."

"Another time it will have to be. You must not be seen."

Red looked at O'Neill, and O'Neill added, "My mourning for dear Siobhan was cut much too short; that I regret."

Red nodded, saying nothing, but turned his gaze on McManus. "I'm told these toes may take time to heal," he said to the physician.

"Keep them dry, warm, and freshly bandaged, pray, and the Lord will do the rest."

"If the Lord chooses not to let them heal—what then?"

"I have seen toes heal entirely. I have seen toes removed. But whether men have kept their toes or lost them, they walk."

"If you lose them or keep them, they'll always be a sign of what the Crown did to you," O'Neill added.

"'Tis well of you to say that, but I want to keep my toes," Red said.

Later, at table—Rose with them now—over venison and ale, O'Neill asked Red to tell them about the escape.

"Art did not make it," Red said at length.

"Hmph," O'Neill commented.

"And Henry ran off."

O'Neill said nothing.

After the meal, Red questioned O'Neill, "'Tis whispered that Henry O'Neill is here?"

Rose caught Red's eye, giving her head a little warning shake.

"Aye," replied O'Neill. "Out of danger, he is."

"Where?"

"The man's soft and so a danger," O'Neill added, noticing Rose's gestures. "In the cell he's no danger. There's no more to be said about it."

"He left his brother to die. And me with him!"

"But you're the man in the gap," asserted Rose, "and here you are, alive as me."

"Ah, Rose. How well you put that. Alive. We are both very much alive! But I must rid the hellish English who desecrate Donegal Friary before showing you how really alive I am. Bloody a few first. Then we shall wed, dear Rose."

Rose looked at him. Her pretty jaw dropped. "What d'you mean, bloody a few English?" she objected.

"Donegal and all of the kingdom must be clean for us," Red said evenly, "if you are going to live in Donegal Castle with me."

"Absolutely!" O'Neill chimed in. "And that is one of the strong matters Red and I shall discuss. It is good to have you back in Ulster, Hugh Roe O'Donnell."

At meal's end O'Neill bade his daughter to say goodnight, her betrothed must bathe and get a good night's sleep; they would have pipers and harpers the next night.

Red begged a little while longer for time with Rose. O'Neill conceded a short time longer, during which he did not leave his chair but appeared to busy himself, drawing figures on the table with a finger. At last, he stood up, Rose sighed, Red sighed, she kissed his cheek and a quick graze of his lips but Red made sure his kiss was tender and lengthy. Then she betook herself to her bed chamber.

Red Hugh tarried four days and four nights at Dungannon, receiving excellent care from McManus. He enjoyed much more the care received from Rose, although her visits were usually interrupted after a short while by the sudden appearance of her father clapping hands and mentioning his need to talk *affairs* with Master O'Donnell.

One early question of Red Hugh's to O'Neill was about the Earl's relationship with the English.

"Well, you make friends with them, like this Moore at Mellifont where you stayed. I want Ulster to stay free of Dublin, but Sir Edward is a friend and a trusted one, too."

"But the dungeon shattered any thoughts of the English being friends for me."

"Red, we need to keep English friends where we find them. If they are not against us, they might even be for us. At all events, they can be very useful."

"I've seen their evil now firsthand. I thought of Alex daily and how the English beheaded him. In what way can they be anything but an enemy?"

"The thing to remember, Red, is that I know them. They think they know me, and I encourage them to think so." O'Neill related, as he so often had, his history in England from the age of eight. How he was taken by the Lord Lieutenant, Sir Henry Sidney, after the murder of his father by Shane O'Neill's men.

"Aye," Red said.

"Whatever regrets I may have now, I certainly learned how an English army can defeat the Irish, like in Munster, but not so easily defeat your mother's Redshanks."

At that they both chuckled. Thus, they conversed each night.

It was only on the third day that O'Neill stated plainly his intent. "The first necessity is to replace Turlough O'Neal as the O'Neill so that I become the O'Neill, king of Tyrone. This is what I hope will happen," he smiled. "Do I have your agreement?"

"That you have. And me mother will be pleased that her mother, Turlough's wife, is too friendly with the English Queen, and thus will no longer be so important," Red chuckled.

The two touched knees in the Irish way of agreement.

"Turlough's an old sot," Tyrone went on, "but dangerous in or out of his cups. Dangerous to me and so dangerous to you. Only his wife—your mother's mother—restrains him at all, so she shall take no harm from me," he said. "Patience is all. Patience. Patience. Time comes to the patient, does it not, Hugh Roe O'Donnell?"

"Patient I am not."

"True. But you had to learn some patience in Dublin Castle. The impatient can also wait till their advantage *ripens*."

"'Tis impatient I am to rid Donegal of this Captain Willis and his ilk."

"I've no doubt you will. But what makes a man the king of his clan is his strength and skill to protect and defend them when the time is ripe. Take some days to prepare, Red Hugh."

"My feet, they don't—"

O'Neill shook his head. "They are your mark of courage. But if you slaughter Willis and his men, more of Bingham's minions will overwhelm Donegal and then all of the land. The kingdom is not united yet. The Crown will be glad to send thousands of heads to Dublin Castle."

Red could not find words to answer, but he forced himself to ask, "What do you have in mind?"

O'Neill began, "You want my help. I need your help. First send Willis and his minions back to Connaught. Then together we shall free all of Ulster, your lands and mine of every Saxon," Hugh O'Neill smiled.

"Aye."

"Your mother and I have addressed such things."

"Mother! When?"

"Over many months."

"So, the two of you—"

"We came up with ideas. And when you arrive in Ballyshannon your mother will give you more details. She will find a way to Ballyshannon to meet you. You know Owen O'Gallagher is yet in Dublin Castle. But the people of Ballyshannon have become loyal since the death of Donal."

Red Hugh found himself almost breathless with sudden emotion that was joy but something else as well. Tears started to his eyes. For the first time, not only in years, but it seemed in his whole life, he was beginning to feel what the prophecy meant for him. It brought a sense of power so strong he thought that if his feet could leave the floor, and if the glass window were only open and wide enough, he could soar into the air. It was also a very strong feeling of gratitude which could never be repaid. That feeling stayed with him all the night into first light.

During the course of that last day, O'Hagan called on O'Neill and Red Hugh with two of O'Neill's men, the first of whom gave Red Hugh a bejeweled dagger, the second a bejeweled sheath for it. The afternoon was uproarious with tales and toasts, avowals of assistance, and compliments to the young man's mother, Ineen Dubh.

That last evening, at the end of supper, O'Neill announced he had too much to do the next day so must retire early, and he said goodnight without sending Rose off to her chamber. Swiftly his footsteps ascended the spiral staircase.

Rose smiled. "You have much to do tomorrow yourself," she said. "Maybe you wish to retire early, too."

"Not yet. Are you so eager to be rid of me, Rose O'Neill?"

"No, no! What I mean is, I know how weary you must be after—everything—and you have the ride tomorrow to Enniskillen, so maybe . . ."

"I am not ready for sleep yet. Perhaps you wish me to take a little more wine?"

"No, what I mean is . . . when you wish to go up . . . I can help you."

"Thank you, I can climb well enough."

"Red. I can help you . . . go up."

Red caught his tongue and said nothing. He looked up at the ceiling; he did not hear his host's footsteps on the staircase any longer and sighed.

"You might be right," he finally said. "Time with you upstairs will assure good sleep tonight."

Rose's smile grew, lips trembling. He returned her smile.

390

"Perhaps cocky of me to think I have learned to go upstairs with these frostbitten toes without slipping. So, yes. Yes. I'll go first, and you . . . behind."

Rose was so near behind him as they climbed. They reached her chamber and did not part till first light.

Next morning, O'Neill managed to avoid the two of them till breakfast was served; but spoke briskly and excitedly of Red's departure for Ballyshannon by way of Maguire's country.

For three days and three nights Red had felt restless to get home, but this morning, Rose at his side, he wished he could tarry a bit longer. He felt a deeper tenderness with her. They squeezed hands, with a silent, keen wish to improve on this happiness.

It was strange, in the morning mist and light snow when he was introduced to the iron-helmeted and armored captain of O'Neill's detachment of English troops, Captain Jenks.

The captain greeted the young man with a stare neither smiling nor committal, addressed him in a strange Gaelic-sounding tongue it took Red a few moments to recognize as Welsh. Jenks was sharp in deference to O'Neill and saluted smartly at the order to escort Red to Enniskillen with a contingent of troops that O'Neill already arranged.

But Red moved away from the soldiers and went over to O'Neill. In a low voice Red, very uneasy, asked O'Neill, "Is it absolutely certain of this man's loyalty you are, for I'm not trusting any Saxon?"

O'Neill looked him in the eye, then answered, "I would not have gone to the trouble and immense expense of securing your escape from Dublin Castle with the help of your mother, especially after one of her arrows is said to have killed Donal, only to sell you back. Besides, most likely the English queen knows by now of your escape, and 'tis best if you leave here with one of my most trusted English."

Red dropped his eyes, face aflame for having asked.

"Don't. For three years Saxon soldiers have bound you to Bermingham Tower. Then another year in the Dungeon. 'Tis entirely to reassure you that we cannot keep Ulster free of Dublin without the assistance of *some* Englishmen that I mean for you to know firsthand that some may be trusted, no matter how justly you doubt it."

Red Hugh reminded himself that O'Neill would not in the least want to call down on his head the wrath of Red's mother, Ineen. After all, the two of them, each in their own way, rescued him from the depths of the hell hole in Dublin Castle.

As he climbed onto the horse held for him, felt the ardor of Rose's embrace and kisses, and saw the passionate tears of Hugh O'Neill in the wet morning light, it became clear to Red how much O'Neill wanted to become the next king in Tyrone.

And yet, Red still wondered if the English were about to take him back to Dublin right there in Ulster when they got away from O'Neill.

XXXIX

Ballyshannon
St. Bridget's Day 1592

O'Neill's runners arrived to obvious effect on a day of fair winds, the clouds high and white in a blue sky. The oarsmen pulled Maguire's boat the short stretch of lower Lough Erne from Enniskillen past Belleek, with cheers raising up along the bankside of *O'Donnell Abu!* Red was safe home and not back to Dublin. Even before the boat neared Ballyshannon, the air roared with *O'Donnell Abu!* Throngs of arms amid blue O'Donnell banners filled both sides of Lough Erne. Nor did the roaring abate when the boat landed below Ballyshannon Castle.

Women stretched out their arms, men waved their pikes. The lad snatched by the English, returned now a man! Children jumped up and down, shouting with joy. And Red waved greetings to all.

In a new mantle gifted by O'Neill, green and rich as emerald, and his red hair looking afire in the sunshine, Red's eyes smiled, *home at last*. Red gently shook off the helping hands from Maguire's captain and the oarsmen and, disdaining the wooden dock, reached one foot over the boat's gunnel into the icy water, almost tottering. The ice-cold seemed to tear his leg like a flame, but his toes still felt nothing. He was practiced by now. He planted both feet like stumps beside each other, then pushed them, splash after splash, up to the path where folk swarmed, trying to hug him.

But they stepped back for Red Hugh's mother as she rushed to him. In a purple mantle trimmed with gold, her long black hair tossing in the wind, 'twas as though she was at a coronation. She threw her arms around her son, squeezing, rocking him to greater and greater cheers. "Red! Red!" she could say no more. Mother and son were both convulsed in tears of joy and laughter, almost dancing, except that Red Hugh could not dance.

Ineen's Redshanks pushed back the crowd, forming a ring about mother and son, and slowly but vigorously moving the two forward up the bank toward the castle.

In front of the castle, cheering with the rest, waited a group of nobles; shaggy-eyed McGroarty, bearer of the *Cathach*, notable among them. Owny broke through the ring to squeeze his Bermingham Tower mate, joining the sobs of joy.

"'Tis with you, Owny, I should have fled Dublin," was the one complete statement Red managed to get out.

"You're here at last," laughed Owny, "and this kingdom is the sweeter for it."

Behind Owny was a lean, tall Redshank with a blonde beard.

"Good morrow, Master Hugh Roe!"

"McAteer!" Red locked arms with him, astonished, as it had been years since he thought of the man who had salvaged Red's rash raid on Bingham's cattle thieves.

"A bonny champion you be. No man escapes Dublin Castle, but twice y'ave done it."

"Once recaptured."

"Na. Sold you were once but a champion twice."

Inside the castle, Ineen held her son back as nobles again flexed knees to him and hastened up the spiral stairs to the great hall. One bag-toting man—Red took him correctly for a physician—lagged behind, following Ineen's gestures.

"And Father?" Red asked his mother.

"At Castle Donegal."

"Ach! Then free him I shall."

"He is in need of you."

"We must not delay. We must expel the English immediately."

"Aye, but first . . ." She kept her arm around her son, steering him toward a dark corner.

"Why do you take me aside? We must go up with the *sub-kings* and nobles."

"As soon as O'Fairon tends your feet."

"Aye," Red conceded, eyeing and lifting, one by one, his muddy shoes and their soaked dressings. "But O'Fairon can do this in the great hall."

"Sit here," she said, pulling up a chair. On a small table covered with a cloth, a candle flickered beside a wine flagon and plate of bacon and cabbage, with apples and hazelnuts. "Rest," his mother said.

"I'll sit," said Red, "but I don't eat till we join the others."

"'Twon't be a moment," the physician mumbled, kneeling, emptying his bag.

Ineen caught her own breath, digging her fingers into her hands behind her, staring at the wounded toes. "Jesus, Mary, and Joseph," she gasped. *Heal him, O Lord.*

Two toes looked black, in the weak candlelight, against the pale skin of the feet. O'Fairon gently gripped the heel of one of Red's feet and raised it for a closer look. "Do the toes feel anything?"

"No," Red answered with a frown. In the thrill of returning home, he was perturbed to be dealing with toes.

"What do we do?" Ineen asked the physician.

O'Fairon dried toes and feet, wrapped them in fresh bandages, told Red Hugh to rest them, but Red cut him off: "We eat and conduct a council to rid the English from the Friary. That's what we do."

And, popping a hazelnut into his mouth, he stood up, rocked to the spiral stairs, and hauled himself swiftly up.

His entry into the great hall was heartily cheered.

Then came the meal at the long table with Red Hugh in the place of honor. His mother sat to his right and Owny to his left, especially as Owny's father was still held in Dublin Castle. Red regaled his long-time Bermingham Tower-mate and others with his adventures after fleeing Dublin Castle. A harper strummed intermittently. At times, Red sat back in the solid oak chair, letting the old familiar songs settle inside him, aware to the core of his being that he was *home*. Mac an Ward, the bard, took in everything so he could regale all with a poem that would go down through the ages.

Red's mother listened and watched, for it was her son's day to shine.

After prayers and toasts, Red rapped the council to order.

"First we free the Friary. Then I free Father, the O'Donnell, in Castle Donegal."

The nobles and sub-kings present roared and pounded.

But not all nobles were present, for the kingdom was not united.

"MacSweeney Doe?" Red asked, looking at his mother.

"'Tis hard put MacSweeney Doe is," she answered. "He could not abandon his country just northwest of where Willis has been snatching cattle and everything else that Saxon can get his hands on. But Doe awaits our signal to join."

After nearly four years in a royal prison, Red gazed round the table, looking every man in the eyes.

"And the *Cathach*, my good McGroarty?" Red asked with good cheer.

"With us," smiled McGroarty, pleased to be singled out.

"Then we prepare to rid the English from the Friary."

So concluded the council, with hearty toasts to Red Hugh and the O'Donnell and curses on Willis, now Sheriff of Donegal as well as entrenched in the Friary.

Aside, Red asked his mother if she feared a spy in their midst.

"No," she said, "but tongues wander. Still, victory depends on your good health. 'Tis not even the first of February, St. Bridget's Day."

Time and rest were not what her son wanted.

Then that first night home he received, like a scapular beneath his shirt, what his mother promised. In a chamber above the great hall, Ineen unwrapped a plain linen cloth. In the guttering flamelight shone the round, gold MacDonnell medallion.

"Alex McSorley's, given to him by your father."

"Yes, my son."

Embossed clearly round the edge were the words he prayed so often: *In Deo Nostra Spes*—In God Our Hope.

Red said, "I remembered these words in the dungeon. And I thought of Alex's head outside."

Ineen pressed cloth and medallion into her son's hands.

Red's fingers trembled a little as he touched the blue waves beneath a boat with tall sails.

"Aye," his mother said. "The medallion of the MacDonnells. And now 'tis yours."

Red still wore the strong cord and he removed it. She strung the medallion upon it then placed it over his head. "You are the hope of Macdonnells as well as a great hope of the O'Donnells." She kissed Red's head.

He raised the medallion and kissed it three times.

Later, walking on the wintry cold sand by the bay, and consulting with those taking part in routing the English, son and mother were still bent on healing Red Hugh's toes. They waited till MacSweeney Doe came and arranged to rid the Saxons from his territory. But come he did, even before the week was out, with a few dozen Redshanks and a hundred kerne.

When MacSweeney Doe first saw Red, he held back.

"My foster father," said a puzzled Red, moving to give him a hug.

"To see you whole again," said MacSweeney, "when I left you in the hands of . . ."

Red interrupted him. "You can join me in routing the English."

Finally, MacSweeney Doe gave his foster son a fierce hug the likes of which Red relished.

"But they have not attacked himself in Donegal Castle," said Red, "knowing I escaped?"

"No," MacSweeney said. "They have only a hundred men, or two hundred at the most."

"Aye. Our troops can handle that!" Red pronounced.

Looking mother and foster father in the eye, Red said, "Donegal Friary shall be cleansed, and Father shall be freed."

MacSweeney and Ineen exchanged glances and nodded.

Then Ineen asked her son to join her for a last walk on the beach.

The sky was dark silver, and silver were the waves beneath a wind Ineen hoped would be cooling for her son in more than one way.

"Is it your intent, my Red," she asked after a few paces in silent thought, "to kill all the English?"

Her son did not respond immediately but soon said, "And aren't they deserving of that!"

"Aye. But I do not want Bingham to set foot this side of the River Erne. Which is what he will do if we kill his minions here at the Friary."

With a quick glance at his mother, Red laughed. "So— we shall attack them in Sligo?"

"Red, Red!"

"Yes, Mother?"

"Did O'Neill explain nothing to you at Dungannon?"

"I hear he explained a lot to you."

She turned fast and furious as she realized in that moment that he would go forward and she must step back. She let her lungs calm. This was too critical after all these years and the suffering, to bring her son home safely, to give way to a mother's passion.

"O'Neill has the right of it, my son," said Ineen. "Harder than you can believe for me to say that. I used to fear he was more Saxon than Irish. But four years of working with him and the two of us trying to keep you alive and escape . . . I have learned there is so much more to him than meets the eye."

"He wants to be king in his part of Ulster," her son said.

"Of course, he does," his mother responded.

Red's intensity eased and instead of speaking further, he laughed.

"'Tis only one vengeance worth obtaining," said his mother, "for their kidnapping you to Dublin Castle—for Alex—aye, and for my brothers at Ardnarea and all our kin at Rathlin Island. One vengeance for all."

"A lovely vengeance 'twill be," Red agreed.

"Aye," she agreed.

Then Red said, "The English will fire when we surround them."

"Fire back. But besiege them, tighter and tighter, till they sue to retreat," his mother urged.

"Ach, Mother!"

"Siege—not slaughter. Drive them out of Donegal!"

"I can make no promises once the firing begins," Red declared.

His mother took his hands into her hands. "But there is a greater promise, my son, '*When Hugh fathers Hugh, and both rule together, the younger shall rule all Erin, and drive out the Gall.*'"

The words stirred Red. He peered into his mother's eyes, then flicked his gaze toward Donegal Bay. "'Tis much you ask . . . Mother."

"Aye, much." Her voice broke. "'Tis all."

XL

Donegal Friary
Tyrconnell, Winter 1592

*T*he next morn in a gentle snow, after a solemn Mass outside not far from the wide path from Ballyshannon Castle, McGroarty's priest bore high the *Cathac,* The Battle Book. He three times processed sunwise round the corps of harpers, pipers, and the ranks of Redshanks and kerne assembled on a small, unplanted field.

On his horse in front of an altar table, Red Hugh sat erect in a fur-collared mantle and padded tunic, jeweled scabbard showing. He addressed all there:

"Men remember! The English Crown, excommunicated by the Pope, deals treacherously with all of us. Me they kidnapped! Me they held four years in prison, in a dungeon. Today they still hold in Dublin Castle the O'Gallagher— your O'Gallagher. They invade our land, they pillage our crops and our cattle, they rape our women, they kill our men. And they say we owe them tribute and allegiance. Never!"

"Never!" cried the men in the ranks.

"Never!" cried Red Hugh, waving a fist.

"O'Donnell Abu!" came wave on wave in response.

"Harpers! Lead on!" Red Hugh commanded. He, Owny, and McGroarty rode just behind the harpers and the kerne.

The harpers filed round, small harps slung on their backs, their swords hanging on their belts. They led the way toward Donegal with soft strings.

At a gallop, a horseman could go the ten miles from Ballyshannon to Donegal in an hour or so by the clear path or beside the few small fields of barley and past huts and stands of oak and ash. On foot, ordinarily, the journey took twice as long. But this taskforce stepped along at a pace, keeping the kerne at a near-trot; nearly three dozen O'Gallagher Redshanks, and close to one hundred fifty kerne. Ineen herself kept fifty of her Redshanks as reserves in the rear.

There was no way Ineen Dubh could keep herself fully away from this. It promised to be the culmination of long, hard years. Clearing out the English would propel her son, who escaped Dublin Castle, to Doon Rock to be proclaimed the next O'Donnell king. But it had to be Red Hugh's triumph, not hers.

Until her hand must be free, Ineen kept her beads in one hand, praying them one by one even as she steered her horse. She wore padded armor, a weapon-boy carried her claymore. Beside her were Captain Crawford, and on her other side, at her request, was McAteer.

"I told Red," Ineen turned to Captain Crawford, "and I warned him, slaughter would be the worst of strategies. But, O, how I ponder! Will the English open fire so strong there will be no question that they must be slaughtered, everyone?"

Captain Crawford said, "I am ready for it."

He knew and she knew, if the Saxons opened fire her son might not survive. Even if he escaped bullets, he may not run to safety on those wounded toes of his.

It was agreed that the stentor in his booming voice would bellow—in English—Red Hugh's demand that the English leave their sacred booty from Donegal Friary behind and remove themselves to the bay and back to Bingham in Connaught or meet death when the bagpipes wailed. A plan so perfect, it could not fail. If Red Hugh was not killed.

At that thought, Ineen dug her heels into the flanks of her horse. A vision of her arrow sticking out of Donal's dying body filled her mind. She shook her head over and over to get rid of the image.

"Anything amiss?" Crawford asked, seeing her shaking her head with a grimacing face.

His voice caused her to catch herself. She slowed her horse and pleaded with the Holy Virgin in the words she had so often said in the Friary: *Ave Maria. Ave Gratia Plena.* Hail Mary, full of grace.

"Be prepared," she ordered Crawford.

As they neared the Friary woods through the pines and birches, she saw the fields ahead, which in the gray light looked trampled or torn up. "Saxon beasts!" she interrupted her *Ave*s to mutter. "Don't even take care of what could feed them."

She pinned her eyes on the kerne, who trod, barefoot in tunics, near the forest edge and could not help a glance behind to make sure of her Redshanks. She chided herself for such womanly fretting.

Meanwhile, MacSweeney Doe and his troops were soon to arrive. It was his task to cross the river Eske and come down into O'Boyle's country, dividing his forces into two.

Ineen's horse startled, sensing his rider's uneasiness. A ragged series of cries sailed back from the forest edge and spread like flames.

But even though the Ballyshannon kerne had reached a long, wide stand of birches permitting freer, faster movement, droves of them fell back there with ebbs and spikes of a never-ending din like a storm in the bay, almost driving Ineen wild with uncertainty.

Where was Red Hugh? She knew he must be in front by the Friary Church. Then, in compliance with the original plan, the sound of the stentor's voice boomed forth in English. She could not hear the words distinctly. But this was Red Hugh's offer: *"The lives of all English who leave Donegal will be spared!"*

What would Red Hugh do? He must do something. And she could not. Would the English leave? Not yet, anyway.

"I go where you go!" McAteer, who noticed how Ineen reined her restive horse, cried to her.

On her other side, Captain Crawford shouted, "I will go only so far as you can see how it goes up front!"

Wild glances they exchanged, and she turned desperately. The rank of Redshanks halted abruptly except for her bodyguards, who followed her. McAteer jogged along ahead of her.

Beyond the trees, morning light of the ruined barley field seemed to beckon like light from an angel of death, but she kept fighting toward it, pleading, *Lord, if one of us must die this day, let it be me! Spare Red Hugh. Let Red be your St. Michael, your St. Michael who drove out devil heretics!*

In front of her, the cross atop the Friary Chapel rose gray and somber.

But she could not help a quick glance left at the round tops of Celtic crosses in the cemetery where O'Donnell kings were buried.

Not this day, Lord. Do not take my son. Her heart beat loud in her ears.

Her Redshanks were there. *Thanks be to God many with Red Hugh!*

Ineen slowed to a more cautious pace till she found a break in the birches. She again heard the stentor's voice chanting Red Hugh's offer.

Beyond the foremost trees—out and clear of cover— was Owny, and in front of him her son sat upon his horse. His back arched and a fresh breeze in his ruddy hair. Utterly exposed to any sniper from Donegal Friary!

"Jesus, Mary, and Joseph!" his mother breathed but kept her post.

As the stentor boomed the offer at the Friary for a third time, a queue of boys marching out from the trees formed a rank, puffing up their bagpipes but not yet blowing. When the pipers piped there would be no more offers from the stentor. No more opportunities for the English to leave the Friary and disappear toward Connaught. The slaughter, God forbid, would begin!

Ineen held her breath, then inhaled and let go, noticing stirrings of bodies. Kerne were now marching out of the woods behind the pipers, some turning left to line the ridge in front of the ruined barley field.

Out of the mist, a troop of specters, led by what appeared to be three horsemen, emerged upon the hill north of Castle Boyle Tower. MacSweeney Doe had arrived. Ineen let herself smile.

Red Hugh held up his hand. "Hold! Hold!"

No sound came from the Friary. Doorways stood empty; and the carelessly boarded windows, with smashed stained glass, were empty, too.

Red Hugh told the Stentor: "One last time before the pipers pipe."

The stentor again stepped forward. "*English soldiers! Your final opportunity before the pipers pipe. Clear out to the bay with your women and your families and shall have no harm.*"

They waited. No sound from the Friary.

Red signaled the row of pipers. "Pipers begin playing!"

A skirl went up. Suddenly four men in English helmets, waving what looked like white altar cloths, ran skulking from the chapel door of the Friary Church. Red motioned the pipers to halt.

*O'Donnell Abu*s rolled north, rolled south, and back into the woods. Then shouts went up from the kerne massed north nearer the river Eske. Ineen dismounted, ran closer, and saw what they saw. Down on the riverbank behind the Friary walls, English-helmeted soldiers swarmed four boats, and were looking for other boats. One was being poled across the river to the O'Boyle side. To roaring cheers, both sides of the river the English rowed hurriedly, pitching sails, in a race to the estuary and out to the bay to head back to Connaught.

Wailing had arisen that turned out to have come from the English women, children.

It was over. Captain Willis and his men were fleeing.

"Thanks be to God," Ineen cried and kissed her beads.

Standing by the pipers and the strumming harpers, Ineen beheld Red Hugh, radiant in victory, still on his horse. His features appeared even more pleasing. And when the early afternoon light shone upon his head, even his red hair became haler and hardier.

"You are the victor today, my son," she said, barely holding in her tears. "You routed the Crown's minions. You are—" she faltered; then held her head up, staring into his eyes that were large with emotions she had not seen in them before. "You are the hero Holy Columcille prophesied."

It was all she could do to keep composed.

"'Tis your son I am," said Red Hugh with a wide smile.

She wanted to kiss him, but not among his warriors.

"I go to bring the joyous news to your father. My runner says no English are at the castle."

"Tell him I will be coming," said Red. Then moved with a sudden, strong emotion, "This victory is for him. 'Tis dedicated to the great O'Donnell king."

Feeling buoyant on the never-ending *O'Donnell Abu*s resounding all about them, and the high-pitched piping of reels and chants, Ineen remounted her horse and turned toward Donegal Castle with her bodyguards.

Himself sat in his chamber by the turf fire, soothed by the glissandos his harper strummed. Father Conan sat on the other side of the fire, tapping his toe in a gentle rhythm, and he looked up with an expectant smile as Ineen emerged atop the spiral stairs. The harper noticed but did not miss a flourish. O'Donnell opened his eyes and looked around.

"Our son has freed Donegal Friary of the English," Ineen spoke before anyone else could.

"Did he now?" said the O'Donnell, white hair tumbling about his brown wool mantle.

"Deo gratias!" said Father Conan, blessing himself and getting up from his chair.

The harper ceased playing but O'Donnell gestured him to continue.

Ineen raised her voice, "Red Hugh freed Donegal Friary, and he has freed *you*."

O'Donnell shook his head in acknowledgement. "'Tis a great deed. Where is my son?"

"*Our* son," said his wife, surprised at how toneless her husband received this news, "will be by shortly."

Ineen recognized that all that this victory meant would take a little time and a more skilled selection of words to penetrate her husband's frailty and defenses.

"Red Hugh's victory over the likes of Willis, Bingham's Sheriff, 'tis as grand a deed as your victory at Farsetmore that avenged my father's murder."

O'Donnell breathed deeply. "Farsetmore," he said. "A magnificent victory, it was."

Ineen turned to the priest and the harper, saying she wished to speak to the O'Donnell before their son arrived. Father Conan bowed and shooed the harper toward the stairs. Ineen told the harper to send one of the few servants remaining at the castle to bring up the best Spanish wine. She set her mantle aside, wearing a saffron léine, having left her padded tunic in the castle kitchen. She positioned a chair in front of her husband and sat down facing him.

"Husband," she said, letting her dark hair fall long around her golden cross. "You know your son's victory is a reason to call the nobles to name Red Hugh your Tánaiste."

"Wife!" O'Donnell all but growled. "I promised you long ago Red Hugh shall succeed me."

"A grand decision, Hugh. Shall we send word tomorrow for the nobles to gather at Kilmacrennan—?"

"Red Hugh is years behind in learning what a Tánaiste must do."

"Very well, Husband. Tomorrow Red shall begin learning."

Her husband gave her a long, silent look. "Donal was my Seneschal. He would have trained Red," he muttered. "I planned for that. It's not to be."

Just Donal's name from her husband's mouth sent sharp pains into Ineen's head and heart. Nonetheless she went on, "For you to be served by such a successor as Red Hugh will ensure that your reputation and legacy are remembered."

"Indeed," O'Donnell said.

"Your Tánaiste must be mighty and inspire terror in his enemies . . . as your son showed this day at Donegal Friary."

After a moment O'Donnell said, "So he has."

"Done!" announced a voice O'Donnell had not heard in four years. "The English out of Donegal Friary and leaving our kingdom!"

Red steadied himself as he entered the chamber. O'Donnell looked at him, thunderstruck, and built himself to his feet, so laboriously he did not notice his son wobble slightly on his own feet. When O'Donnell stood as tall as his back permitted, his son bowed, gingerly lifting one knee in homage to his king. Then he raised a face bright and bursting into tears. "Father!" He embraced the old man.

"'Tis God's will," his father said.

"'Twas for you, Father," Red Hugh said.

"And sure," O'Donnell, tears streaming down his face, said, "would I be expecting anything less of my son? Gone—stolen—four years, is it, son? And you coming back a hero. Worthy—worthy—to succeed me." He could barely make his voice finish the declaration.

Ineen rose.

"Mother!" Red reached to hug her. "Alex knows this victory, I *feel* Alex McSorley knows it!"

"Certain he does." Ineen kissed Red's cheek then lifted and kissed the MacDonnell medallion beneath his padded tunic.

"Let me hold you, son. Let me hold you with the wonder I felt the night you were born, the night of the great comet."

"Aye, Mother." Then Red straightened up. "We must send word to Hugh O'Neill, Father."

"You mean you have not already?" came O'Donnell's rather gruff response.

"No, Father. First I have come to you."

O'Donnell let his stern countenance smile and his memory came back as if it had never left him. "Now, if myself in my day chased the English out of Donegal Friary, I would have sent pipers, drummers, and chanting friars to Hugh O'Neill—and all of Ulster—before I swung off my horse."

Son and wife smiled.

A servant arrived, proffering a tray with goblets and bottles of Spanish wine. Another came with a tray of salted salmon and beef.

For the rest of that day into night, to the soft glissandos of the harper, whom Ineen summoned back, O'Donnell, Red, and his mother shared wine, fish, and beef at trestle tables as Red recounted the rout and the condition of Donegal Friary. It turned out not to be at all an utter ruin. The Friary Library, for one, was surprisingly intact, surely still the best library in all of Ireland.

"Holy Columcille saw all this a thousand years ago," said Ineen, looking on husband and son together. "The English have not wiped us out! *Not* destroyed our sacred places. O'Donnell lands do *not* belong to the Queen of England."

In the glow of the conversation, and the warmth from the fireplace, Ineen also thought of her MacDonnells, whom she fancied hovering in the twilight shadows of this star-pierced chamber.

Then Ineen repeated the old lines of prophecy, *"When Hugh is fathered by Hugh . . ."*

Her Red would now go forward without her. She would need a courage she was not used to—to endure events she could not herself control. She clutched her gold cross. What began at the Friary must go beyond their kingdom—must go beyond Bingham in Connaught. She believed the day would come when Ireland would be free.

When Red Hugh left them to return to Ballyshannon, for he knew his frost-bitten toes must be tended to, he did not mention anything about them to his father.

414

O'Donnell looked long at his wife as the sound of Red's boots echoed from down the curved stone steps.

The winter dusk grew darker, and flakes of snow began to cover the bawn. Some sparkled in the torchlight as if in celebration of the victory. Ineen could no longer see clearly the expression in O'Donnell's eyes.

O'Donnell raised his goblet of wine and refilled his wife's. "Sláinte. We shall summon the nobles to Kilmacrennan, Ineen. Our son is advanced in skills. Tell them when you go to gather them that I will step down. When Donegal Friary is readied, I shall live there as my forebearers did." Then he said, "I'll bring my grandson Donal Oge with me to be educated by the holy friars."

There it was—this momentous moment of Ineen's life, what she had dreamed and hoped and fought and prayed for Red Hugh, and she was reminded of Donal and his fatherless son, Donal Oge. Would it forever haunt her?

Nevertheless, Ineen reached over and placed her right hand upon her husband's. She smiled at him and proclaimed, "Our Red Hugh will be given the white wand of kingship. He will become *king*."

Epilogue

*I*n May 1592, on a day ablaze with sunshine, Ineen Dubh looked upon Red Hugh as he stood by the Rock of Doon with his father beside him. In a religious ceremony at Kilmacrennan Abbey, the inauguration ceremonies began. The inaugural stone of generations of O'Donnell kings had been brought from the Abbey to the Rock of Doon where Red Hugh was to be inaugurated king. The stone itself was a rough, gray piece of granite with two carved impressions. MacSweeney Doe lifted Red Hugh upon it. Red's bare feet, minus two big toes, symbolized his courage when escaping the English. Proudly, he slipped his bare feet into the noble imprints of the first O'Donnell who ruled these lands, Eigneachan, in 1200.

The scribe read the Brehon laws. Abbott O'Friel, the Inaugurator, administered the oath of office. He handed Red Hugh the straight, white hazel rod that stood for purity, honor, and judgment. MacSweeney Doe put a sandal upon Red's foot, then threw the other sandal over his own shoulder as a sign of submission to the new king.

The Abbott pronounced one word: "O'Donnell."

"O'Donnell," repeated the clergy, including the Bishop of Derry (successor of Columcille), and the nobles. The word carried throughout the crowd.

Ineen Dubh joined her voice in crying out "O'Donnell." It mattered little that Niall Garbh and others who had gone over to the English did not attend. Her son was *king*. The prophecy, fulfilled.

Before Red Hugh stepped down, he turned three times forward and three times backwards, viewing his lands and his people in honor of the Holy Trinity.

After the celebration, Ineen returned to Mongavlin while her husband went to live at Donegal Friary. He brought Donal Oge with him. Before that, Red's father was known to live in Ballyshannon and to have been there when Red Hugh's two big toes were amputated.

In a church wedding held in December 1592, Rose O'Neill and Red Hugh married. And in 1593, Turlough O'Neill abdicated, and Hugh O'Neill was inaugurated in the ways of Gaelic kings.

In March of 1603, Elizabeth I died. James the VI of Scotland, son of Mary Queen of Scots and relative of Ineen Dubh, became James I, King of England.

Red Hugh, burning with a desire to avenge what the English did to him by imprisonment, asked his mother to go to Scotland in September to procure Scots' mercenaries for him. He and Maguire banded together to attack the English in the south of Ulster. Thus began the Nine Years' War, though Hugh O'Neill concealed his role in obtaining arms for Red Hugh.

The Nine Years' War was fought from 1593–1602, and Hugh O'Neill openly acknowledged his position in January 1595. In fact, Donal Oge was among those who fought with Red Hugh in the war.

Ineen did not spend her days at her castle crocheting. Red Hugh welcomed his mother's abilities, and she continued to supply him with Redshanks. In 1597, Red sent Ineen to Scotland to negotiate with her brother Angus that he not take revenge on Hugh O'Neill. And in 1599, Ineen bought arms and Redshanks for Red Hugh and Hugh O'Neill. For her fidelity, Red appointed his mother Governor of Sligo Castle after his troops succeeded in taking Connaught and destroying Bingham and his minions there.

Regardless, hard times persisted as the English prevailed at the Battle of Kinsale. Red Hugh went to Spain in 1602 to seek further help from the Spanish. He died September 10, 1602, in Simancas and was buried in a Franciscan monastery in Valladolid. A number of historical records tell us his untimely death was due to poisoning by an English agent.

Donal Oge was among the beneficiaries of Red Hugh's will.

Red Hugh's brother Rory was inaugurated a king and later became an Earl, though he left Ireland in 1608 with Hugh O'Neill and Donal Oge. They left from Rathmullen with a group of ninety-nine. Among the nobles were Nuala

O'Donnell and Caffar O'Donnell in "The Flight of the Earls." They lived as exiles in Europe where they were helped by the Irish College in Louvain as well as by patrons in Rome and Spain.

Amazingly, with the advent of the Ulster Plantation in 1607, Ineen Dubh, as a Scots noble, was permitted to live in Mongavlin Castle. All her sons preceded her in death. She died after 1608 in Ireland. Her daughters, grandchildren, and Donal Oge were still living.

Over four hundred years later, with the Easter Rising in 1916 and the Good Friday Agreement in 1998, Ireland finally achieved much of what Ineen Dubh, Red Hugh O'Donnell, and Hugh O'Neill envisioned and fought tirelessly for—the right to be independent.

Glossary

Arquebus	Handgun of the 16th century that resembled a musket
Athwart	Across
Bawn	Defensive enclosure around an Irish castle
Behindhand	Unaware of recent events OR late paying a debt
Blackguards	A contemptible person; a scoundrel
Bodrhan	A frame drum of Irish origin
Caman	Hurley stick
Claymore	Scottish sword
Columcille	O'Donnell ancestor, Irish abbot, who prophesized life of Red Hugh O'Donnell
Currah	Irish and Scottish for small boat
Dirk	Thrusting or stabbing straight-bladed dagger
Fubun	Shame in Gaelic
Garderobe	Castle toilet
Gille	Scottish Gaelic for servants
Glib	Male hair in Ireland in the 16th century, in which a fringe fell over the face
Glissandos	A sound emitted by a harp, generated from a slide upward or downward between two notes
Gyves	Shackles
Harquebus	A portable gun supported on a tripod or a forked rest

Halberd	A weapon dating from the 14th-16th centuries consisting of an axe blade topped with a spike on a long staff
Hurley	An Irish game in which players use a hurling stick to hit a small ball
Kerne	Irish foot soldier
Léine	Main garment worn by Gaelic women
Misneach	Possessing courage, spirit and a feeling of well-being
Pale	Area of English control in Ireland
Prie-dieu	A piece of furniture used during prayer
Redshanks	Scottish mercenaries
Senechal	A royal advisor handling administration and justice for a king
Sliotar	A small ball for use in hurling and other Gaelic games
Tánaiste	Successor or heir presumptive
Trews	Tartan trousers from Scots Highland dress

Notes on the History and Suggestions for Historical Source Materials

An ancient primary source provided the Irish version of Ineen and the O'Donnell and their son, Red Hugh, who was kidnapped by the English and escaped from Dublin Castle: The *BeathaAodh Ruaida Ui Dhomhnaill, Prince of Tyrconnell (1586-1602)*, written by Lughaidh O'Clery. O'Clery was a relative of the O'Donnell's scribe. This true story was written in Gaeilge (Irish Gaelic) and scarcely known before 1893 when Reverend Denis Murphy translated it into English. O'Clery was one of the writers known as the Four Masters who wrote *THE ANNALS OF THE FOUR MASTERS* about Ireland from the earliest times into 1616 AD.

Sources relevant to the history of Elizabeth I, Ineen Dubh, the O'Donnell, Red Hugh, Hugh O'Neill, and Donal as presented in this novel include the *Calendar of State Papers Relating to Ireland in the Reign of Elizabeth 1, Volumes 4 – 11* (1586–1602), London: HMSO. These papers provided numerous insights into Queen Elizabeth I, who referred to Ineen Dubh as "that Scotswoman." The many references to Ineen Dubh, the O'Donnell, Red Hugh, Hugh

O'Neill, and the Redshanks revealed the way the English Crown operated in Ireland and London. While at times what the English wrote and what the Irish wrote about dates, events, and their interpretations of them were similar, frequently they were not.

From the sixteenth century into more recent times, numerous nonfiction books were written that relied on significant information from the O'Clery book and the Elizabethan State Papers. Over the centuries, more research became available. Darren McGettigan's *Red Hugh O'Donnell and the Nine Years War* (Dublin: Four Courts Press, 2005) proved helpful. Although the main subject matter is the Nine Years' War, much detail leading up to that war helped to provide context for this work of historical fiction. Other valuable nonfiction works read in the authors' research: Francis Martin O'Donnell's *The O'Donnells of Tyrconnell: A Hidden Legacy* (Washington DC: Academia Press, 2018). This work was essential to understanding the importance of the first family of Hugh O'Donnell. Both Donal, Ineen's nemesis, and Siobhan, Hugh O' Neill's wife, were offspring of that first family, born of an Irish mother unlike the O'Donnell's children by his second wife, Ineen Dubh, who was Scottish.

Hiram Morgan, a noted Irish historian born in Belfast, became an expert on Hugh O'Neill. His work continues to provide scholarship regarding O'Neill's role and his union with Red Hugh. Among his works, *Tyrone's Rebellion*

(Woodbridge: Suffolk, Brydell and Brewer, 1993) is critical to understanding the role of the Earl of Tyrone.

Vincent O'Donnell, longtime leader of the O'Donnell Clan Association, planned O'Donnell Clan gatherings and author Mary Pat Ferron Canes' trips related to O'Donnell heritage, providing the opportunity to obtain significant oral histories from descendants of the historical characters in *Dark Queen of Donegal.* Vincent O'Donnell wrote *O'Donnells of Tyrconnell* (Inver: Dalach Publications, 1989).

Carolyn Erickson's *The First Elizabeth* (New York: Summit Books, 1983) contributed to in-depth insight into the life of Elizabeth I. Also, Antonia Fraser's *Mary Queen of Scots* (New York: Dell Publishing Company, First Laurel Printing, 1984) contained information regarding Elizabeth's view of the Scots, particularly of Mary Stuart, a relative of Ineen Dubh.

About the Authors

Mary Pat Ferron Canes

Mary Pat Ferron Canes wrote a Master's thesis in anthropology dealing with Gaelic women and men going back to ancient sagas. Ever since conducting her research, Canes fell in love with the Emerald Isle and has visited numerous times over the years. She holds a graduate degree in anthropology from George Washington University and an undergraduate degree from St. Catherine University.

Since teaching at the Rochester Institute of Technology as an adjunct professor, the author has continued writing about Irish history. Her discoveries about the Queen of Donegal, an historical woman of Ireland whose son, Red Hugh, is considered one of Ireland's heroes, intrigued Canes. This discovery, coupled with appreciation for her grandmother's fascination with her Irish heritage, led Canes to narrate the stories in this novel.

Canes' research included attending a clan reunion in Donegal and interviews with descendants of the real-life characters in her book. She has stood in the footsteps of the characters at Donegal Castle and other significant locales in the historical novel.

The published author has written a series of booklets, poems, articles, and had her work appear in numerous journals. Canes is a member of the National League of American Pen Women (NLAPW) and currently serves as the fourth vice president for the National organization. Raised in the Midwest, she now resides in Northern Virginia.

About JR Foley

JR Foley is a descendant of the O'Donnell Clan. He has an MFA from the University of Iowa Fiction Workshop as well as a Ph.D. in English. A member of the Dramatists Guild, he is also Fiction editor of Flash Point: A Multidisciplinary Journal of the Arts and politics.

http://www.flashpointmag.com

CPSIA information can be obtained
at www.ICGtesting.com
Printed in the USA
BVHW081145030522
635994BV00029B/755

9 781950 251070